COMPARATIVE
POLITICAL
PHILOSOPHY

Border Crossings: Toward a Comparative Political Theory, edited by Fred Dallmayr
Race and Reconciliation in South Africa: A Multicultural Dialogue in Comparative Perspective, edited by William E. Van Vugt and G. Daan Cloete
Gandhi, Freedom, and Self-Rule, edited by Anthony J. Parel
Beyond Nationalism? Sovereignity and Citizenship, edited by Fred Dallmayr and José M. Rosales
Conversations and Transformations: Toward a New Ethics of Self and Society, by Ananta Kumar Giri
Comparative Political Culture in the Age of Globalization: An Introductory Anthology, edited by Hwa Yol Jung
Hinterlands and Horizons: Excursions in Search of Amity, by Margaret Chatterjee
New Approaches to Comparative Politics: Insights from Political Theory, edited by Jennifer S. Holmes
Comparative Political Philosophy: Studies under the Upas Tree, edited by Anthony J. Parel and Ronald C. Keith

Comparative Political Philosophy

Studies under the Upas Tree

Edited by
Anthony J. PAREL
Ronald C. KEITH

LEXINGTON BOOKS
Lanham • Boulder • New York • Oxford

Dedicated to the Memory of
Yusuf K. Umar
1948–1991

LEXINGTON BOOKS

Published in the United States of America
by Lexington Books
A Member of the Rowman & Littlefield Publishing Group
4501 Forbes Boulevard, Suite 200, Lanham, Maryland 20706

PO Box 317
Oxford
OX2 9RU, UK

Copyright © 1992 by Anthony J. Parel and Ronald C. Keith
Introduction to the second edition copyright © 2003 by Lexington Books
First Lexington Books paperback edition published in 2003.
Originally published in 1992 by Sage Publications.

British Library Cataloguing in Publication Information Available

The Sage Publications edition of this book was previously catalogued by the Library of Congress as
follows:

Comparative political philosophy: studies under the upas tree
 Editors, A. J. Parel, R. C. Keith
  p. cm.
 Includes index.
  1. Political science—History. 2. Political Science—Philosophy. I. Parel, Anthony J. II. Keith,
Ronald C.

 JA81.U46   1992   320.01—dc20   92–9115
 ISBN 0-7391-0610-4 (pbk.: alk. paper)

Printed in the United States of America

⊖™ The paper used in this publication meets the minimum requirements of American National
Standard for Information Sciences—Permanence of Paper for Printed Library Materials,
ANSI/NISO Z39.48– 1992.

Contents

Introduction to the Second Edition   vii

Preface   7

Acknowledgements   9

1. The Comparative Study of Political Philosophy   11

    Anthony J. Parel

2. Classical Western Political Philosophy   29

    Barry Cooper

3. Modern Western Political Philosophy   45

    Barry Cooper

4. Law and Society in Confucian Thought   71

    Ronald C. Keith

5. Mao Zedong and his Political Thought   87

    Ronald C. Keith

6. What Good is Democracy? The Alternatives in China
    and the West   113

    Robert X. Ware

7. Of *Artha* and the *Arthasastra*   141

    K.J. Shah

8. Mahatma Gandhi's Critique of Modernity   163

    Anthony J. Parel

9. Farabi and Greek Political Philosophy 185
   Yusuf K. Umar

10. Khomeini's Doctrine of Legitimacy 217
    Majid Tehranian

Contributors 245
Index 247

Introduction to the Second Edition

Comparative political philosophy is both a historical and a philosophical discipline. As a historical discipline, it is context sensitive. In the first edition we were sensitive to the emergence of the towering figures of Mao, Gandhi, and Khomeini in modern China, India, and Iran, respectively. Since the first edition appeared in 1992, however, the context of politics in China, India, and Islam has undergone notable changes. India, under the impact of *hindutva* (hinduness) has taken an ominous turn to the extreme right. Sunni fundamentalism, which we had not considered in the first edition, has given rise to the Taliban and al-Qaeda movements.

Meanwhile in China there has been a resurging interest in China's traditional moral culture as China's secular state grapples with the deep implications of an unprecedented transition to a "socialist market." The distinction between "socialism" and "capitalism" has been increasingly obscured in open-ended subscription to societal experiment, rationalized in unqualified reference to praxis. And the Chinese Communist Party has been struggling on a number of fronts to save "socialist spiritual civilization" from "evil cults," such as the Falun Gong; from "blind Westernization"; and from foreign sponsored "disintegration" of the people's democratic dictatorship.

To do justice to these contextual changes we add this new introduction. In part I Ronald Keith analyses the situation in contemporary China; in parts II and III, Anthony Parel does the same for Sunni fundamentalism and the extremism of *hindutva*.

PART I—THE DILEMMA OF CHINESE "SOCIALIST MODERNIZATION"

The original edition of the present volume asked, What is happening to the revolutionary élan of Marxism-Leninism in contemporary

China?[1] This question is now even more pressing in light of the 2002–2003 transition in the top Party leadership as China begins to move from the "third generation leadership" of Jiang Zemin to the "fourth generation" of Hu Jintao.

Corruption continues to eat at the legitimacy of the Chinese Communist Party (CCP) even as the Party stakes its claim to govern on the basis of highly successful economic growth and improvement in the people's material and cultural life. Even as the Party attempts to bring private entrepreneurs into its membership it is struggling to reassert "socialist spiritual civilization" (*shehuizhuyi jingshen wenming*) in the face of rampant materialism.

The contemporary Chinese socialist state fears "disintegration." "Socialist spiritual civilization" is in decline as China struggles with the widening sociocultural impact of economic globalization. In the view of the Party, globalization represents a duality of political and economic liabilities and opportunities that could either support the growth of the world's developing economies, or reinforce the developed world's hold over international markets. There is a real question as to whether the Party can master this duality. Certainly the prospect for "socialist spiritual civilization" seems increasingly dim in light of the transition to the "socialist market," which is accompanied by spreading immorality and a widely recognized "crisis of faith" (*xinyang weiji*).

Concurrent with the spread of market materialism there have been radical changes in the form of spreading domestic violence, rapid development of organized crime in the drug and sex trades, the phenomenal growth of "heretical cults" as well as of "official religion," and overwhelming political and social cynicism. In 2000, Jiang Zemin lamented the terrible fact that leading cadres had "failed the test of power, money, and the temptation of beautiful women."[2] Unlike the *junzi* ("superior man") in imperial Chinese history, they are not really focused on providing personal moral example as the basis of good governance.

Since the late 1990s, CCP leaders have increasingly spoken about morality, calling for a new "rule of virtue" (*dezhi*). The latter was combined with the recently constitutionally sanctioned "socialist rule of law" (*shehuizhuyide fazhi*). Even as the rule of virtue was given express constitutional sanction in 1999, the Party moved to suppress the Falun Gong. The Falun Gong had allegedly not only committed crimes, it was also accused of negating "socialist spiritual

civilization." The Falun Gong was, therefore, an affront not only to the "rule of law," but also to "socialist modernization."

In the mid-1980s, there had been debates about the need to adapt the foreign concept of the "rule of law" and its focus on the "rule of man"[3] to Chinese culture. In the face of the resurgent "feudalism" of the Falun Gong and its challenge to the Party's emphasis on science and modernization, and in response to the rule of law's failure to keep up with rampant corruption, which was threatening to undermine the justice system, Jiang has argued that good laws need good people to ensure the genuine and true implementation of the law as it reflects the morality in society:

> we should persistently strengthen the construction of a socialist legal system and govern the country according to law. It is equally important to govern the country with high morals and persistently strengthen socialist moral construction. Ruling the country according to law and governing the country with high morals complement and promote each other. Neither is dispensable, or should be overemphasized to the neglect of the other. Ruling the country according to law belongs to political construction, or political culture, while governing the country with high morals belongs to ideological construction, or spiritual culture. Though belonging to different categories, they are equally important in status and function. We must closely combine legal construction with ideological construction and ruling according to law with governing with high moral principles.[4]

On the ideological/moral front, internal Party rectification campaigns required that Party cadres undergo education based on "three emphases," namely, emphases on theoretical study, political awareness, and moral rectitude.[5] While pledging fidelity to "the decisive role of material production in social development," Jiang gave "full credit to the motivating role of spiritual activity of people in the process of transforming the objective world."[6]

The CCP has, however, a hard-and-fast formal view on what types of "spiritual activity" actually support socialism. In 1999, Jiang Zemin, recalling his personal leadership in suppressing dissidents in Shanghai in 1989, rallied the CCP in the suppression of the Falun Gong.[7] He dealt with the contemporary challenge to "socialist spiritual civilization" by lumping together the spreading of inter-

nal feudal "evil cults" with the hostile capitalist "Westernization" and "disintegration" (*jieti*) political strategies, all of which were designed to undermine socialist China as led by the CCP.[8]

As Party leader, Jiang Zemin urged the Party to engage in a comprehensive study of a number of truly soul-searching questions relating to "historical and contemporary factors" involving "material and technological developments and the spiritual and cultural domains":

> We have done a lot of work in publicizing Marxism and establishing socialist ideals and belief in both the Party and society, and have achieved great results. Then, why do Marxist theories and socialist ideals . . . have little effect on some people? Why have absurd fallacies, such as "Falun Gong," been able to have a strong impact on some people and even a few senior intellectuals and cadres? Why have some Western capitalist theories and corruptive ideologies, culture and living styles had strong attraction for some people?[9]

What is the CCP's approach to change within the context of deepening so-called "socialist modernization?" For some time now Western critics have wondered whether Marxism in China has become simply an "ideology of modernization."[10] One might generalize that the Party has dealt with related ideology in an essentially conflicted manner. While there has been exceptional emphasis on the ideological necessity of praxis so as to greet change with rational new policy, good leadership style (*fengdu*) is still predicated in the principled continuity of ideological principle, and in the classical insistence on words only following upon deeds.

From the inception of reform in 1978 to the present, various senior leaders have stressed the importance of "liberating the mind" and "seeking the truth from the facts" as these notions are featured in Mao Zedong Thought and its particular exegesis on praxis. Historically, the latter had served as the basis for the victory over the material superiority of both the Japanese and the Guomindang of Chiang Kai shek. At one point, Mao Zedong had protested, "No, we are not insane; we are pragmatists [*shijizhuyizhe*]. We are Marxists seeking the truth from the facts." His praxis was, however, enlisted in the cause of socialism, and was therefore fundamentally different from the "pragmatism" of bourgeois thinkers such as John

Dewey.[11] Is it this same praxis that is now to save the CCP from the "disintegration" that forced the collapse of the Soviet Union? One might argue that despite CCP denials this praxis is taking on the character of Western "pragmatism," which, in its exclusive focus on expediency, places ideology in antithesis to modernization.

At the Fifteenth Party Congress in October 1997, Jiang Zemin took over the responsibility for ideology from Deng Xiaoping. Rather than declaring a self-consciously new direction, he was content with evolving Mao Zedong Thought with revered reference to the theoretical achievements of Deng Xiaoping. "Deng Xiaoping Theory" was canonized as the "continuation and development of Mao Zedong Thought." Essentially, it was a theory designed to guide "socialist modernization in the process of reform and opening to the outside world." This theory, as Jiang explained, seemingly represented principled continuity even as it encouraged new praxis: "First, Deng Xiaoping Theory, upholding the principles of emancipating the mind and seeking the truth from the facts, not only inherits the achievements of predecessors but also breaks with outmoded conventions on the basis of new practice, and explores a new realm of Marxism."[12]

Recent emphases on the "diversification" of ownership and distribution and on "innovation" to meet the new world of high technological revolution are seemingly justified in the tradition of ideological principles that dates back to the 1940s Yan'an principle of "seeking the truth from the facts." Building on "Deng Xiaoping Theory," Jiang emphasized the importance of promoting science within the Party and general public, and he insisted, "Making innovations is the soul of a nation."[13]

Deng had earlier accelerated economic reform in 1992 based on his "southern tour theory." Jiang, in his subsequent tenure as leader, built on this theory's distinction between the "liberation" and "development" of the productive forces.[14] While Jiang's leadership has been considered by many in the West as quite bland, and while he did claim a principled continuity based on the Mao–Deng legacy of praxis, some of his apparently supplementary emphases constitute quite a radical departure from the mainstream assumptions of dialectical materialism. He supported, for example, the clarification of "property rights" within the reform process that was to facilitate "diverse forms of ownership with public ownership in the dominant position." Arguably, in the name of praxis, he fundamentally revised the Marxist-Leninist principle of distribution, moving from "each according to his/her work" to "combining remuneration according to work and remuneration according to diverse factors of production put in" (*an lao fen pei yu duozhong fenpei fangshi xiangjiehe*).[15] While Party policy continued to extol the "three favourables" (common prosperity, development and liberation of productive forces, and preventing polarization in society, or *sange youli yu*), the changes in distribution were rationalized in terms of "efficiency is in the first place, while justice is supplementary" (*xiaoyi wezhu, gongzheng weifu*).[16]

Social justice, in other words, can only follow upon the efficiency of the "socialist market." As a consequence class struggle has been progressively narrowed to a point of theoretical obsolescence. Instead, the Party and the state have been involved in political discussion and law-making that recognize newly emerging "rights and interests" (*quanyi*) in society.[17] The "diversification of material interests" is recognized as "unavoidable with the deepening of reform."[18] The subjective content of these interests is accepted even if leaders make occasional reference to the objective dimensions of class struggle as it is understood on the ideologically conventional basis of dialectical materialism.

At the formal level of state legislation, the new focus on the legal protection of "rights and interests" of women and children, the handicapped, and elderly in the traumatic context of modernization has witnessed a new political focus on the rule of law as it relates to the protection of human rights.[19] This convergence is not easy in China, but as suggested in the following remarks by Jonathan Hecht to the U.S. Congress, it is promising:

> Whereas under Mao, law was viewed solely as a "tool of proletarian dictatorship," it is now being called upon to play multiple roles in economic and social life including defining rights and establishing institutions for their protection. In many respects Chinese law still falls short of international human rights standards. We see this every day in the Chinese government's use of the legal system to suppress political dissidents, religious group activities. . . . However as paradoxical as it may seem, law is simultaneously the principal medium through which the Chinese are engaging in debate and experimentation about human rights and closely re-

lated issues of predictability, transparency, and accountability of state action.[20]

While the Party has by and large found it necessary to subscribe to the legal protection of "rights and interests," it is locked in related controversy over social justice and the fundamental distinction between capitalism and socialism as that distinction originates with thinking on the nature of ownership and distribution. Inner controversy about the modified principle of distribution did not cause great waves of reaction, and yet these other "diverse factors" included recognition not only of technological and scientific skills but also of once dreaded capital. Dead capital was once thought to have reigned over live labour. Certainly, current "diversification" of distribution would seem to represent a backsliding into the former stage of capitalism. In the Cultural Revolution period of the late 1960s and early 1970s such revision would have been bitterly condemned as a "theory of productive forces" that was designed to foster "capitalist restoration."

Theoretical change sanctioning diversified ownership and distribution paved the way for the recent controversy over the induction of private entrepreneurs into the ranks of the Party. This is potentially the most controversial element in the ideological legacy of the "third generation." Apparently, it was for the purpose of developing common prosperity under socialism that the Party originally acquiesced to the idea of some people "getting rich first." The contemporary induction of private entrepreneurs into the Party is, nevertheless, a radical continuation of this line of thinking as it relates to Jiang Zemin's theory on the "three favorables."

Even as China enters the World Trade Organization (WTO), the CCP hopes to colonize fast growing private enterprise. Jiang Zemin has clearly stated his wish to colonize private enterprise by installing within its newly tailored Party organization. His statistics indicated that there were no Party members in 86 percent of the private enterprises across the country and that actual Party organization was present in only 0.9 percent of private enterprises. Jiang explained this related aspect of his "three favorables" theory:

Because the relations of proprietorship in non-state enterprises are not the same as those in state-owned and collective enterprises, Party organizations are required to adapt the approaches to their role as the political core, their actual setups, the content and modes of their activities, and their work methods to the peculiarities of these enterprises and combine them closely with production and management; and they are also required to promote material and cultural progress with flexible, diverse measures and pay due attention to actual results. The private business owners of today have come to the fore by responding to our Party's policy of reform and call to get rich first, and many of them were laborers in the first place.[21]

Obviously the Party leadership plans to colonize newly emerging private market forces, but it is not clear in the long run who will colonize whom. Perhaps this induction process will result in even more leading Party cadres succumbing to "power, money, and the temptation of beautiful women." It is possible that such a plan may backfire, or that it may aggravate an already profoundly serious pattern of Party corruption.

Traditional political culture had always expected politics to adapt to moral principle, as it flows through the cosmos into human society. In Chinese culture, words were considered honest only if they followed upon the commission of honest deeds. In the contemporary context of deepening corruption, the CCP has sensed the spiritual angst that accompanies even "socialist" modernization. In the grips of a "crisis of faith," and in response to "blind Westernization" and "disintegration theories," the CCP leaders have recently called for a "rule of virtue" that is to be entwined with the "rule of law." A critic might suggest, however, that the CCP is engaged in transparently superficial political exercises to recapture its revolutionary élan in the nonrevolutionary context of "socialist modernization" and furthermore that praxis, as it has been used either to justify "diversification" and "innovation," or to subordinate, at least in the short term, social justice to "efficiency," has become a form of casuistry that undercuts the CCP's own ideological focus on morality and "socialist spiritual civilization."

PART II—THE TALIBAN, AL-QAEDA, AND SUNNI FUNDAMENTALISM

Modern Islamic fundamentalism is not a monolith. There are first of all the Shiite and the Sunni versions of it. The Shiite version, as we saw in the first edition, has its source mainly in the teachings of Ayatollah Khomeini. The Sunni version, which we did not examine in the first edition but which we are examining now, has received much notoriety recently with the rise of the Taliban and al-Qaeda. It has its sources in the teachings of several masters. The influence of Muhammad ibn Abd al Wahhab (1703–1792), the founder of the virulent Wahhabi movement, is felt throughout the Sunni world. It is now being exported to many parts of the world from Saudi Arabia with the munificent support of petrodollars. Equally influential is the militant Pakistani version of Deobandism. The original Deobandism, which was taught in the Muslim Academy at Deoband, in India, was a nonmilitant form of fundamental Islam. However, as it crossed the Pakistani border it became militant. The *talibans* (students) are products of the thousands of the *madarassas* (petit seminaries) run by one or other of the factions of these Deobandis, supported by the Pakistani state.

But the deep theoretical roots of modern Sunni fundamentalism are traceable to the writings of three major figures, Abul Ala Mawdudi (1903–1979), Sayyid Qutb (1906–1966), and Abul Hassan Ali Nadvi (1914–1999). Each is a major modern Islamic fundamentalist thinker in his own right, read throughout the Islamic world. They admired each other and, on particular doctrinal points, were influenced by each other. They shared several core fundamentalist values, as we shall see presently. All the same, interesting differences in emphasis are discernible between them, which are important to notice, if only for the sake of accuracy.

Qutb, who hailed from Egypt, is the most radical of the three. He represented the militant fundamentalism of the Muslim Brotherhood of Egypt of the 1960s. Though he was highly critical of the West, his immediate target was not the West but his own, not so fervent, fellow Muslims. It is important to bear in mind that in Egypt the first target of the fundamentalists is the Egyptian state. President Nasser and his followers were the targets of the Muslim Brotherhood. It was for his alleged role in the plot against Nasser that Qutb was convicted and executed. Bin Laden and his al-Qaeda movement now carry Qutb's ideas one step further, applying them to non-Muslim states whether in Kashmir, Chechnya, the Philippines, Singapore, or the United States.

Mawdudi, born in Aurangabad, India, had spent the first forty-four years of his life in India and the last thirty-two in Pakistan. He died in Buffalo, New York, while on a visit to that city for medical treatment. His fundamentalism had its origin not in a Muslim country but in India of the 1930s and 1940s. His confrontation with Hinduism had a decisive influence on the formation of his philosophy.[22] He viewed that confrontation as nothing less than a life-and-death struggle for Islam. The dichotomy between Muslims and Hindus became axiomatic to his thinking. After his migration from India to Pakistan in 1947, the focus of the dichotomy shifted from Hindus to non-Muslims as such. To survive in a world divided between Muslims and non-Muslims, Islam had to become politicized and turned into a modern Islamic state. Moreover, it needed the help of a vanguard party, the *Jamaat i Islami* that he himself founded in India in 1941. Islam should be willing and able to capture state power and to establish a truly shariah state—in Pakistan first, and elsewhere later. The Islamization of the civil society had to proceed *pari passu*: all non-Muslims had to be either converted to Islam or brought under Muslim subjection.

Nadvi, born in Re Bareli, India, died in Lucknow, where he was the head of the Islamic Academy. The mildest of the three, he was no less fundamentalist that the other two. Yet he strove to give fundamentalism a truly humane face. Fundamentalism for him meant above all, a psychological and spiritual return to the times of the Prophet. Its goal was spiritual renewal of individual Muslims. That is why he remained a fervent supporter of the early twentieth-century *tabglighi* or "evangelical" movement within Indian Islam, started by his hero Maulana Muhammad Ilyas (1885–1944).[23] That movement had as its object the conversion not of non-Muslims but of the not-so-fervent Muslims, to a pure, fundamental kind of Islam. So long as the Muslims were permitted to live a pure Islamic life unmolested, they were prepared to live in peace anywhere, including non-Muslim countries. Only when non-Muslim states prevented the possibility of such a life were they to think of other options. Not for Nadvi the violence directed against the state per se, whether Muslim or non-Muslim. Of course on doctrinal grounds he could not deviate from the orthodox teaching on jihad. On practical grounds, however, he did not look upon jihad as the first option for the fundamentalists.

We have before us four different visions of Sunni fundamentalism: the Saudi Arabian, the Egyptian, the Pakistani, and the Indian. Their social settings explain their behaviour towards non-Muslims and

Muslims alike. Violence and terror are not necessarily endemic to Islamic fundamentalism. They become such only under certain social and moral conditions. Whereas Nadvi was willing to live in peace in a secular state such as India, Mawdudi, and Qutb were quite unwilling to live in peace in Pakistan and Egypt.

That said, we must now examine the ideas that Mawdudi, Qutb, and Nadvi have in common. Of these the most important is their philosophy of history, which provided them with a common Islamic vision of the world. Within that broad vision they were able to accommodate their slightly differing fundamentalist approaches to modernity, jihad, and the Islamic state.

The Fundamentalist Philosophy of History

What ties everything in fundamentalism together is its philosophy, or more accurately, its theology of history. It is remarkable that the thinker who has given a sustained account of it is Nadvi, the least militant of the three. A view of history is certainly present in the writings of the other two as well, but not in one place, in a concentrated manner. Nadvi's *Islam and the Modern World*, written in Arabic and first published in 1950 in Cairo, is a work of major importance.[24] Qutb himself wrote a significant foreword to its second Arabic edition of 1951, and it has gone into numerous editions in a number of languages, including English, French, Turkish, Persian, and of course Nadvi's own native Urdu. Those who wish to understand modern Islamic fundamentalism can hardly do better than starting with this work.

Nadvi's focus is on history as such, not just Islamic history. History has a beginning and an end. It begins with Creation, and ends with the Resurrection and the Last Judgement that leads to either Paradise or Hell. Between these two cosmic points lies the stuff of history, which is the struggle between those who disobey God's plan for history and those who willingly obey and carry it out in time and place. The first category of humans mentioned above constitutes the unbelievers. They are led by paganism of one kind or another, comprehensively called *jahiliyya*. The second category constitutes true Muslims. The highpoint of history was reached in seventh century A.D. when God revealed His final plans for history to the Prophet Muhammad. From then on the Koran and the *hadith*, together with the shariah, are the only repositories of the true knowledge of the laws of history. The *hijra*, the flight of Muhammad from Mecca to Medina, was the key event of history. It revealed that faith in God was not only a matter of private belief but also a matter of public expression and organization, to be defended by arms. Even today it symbolizes the perpetual fight that must be waged between forces of Islam and those of *jahiliyya*. Speaking of the crucial importance of the *higra*, Nadvi writes as follows: "So far Islam was no more than a religious movement, but henceforth it emerged as a complete civilization—refined, progressive, and full of glory."[25] After the *higra*, the leadership of all humanity was placed in the hands of true Muslims whose task in history become nothing other than turning humanity into "a single divinely-guided society."[26] In Nadvi's words, Muslims were to be the "shepherds of mankind."[27] Or as Qutb states in his foreword, "The teaching of Islam is essentially a teaching for leadership and world welfare." Their faith requires that they should shoulder "the responsibility of humanity at large" and take on "the trusteeship of the entire human race."[28] Assuming "world leadership" is part of the duty imposed by the revelation to Muhammad.

Muhammad and the first four Caliphs who followed him set an example of how world leadership should be exercised. First, they won a decisive victory over *jahiliyya*. Their period was the golden period of all history. Second, they brought the whole of Arabia, parts of the Eastern Roman Empire, and the Persian Empire under the rule of God. The period of Muhammad and the first four Caliphs, therefore, has a unique normative value for all periods of history. What came before has now become redundant. Thus in one fell sweep the great civilizations of Egypt, Greece, Israel, Rome, Persia, India, and China lost whatever meanings they might have had before the rise of Islam. After the rise of Islam they have lost their historical reasons for being. They have to be either eliminated or kept under strict Islamic control. This is the truth about them from the point of view of the fundamentalist interpretation of history.

It follows that the historical legitimacy and validity of pre-Islamic religions such as Judaism, Buddhism, Hinduism, and Christianity have also lapsed. The teachings of Moses and Jesus belong to a special category: they had their legitimacy and validity in their own times, and fundamentalist Islam readily concedes this. But it does not follow that historical Judaism and historical Christianity still enjoy any historical validity. With the rise of Islam, they have forfeited their right to continue. They are waiting to be surpassed and, if necessary, to be eliminated.

Unfortunately, however, even historical Islam is not immune to the ravages of *jahiliyya*. Greed and lust can corrupt even the just regime of Islam. Why this is so is not explained. The degeneration of the Islamic civilization is presented as a fact. Thus the caliphate degenerated into a hereditary system. Corrupt Muslim rulers—the sultans, the nabobs, and the like—sprang up wherever Islam spread. The cumulative result of this was that Muslims lost the divinely entrusted leadership of the world.

To add insult to injury a new form of *jahiliyya*, spreading from a de-Christianized, pagan West, wrested the leadership of the world from the Muslims. Modern science and technology, politics and economics, trade and commerce, helped the West here. What is more, the Muslims, instead of resisting Western modernity, became willing victims of its allurements. They began to introduce into their political and economic ideas elements taken from the West. Modernity only reinforced the natural tendency of *jahiliyya* towards human corruption.

According to the fundamentalist theory of history, Islam today finds itself facing two challenges. The first comes from without, from the West, in the form of materialism with its corresponding loss of "the spiritual sense." [29] The second comes from within corrupt Islam itself, attracted as it is by secularism, nationalism, capitalism, socialism, and the like. Moreover, an ever increasing number of Muslims, forgetting the meaning of the flight of the Prophet from Mecca to Medina, are now leaving Muslim societies and flocking to "corrupt" Western societies. A greater humiliation could hardly befall a people who are destined to be the divinely appointed "shepherds" or "trustees" of humanity.

From the point of view of the fundamentalist theology of history, then, the first task facing Muslims is to undergo conversion towards fundamentalism, that is, to become pure Muslims according to the rules of the normative period of history. Personal conversion is obviously necessary, and the *tablighi* movement, already alluded to, went part of the way in meeting this need. But from a historical perspective, and speaking for world Islam as a whole, Nadvi is obliged to adhere to the orthodox position. Islam must do more and revive the methods of jihad and *ijtihad* (prudence). [30]

Jihad is of two kinds, inner and outer. Inner jihad is self-purification and total submission to God. The outer jihad is the public activity of resisting those who resist God's rule. "The law of the enforcement," writes Nadvi, that Muslims have to implement, was brought into the world by the Prophet. "Opposition to this Law will not cease as long as the world endures. There will always be some force or other to resist and to reject it. Jihad, is therefore, an eternal phase of human life. It may take various forms, one of which is war, which may sometimes be the highest form of it to take."[31]

To fight modern *jahiliyya* effectively it is necessary to know both the Koran and the philosophies of *jahiliyya* itself. The fundamentalist has to know, for example, what economic "pantheism" and pansexualism (the philosophy that teaches that "nothing exists except sex and hunger") mean.[32] To drive home the point that the West is spiritually bankrupt, Nadvi uses the testimony of such critics of the West as C. E. M. Joad and Alexis Carrel, names hardly remembered in the West today.[33] To secular knowledge should be added the power of inner spiritual regeneration. Muslims must return to their sources. Together with spiritual renewal, they should acquire educational, scientific, industrial, and military strength. They must make themselves independent of the West and regain "intellectual superiority" and "world leadership for Islam."[34]

Nadvi concludes his analysis of world history by reflecting on the role that the Arabs have played in the past, and ought to play in the future. This is all the more striking, considering it is an Indian Muslim who is writing this. As Nadvi sees it, Arabs have a special place in God's plan for history. The revelation, and with it the laws of history and the trusteeship of humanity, is first entrusted to them. It is imperative that they should wake up from their present lethargy, and resume their "martial and manly spirit" and regain leadership of the Muslim world. The references to the need to combine economic, technological, military, and political powers are highly significant. They also cast a dark shadow on the notion of jihad. How are the Arabs to wrest leadership from the West and to lead the Islamic world, except, at some point, with the help of outer jihad? Inner purification may be sufficient in certain societies under certain conditions. But taking history as a whole, inner purity without the readiness to engage in outer jihad is not enough.

This idea comes out clearly in Nadvi's passing analysis of Mahatma Gandhi. Gandhi is the only non-Muslim, other than Moses and Jesus, of whom he speaks approvingly. But compared to the Prophet's "methodology," Gandhi's methodology was defective. According to Nadvi, Gandhi depended on the voluntary cooperation of individuals and societies. He had set two moral objects before himself—nonviolence and the removal of untouchability. Admirable though these objects were, he could not produce "that fundamental change in the minds of his people, which is essential to the success of a moral movement." This was because his approach was different from that of the prophets—"the only sure and successful way of bringing about a radical change for the better in the religious and social affairs of humanity at large."[35]

What is Nadvi hinting at here? Who was the prophet whose methodology brought about permanent and radical changes in both religion and polity? It could not have been Moses or Jesus, because their methodologies, according to the fundamentalists, were time and place bound. The only prophet whose methodology has permanent and universal historical value is of course Muhammad. And he accomplished what he did with the help not only of spiritual means, but also of military means.

There is a strange similarity between Nadvi's and Machiavelli's analyses of the methodology of prophets. The latter had famously declared that all the armed prophets win and unarmed prophets lose.[36] Innovators who do not have the support of arms ultimately fail. For innovations to be lasting, people have to be changed *by force*. Mere advocacy produces no lasting results. Seen from this perspective, Gandhi appears to be failed innovator. According to Nadvi, Gandhi failed, not because he lacked a spiritual vision, but because he lacked arms. Only if he had *forced* his followers to be nonviolent, could his nonviolence have succeeded. Such seems to be the twisted fundamentalist reading of Gandhi.

Even Nadvi has to defend the necessity of armed support of religious causes. Exceptions may be possible. But in this case, as in others, exceptions only prove the rule, which is that belief without arms cannot last long. Such is the chilling conclusion of the Muslim fundamentalist analysis of history.

The Doctrine of *Jahiliyya*

Belief in the doctrine of *jahiliyya* is a *conditio sine qua non* of Muslim fundamentalism. It enables the fundamentalist to divide the world into two warring camps (the believers and the unbelievers), to appropriate God exclusively for themselves, and to generate the necessary motivational force to fight the unbelievers. Though Mawdudi and Nadvi recognized its importance for Islamic revivalism, it is Qutb who gave it the most elaborate and closest attention. His three books—*Milestones, Islam the Religion of the Future,* and *This Religion of Islam*—remain indispensable sources of information here. And Roxanne L Euben's *Enemy in the Mirror* is the best available sustained study of Qutb.[37]

Jahiliyya is the moral and spiritual condition of rebellion against God. Not God as such, it must be pointed out, but the God of the Koran. It is therefore a strictly Koranic doctrine, even though it is paraded as enjoying universal validity. Rebellion and disobedience against any divine mandate are presented as an aspect of the unregenerate human condition. *Jahiliyya* is a sort of original sin— something that will always be there, and something that should always be fought against. Under its influence humans seek to appropriate for themselves what truly belongs to God, and God only, namely, the sovereignty over things, persons, and peoples.[38] It is this illegitimate appropriation that enables some humans to gain mastery over others and create conditions of tyranny and inequality.[39] It affects our thought systems also, so much so, that under its influence, human thought is given "the status of a god."[40] All the injustices in the world are ultimately traceable to *jahiliyya.* And Islam was created to fight precisely this fundamental evil.

Thanks to this doctrine, Qutb is able to divide societies into Islamic and *jahili* societies.[41] The first is nourished by divine wisdom, and the second, by the cravings of human desires. *Jahili* societies are those that do not submit to the God of the Koran with respect to their beliefs, ideas, laws, and modes of worship.[42] On the basis of this definition, he is able to present a remarkable list of such societies. First, there are the communist societies (he was writing in the 1960s). Then there are the idolatrous societies of India, Japan, the Philippines, and Africa. They are followed by Jewish and Christian societies. Last but not least, there are "the so-called Muslim societies" that are attracted to such things as modern social, economic, and political philosophies.[43] Special attention is given to the societies of the West, notably America. They are morally exhausted; they live on the fast-vanishing capital of Christianity; they practice the new paganism of material success, sexual excess, and compulsive con-

sumption. As witnesses for the prosecution, he summons such figures as Alexis Carrel (a favourite of all three of our fundamentalists)
and, *mirabile dictu*, John Foster Dullés himself, a former American
secretary of state. Carrel's *Man the Unknown* and Dulles's *War or
Peace* are given some forty pages of careful scrutiny.[44] Qutb agrees
with Dulles: the FBI cannot save the West; only a spiritual regeneration could. But the West is too bankrupt morally and spiritually to
bring that about. Into this moral and spiritual vacuum, argues Qutb,
fundamentalist Islam should step in; only it has the necessary moral
and spiritual resources to meet the West's needs.

To fight the forces of *jahiliyya* Islam must become not only a
system of beliefs but one of action and not a source of a deeply felt,
aesthetic experience. The introduction of aesthetics into Islam, he
believed, would add to the motivational force of the believers and
would prepare them for martyrdom.[45]

Given the doctrine of *jahiliyya*, it is not possible to have any
peaceful coexistence between fundamentalist Islam and the rest, including moderate Islam. It therefore becomes the foremost duty of
the fundamentalists to depose *jahiliyya* wherever it is found.[46] Only
one of the two can survive, not both: either Islam lives or *jahiliyya*
lives. Fundamentalism cannot accept "a situation which is half-
Islam and half *Jahiliyya*."[47] Dialogue between the fundamentalists
and the rest is forbidden. "The chasm between Islam and *Jahiliyya*
is great, a bridge is not to be built across it so that the people on the
two sides may mix with each other, but only so that the people of
Jahiliyya may come over to Islam."[48] The dialogical possibilities
being absent, the only meaningful contact that the fundamentalists
can have with moderate Muslims and non-Muslims is confrontation
and violence. Hence the need to rethink the doctrine of jihad.

Jihad Modernized

Making jihad a part of the current international conflicts is one of
Islamic fundamentalism's more sinister achievements. The person
responsible for initiating the trend was Mawdudi. Qutb and Bin
Laden only took his lead one step further by linking it with martyrdom and suicidal terror.

The motive that moved Mawdudi, as we have already noted, was his Indian experience, including Hindu phobia. It is no accident that his influential treatise on jihad first appeared in 1927 in an Indian weekly, the *Al-Jamiat*. In it he sought to make jihad legitimate and respectable for the times.[49] This step was needed since jihad had not been resorted to by any Muslim state since the nineteenth century. Within Indian Islam itself there were those who thought that the faith had to become more peaceful and that jihad better be dropped. Others felt that it should be treated as a historic relic that made sense in the past, but not in the present or the future. Mawdudi was reacting to these internal Islamic questionings. In 1939 he followed his first book on jihad with a second one, *Jihad in Islam*, in which the same argument was made but more succinctly.

Mawdudi starts with the assertion that Islam is a world revolutionary movement promoting radical monotheism. It was revolutionary in the seventh century, and it must remain so in the twentieth. Being revolutionary meant (and here he betrays his indebtedness to Marx) seeking "to alter the social order of the whole world and rebuild it in conformity with its own tenets and ideals."[50] In order to achieve this Islam needed a vanguard party. The *Jamaat i Islami*, as noted already, was to be that party. And jihad was nothing other than "that revolutionary struggle" which that party was to bring into play to achieve Islam's revolutionary objective.[51] The scope of this struggle was to be humanity-wide. For Islam wished "to destroy all states and governments anywhere on the face of the earth" that were opposed to it: "Islam required the earth—not just a portion, but the whole planet."[52] Jihad also sought to change "the outlook of the people" and to initiate "a mental revolution among them through speech or writing." To alter the old social system and to establish a new one, "by the power of the sword" was jihad. To expend goods and exert physically for this cause was also jihad.[53] Jihad involved a process of "destruction and reconstruction, revolution, and reform" affecting not just one nation or a group of people, but all humanity." And the revolutionary party that would carry out such a program was called *Hizb Allah* in the Koran.[54]

Mawdudi makes it clear that jihad is not war but struggle. War, a secular activity, is between states; its motive is material—economic, political, territorial, etc. Jihad, a religious activity, is not between states, but between the universal Islamic *umma* and the forces of *jahiliyya*, wherever they are to be found, whether among Muslims or non-Muslims. It had nothing to do with territorial gain, but everything to do with regime change in favor of the shariah. For practical reasons, however, regime change was best achieved in one's own country first—Pakistan or Egypt, for example. Once that was achieved, the experiment could be repeated elsewhere.

Jihad therefore had to be both offensive and defensive, simultaneously. Offensive, because the vanguard party assaulted the rule of its opponents. It had to be defensive, because the vanguard party had to acquire the necessary power in order to capture power.[55]

Mawdudi was careful to point out that jihad forbade the unnecessary shedding of blood. Islam allowed only for "the minimum essential" sacrifice of life and property. But he also stated that jihad was the "greatest sacrifice in the way of God" for in it a man sacrificed not only his own life and property but destroyed those of others also.[56] It is unlikely that he foresaw that a modernized revolutionary jihad could become both suicidal and homicidal simultaneously. All the same, his writings on jihad, as John Esposito rightly points out, had "unforeseen consequences."[57] In any case, Mawdudi helps to throw useful light on Bin Laden's two declarations: "The Declaration of War against the Americans Who Occupy the Land of the Two Holy Mosques" (1996) and "The Declaration of the World Islamic Front for Jihad against the Jews and the Crusaders" (1998).

The Fundamentalist Theory of the State

Islamic fundamentalism has developed its own theory of the state, and here too the seminal thinker is Mawdudi. His *Political Theory of Islam*, published in India in 1939, still remains an important source of information.[58]

Without a shariah state it is impossible for fundamentalism to carry out its mission in the world. Faith is so closely tied to the state, that when the state fails, the faith falters. So what kind of a state is the fundamentalist Islamic state? First of all, it is modeled on the state that operated in the first decades of Islam in the seventh century A.D. It is therefore "the very antithesis of secular Western democracy."[59] The reason is not far to seek. For modern democracy rests on the theory of popular sovereignty. This to the fundamentalist is nothing but a *jahili* doctrine. For sovereignty belongs to God, and God alone. Any theory that thinks otherwise is un-Islamic. Political power is vested in the entire Muslim community—the *umma*. The Caliph, or the Amir, is only God's viceroy. The power that the Caliph exercises is the delegated power of the *umma*. In this sense Islam, according to Mawdudi, is a "theodemocracy."[60]

It follows that Muslim monarchies, Muslim nation-states, and Muslim states based on socialism, etc., are all un-Islamic; they need to be overthrown and replaced by strict shariah states. An Islamic state cannot have such "accursed methods" of Godless democracy as multiparty elections and assemblies.[61] Its laws must be based on the shariah, the divine law. The traditional *hudud laws*, the laws of "divine limitation" as they are called, must be reintroduced. Thus property rights must be limited by the obligation to pay *zakat* (poor dues). Family laws must put limits on women regarding their dress, status vis-à-vis their husbands, etc. The "retaliatory laws"—the laws that demand such things as cutting off the hands for theft, stoning for adultery, etc.—are all unchangeable, and must be restored.[62]

It follows that the first task of Islamic fundamentalism is to bring about regime changes in existing Muslim societies. Dynastic rule must end; so must the Muslim nation-states, not to mention Muslim socialist or secular states. The Taliban state came closest to Mawdudi's idea of an Islamic state. It had an Amir and a council; its laws were all in conformity with the shariah. And it was ready to recruit volunteers from the entire *umma* for the purpose of training them for jihad, whether in the United States or Chechnya or Kashmir or the Philippines. The Taliban and al-Qaeda are the forerunners of things to come.

It is obvious that the theory of the Islamic state poses more problems to existing Muslims states than it does to non-Muslim states— unless the latter have significant Muslim populations. It is no secret that the fundamentalist theory of the state is both an embarrassment and a threat to moderate Muslim states everywhere. At the very least, it seeks to create conditions of civil unrest if not civil war, as is the case in Afghanistan and Algeria. It also puts the moderates on the defensive, for the latter do not have a counter theory that is rooted in Islamic principles—which raises the question of whether it is possible for them to come up with an alternative to fundamentalism that is theoretically legitimate. Any introduction of modern ideas into Islamic theory is open to the accusation of introducing elements of *jahiliyya* into Islam.

The fundamentalist theory of the state can foment not only civil unrest but also apply blackmail. It can blackmail moderate Muslims for being insufficiently Islamic. The moderates find themselves unable either to fight back or to offer an alternative.

The possibility of blackmail places moderate Muslim politicians in an awkward position. Often they, like Benazir Bhutto, are forced to curry favor with the fundamentalists in order to make short-term political gains, even though they themselves may not believe in fundamentalism. As they lack a solid theory, they are obliged to vacillate opportunistically between supporting and opposing them. In doing so, they betray the embarrassing theoretical poverty of the moderates.

To conclude, we have examined four basic elements of modern Islamic fundamentalism—theories of history, *jahiliyya*, jihad and the state—all interacting with one another. Fundamentalism sees itself as a revolutionary force, even though its gaze is fixed on the past. It brooks no opposition nor is it interested in dialogue. Given this, it has either to exhaust itself as all revolutionary forces tend to do, or be stopped by forces, both moral and physical, external to it.

PART III—THE IDEOLOGY OF *HINDUTVA*

Hindutva (hinduness) is an ideology of Hindu ethnic nationalism that seeks to transform India into an exclusively Hindu nation. It also seeks to make the Indian state the instrument of realizing its goals. Its ultimate end is the revival of Hindu greatness, but the means it uses is, unfortunately, the suppression of India's minorities. The choice of such a means threatens India's religious pluralism and political liberalism, a state of affairs that Gandhi, Nehru, and the other founders of modern India had so laboriously, and so successfully, built over the last century. From the West it takes its theory of power, but rejects its humanism. Inasmuch as it is an ideology directed against minorities, it weakens India's internal stability and jeopardizes its external peace with Muslim Pakistan and Muslim Bangladesh, and the predominantly Buddhist Sri Lanka.

The ideology of *hindutva* was first articulated by Vinay Damodar Savarkar (1883–1966) in 1923. It was further refined in 1939 by Madhav Sadashiv Golwalkar (1902–1973). Its organizational support system called the Rashtriya Swayamsevak Sangh (the RSS) was created in 1925 by Keshav Baliram Hedgewar (1889–1940). The RSS is not a political party but an organ of civil society that attempts to create militancy among extremist Hindus. This it hopes to achieve by promoting solidarity among the castes, a martial spirit among the youth, and a confrontational psychology against the minorities. In 1964 the RSS spawned the Vishva Hindu Parishad (the VHP)—a pan Hindu organization representing the interests of the princely, business, and priestly classes, with financial support coming from the extremist elements in the Hindu diaspora in the United States, Great Britain, Canada, and elsewhere. The Bharatiya Janata Party (the BJP), founded in 1980, is *hindutva*'s political arm. At the present time, it holds power at the federal level as well as in some provinces. The RSS, the VHP, and the BJP, taken together, form a family of organizations, a *sangh parivar* ("a family compact"), as it is called, sharing a division of social and political labour between them. In what follows I shall give a brief account of *hindutva* as expounded by Savarkar and Golwalkar. It will become apparent that the ideology of *hindutva* parallels the ideology of Muslim fundamentalism of Mawdudi, and that both these ideologies in their respective ways are seriously undermining moderation in politics and toleration in religion, which was the substance of Gandhi's political philosophy.

Savarkar's Theory of Hindutva

The basic text of the theory of *hindutva* is Savarkar's *Hindutva: Who Is a Hindu?*[63] A brief account of the author's ideological background is necessary for an understanding of the book's argument. Already as a young man, he was actively involved in an underground terrorist organization called Abhinav Bharat. In 1906 he went to London to study law, but was soon distracted by the revolutionary activities of the Indian expatriates living there. During this period he had met Gandhi who was visiting London from South Africa. They had many discussions on Indian politics, nationalism, and the question of Indian identity. Even in those early days they agreed to disagree on all these issues. In July 1909 he was implicated in the assassination of Sir William Curzon-Wyllie, a senior Indian civil servant. He was arrested and sent to the penal colony of the Andaman Islands and later to a jail in India. And while in jail, he published anonymously, *Hindutva, Who Is a Hindu?*, his political manifesto.

A highly gifted intellectual, he was widely read in modern European history and politics. While in London he had published, also anonymously, *The Indian War of Independence of 1857*, an incendiary interpretation of the Indian Mutiny.[64] There was no doubt in his mind that only an armed Indian uprising could bring colonialism to an end. After his release from jail, he was made president, for five years (1937–1942), of the Hindu Maha Sabha, the party of Hindu ethnic nationalism, opposed to both Gandhi's Indian National Congress, the party of Indian civic nationalism, and to Jinnah's All-India Muslim League, the party of Muslim religious nationalism. The famous trio—Savarkar, Gandhi, and Jinnah—presented to the public three conflicting visions of Indian identity. Declining health forced Savarkar to leave active politics. Though suspected by some of having an indirect hand in Gandhi's assassination in 1948, he was never charged with any crime. To the end he remained convinced that only Hindu ethnic nationalism backed by overwhelming military strength could preserve India as a nation. "Hinduize all politics, and militarize Hindudom" was his favorite mantra.[65]

Hindutva, Who Is a Hindu? is part reflection on India's past and part a manifesto for its future. As a reflection on Indian history, it takes the reader three millennia back, to the time of the Aryan invasion of India. The Aryans had developed a magnificent civilization that flourished for several centuries. Their political sway extended from the Himalayas to the seas. As the great epics the *Ramayana* and the *Mahabharata* attest, India's institutions were Hindu and vigorous, the people prosperous, and the rulers both just and warlike.

Into this idyllic state of affairs Buddhism sowed for the first time seeds of national decline and decay. Though respectful of the Buddha and his "wheel of the law of righteousness,"[66] Savarkar had nothing but contempt for historical Buddhism, with its monasticism, pacifism, and universal love. In his judgement, it had sapped India's military vigor and had left the people ill prepared to meet "the strange bible of fire and steel" of foreign invaders. People got tired of "the mumbo jumbo of universal brotherhood" of Buddhism, while invader after invader ravaged the country "that had in utter confidence clad in a *Bhikku's* (mendicant's) dress, changed her sword for the rosary and had taken to the vows of *ahimsa* and non-violence."[67] India, under Buddhism, had lost the capacity to maintain even internal peace.

Then came the Muslims, and with them began "the conflict of life and death."[68] However, the spirit of *hindutva* began to reappear in the Sikhs, the Rajputs, and, above all, the Marathas.[69] However, with the defeat of the last group in 1818 in the battle of Panipat, the ancient *hindutva* was once again extinguished.

British rule forced the Hindus to rethink their identity and reform their institutions. The caste and the maharaja systems were no longer suitable for modern life. It became clear that a modern form of *hindutva*, based of the triple foundations of race (*jati*), nation (*rashtra*), and civilization (*sanskriti*), was needed if India was to take its rightful place in the world.[70] This insight led Savarkar to define an Indian as one who possessed *hindutva*, a quality inherited by birth enabling him or her to claim India to be both the fatherland and the holy land.[71] To be an Indian, it was not enough to have India as the fatherland. It was also necessary to have India as the holy land. Thus in his thought the idea of the holy becomes inseparable from the ideas of the land and the nation. Only if nationalism could be grounded in the idea of the holy could national cohesion be guaranteed. "The ideal conditions, therefore, under which a nation can attain perfect solidarity and cohesion would, other things being equal, be found in the case of those people who inhabit the land they adore, the land of whose forefathers is also the land of their Gods and Angels, of Seers and Prophets; the scenes of whose history, are also the scenes of their mythology."[72] *Hindutva* is supposed to produce in its adherents a certain mystical bond with the land. It is so mystical, that it definitely excludes Indian Muslims and Indian Christians from being part of the Indian nation. The reason is clear: their holy lands lie outside India. Their presence in India would pollute the nation. They therefore deserve to be treated as the new untouchables of Savarkar's India.

In addition to the idea of the holy, Savarkar employs the idea of a founding people as being essential to India. A nation, he writes, "requires a foundation to stand upon, and the essence of the life of a nation is the life of that portion of its citizens whose interests and history and aspirations are most closely bound with the land and who thus provide the real foundation to the structure of their national state."[73] This, he points out, is true of Turkey where Muslims, not the Armenians, are the founding people. It is also true of the United States, where the Anglo-Saxons occupy that privileged position. And in India, the Hindus have no choice but to consider themselves as its founding people. They constitute "the foundation, the bed rock, the reserved forces of the Indian state."[74]

The idea of civilization is as equally important for a nation as that of the holy. Savarkar defines civilization as "the expression of the mind of man . . . ; the account of what man has made of matter." "The story of the civilization of a nation is the story of its thoughts, its actions and its achievements. Literature and art tells us of its thoughts; history and social institutions, of its actions and achievements."[75] Epics and their heroes, architecture, philosophies, laws and rituals, feasts and festivals, places of pilgrimage and worship— all these are the component parts of a nation's civilization. In India these were created by the Hindus, and therefore the latter should remain their exclusive guardians.

By focusing on race (*jati*), the holy, and civilization, Savarkar has produced a very powerful set of criteria of national inclusion and national exclusion. He does not see that the ideas of "the holy" and "civilization" when properly understood have the power to transcend the limitations of *jati*. On the contrary he interprets them as being bound and limited by the idea of *jati*. This has disastrous implications for the idea of holy as expressed in traditional Indian spirituality. He makes it appear as though the revelations that occurred at the Sinai, Galilee, and Mecca are in irresolvable conflict with those that occurred along the Ganges. Savarkar's theology—if we can call it that—is wholly bound by his nationalism. The holy is merely a principle of social and national solidarity, and not something that opens up the mind and the heart, much less something that elevates the spirit. Given such a notion of the holy, it is not surprising that *hindutva* can only dispose its adherents to attack, not conciliate, religious minorities.

The fact is that the theory of *hindutva* is in reality a theory of national power that uses the idea of the holy instrumentally and for punitive purposes. That Savarkar is deluded by his vision of the grandeur that *hindutva* is supposed to bring becomes apparent towards the end of his argument. If only extremists Hindus could achieve solidarity along the lines of race, nation, and civilization, he claimed, they would be able "to dictate their terms to the whole world. A day will come when mankind will have to face the force."[76]

Golwalkar's Theory of Nationalism

Golwalkar, a follower of Savarkar, added two elements to the ideology of *hindutva*. First, he narrowed the broader concept of "the holy" to the more concrete reality of the Hindu "religion." And second, he underscored the neofascist tendencies inherent in *hindutva* and the RSS.

In this basic work, *We or Our Nationhood Defined*, published in 1939, the same year that Mawdudi published his *Political Theory of Islam and Jihad in Islam*, he argued that in India "nation" means "the Hindu nation and naught else."[77] The term "Hindu" in the concept "Hindu nation" gives the "religion" of Hinduism a new meaning. Religion here is not so much a matter of belief as of birth, something that one inherits with the transmission of life itself. Hindus are born, not made. "We are Hindus even before we emerge from the womb of our mother," writes Golwalkar. "We are therefore born as Hindus." Others are born "as simple unnamed human beings."[78] Religion for a Hindu, asserts Golwalkar, is not a matter of choice; it is something that one is born with, something, for that reason, one may not change.

This postulated connection of religion to nation explains to some extent the national phobia about religious conversions. The loyalty of a convert cannot be trusted. Conversion is a form of cultural treason. Such a view of religion poses difficulties for Muslims, Christians, and Buddhists, all of whom recognize the legitimacy of conversion. In Golwalkar's absurd logic, they have no place in the nation, unless they *convert* to Hinduism. Otherwise they should remain "wholly subordinated to the Hindu nation," having no privileges, "not even citizen's rights."[79] Jews and Parsis are welcome as guests, but Buddhists must remain "traitors to mother society and mother religion."[80] After all, it was the Buddhism of Kandahar, once a province of India, that made it easy for Muslims to Islamize it completely.[81]

Given the natural connection of religion to nation, it is unnatural to create a multireligious state. Golwalkar likens such a state to a new animal, one with the head of a monkey, the legs of a bullock, and the body of an elephant.[82] It is *hindutva's* responsibility to see to it that modern India does not turn out to be such a grotesque creature.

The second element that he added to *hindutva* was its neofascist orientation. *We or Our Nationhood Defined* spoke approvingly of Nazi nationalism. "To keep up the purity of the race and its culture, Germany shocked the world by purging the country of the Semitic race—the Jews. . . . Germany has also shown how well nigh impossible it is for races and cultures having differences going to the root, to be assimilated into one united whole—a good lesson for us in Hindusthan to learn and profit by."[83]

As the Raj Guru of the RSS, from 1940 to 1973, Golwalkar presided over its highly questionable activities. Following Gandhi's assassination in 1948, the RSS was banned and 20,000 of its members and Golwalkar himself were arrested. As Nehru, the prime minister, had warned already in 1947, the RSS did pose a neofascist threat to India. He wrote to the heads of the provincial governments that he had "a great deal of evidence" to show that the RSS was an organization that was "in the nature of a private army," proceeding "on the strictest Nazi lines."[84] The RSS was banned again in 1975, this time together with *Jamaat i Islami*, and again in 1992, in connection with anti-Muslim riots that resulted in the demolition of the famous mosque in Ayodhya. And of course it was accused of being heavily involved (together with the VHP), in the more recent riots in Gujarat that saw the burning of churches and mosques and the killing of hundreds of innocent civilians.

I conclude this brief introduction to *hindutva*, as expounded by Savarkar and Golwalkar, by asking what is ominous about it. The first thing ominous about it is its contempt for liberal democracy, civic nationalism, and religious pluralism. It takes from the West its power politics without its deep humanism. Its readiness to use the power of the state to carry out its ideological ends is and ought to be alarming. The individual for these thinkers is subordinate to the state and the nation. All this smacks of neofascist tendencies. Secondly, *hindutva* scapegoats religious minorities, and is willing to punish them for being what they are. Thirdly, it deliberately distorts Indian history, especially the contributions that the Muslims and the Christians have made to India. It reads history as if the Taj Mahal and the Red Fort do not belong to Indian history. Fourthly, it distorts the Indian idea of the holy, especially its reflective and contemplative aspects. Instead of allowing the pursuit of the holy to do what it is supposed to do, namely, moderate the appetite for absolute power, it attempts to use it as an instrument of the pursuit of absolute power. Finally, it attempts to dismantle all that Gandhi and the other founders of modern India had built over the last hundred years. Its complicity in the demolition of the mosque in Ayodhya is symbolic of its desire to demolish Gandhi's India.

CONCLUSION

The foregoing introduction to the state of political philosophy in the most recent decades in China, India, and the Islamic world reveals the following.

China, despite its adherence to the Marxist worldview, appears to be open to a constructive dialogue with non-Marxist ideas. The Chinese Communist Party's legitimacy has been irrevocably tied to the promise of continuing economic growth, and the government has maintained an "open door policy" (*kaifang zhengce*) vis-à-vis foreign culture and investment so as to facilitate national economic development in the context of globalization. Even as the Party continues to struggle with the potentially pathological implications of Western materialism, it has not yet surrendered to the temptations of extreme cultural nationalism.

The India of *hindutva* and the fundamentalist Islamic world, on the other hand, are not open to a constructive dialogue with political ideas different from their own. They refuse to look upon political philosophy as a means of finding a common ground between themselves and their opponents. They compare philosophies other than their own only for apologetic ends, and to condemn and ridicule. The comparative study of political philosophy, in their case, does not lead to dialogue and peaceful co-existence.

It appears then that comparative political philosophy is not always and everywhere dialogical. While all dialogical political philosophy is comparative, not all comparative political philosophy is dialogical. Comparative political philosophy can become dialogical only when certain moral and political conditions are present. Fundamentalism and extremism prevent such conditions from arising. Because of this, violence remains for them their medium of communication with their opponents. This alas is borne out by the events of 9/11 and by what is happening now in Afghanistan, Kashmir, Chechnya, the Philippines, Indonesia, Palestine, and elsewhere.

NOTES

1. Anthony Parel, "The Comparative Study of Political Philosophy," A. Parel and R. C. Keith, eds., *Comparative Political Philosophy: Studies under the Upas Tree.* New Delhi: Sage, 1992, p. 20.
2. Jiang Zemin, "How to Attain What the 'Three Represents' Requires of Our Party under the New Historical Conditions," 25 January 2000, *On the "Three Represents."* Beijing: Foreign Languages Press, 2001, p. 12. In the new era, according to Jiang, the Party is to focus on representing the development of the advanced productive forces, advanced culture, and the fundamental interests of the broad masses of people in China.
3. For the debates on "combining law and li" (or law and decorum) see R. C. Keith, *China's Struggle for the Rule of Law.* London & New York: Macmillan and St. Martin's Presses, 1994, pp. 40, 43, 51.
4. Jiang Zemin, "Speech at the National Conference of Publicity Directors," *On "The Three Represents,"* pp. 162–63. For further analysis of the contemporary relation of the "rule of law" and "rule of virtue" see Randall Peerenboom, *China's Long March to the Rule of Law.* Cambridge: Cambridge University Press, 2002, pp. 224–25.
5. Jiang Zemin, "Promote the Develop of the Party's Workstyle, the Building of a Clean Government and the Fight against Corruption," 26 December 2000, in *The "Three Represents,"* p. 145.
6. Jiang Zemin, "Speech at the National Conference of Publicity Directors," in *On the "Three Represents,"* p. 158.
7. For discussion of the Falun Gong, morality, and the rule of law see R. C. Keith and Zhiqiu Lin, "The 'Falungong Problem': Politics and the Struggle for the Rule of Law in China," *The China Quarterly,* forthcoming article, scheduled for the September 2003 issue.
8. While "Westernization" includes bad phenomena such as hedonism, materialism, and egoism, "disintegration" seems specifically to invoke the replay of the West's cultural infiltration of Eastern Europe and the former Soviet Union. Jiang Zemin, "The New Situation and New Circumstances Facing Ideological and Political Work," *The "Three Represents,"* pp. 69, 74–75. It should be noted that the policy and ideology of "seeking the truth from the facts," nevertheless, allows China to at the same time assimilate "the outstanding cultural achievements of foreign countries" in so far as these help to build China's distinctive "socialist culture."
9. Jiang Zemin, "Speech at the National Conference of Publicity Directors," *The "Three Represents,"* p. 162.
10. Refer to Keith's discussion in the original edition of *Comparative Political Philosophy: Studies under the Upas Tree* on Mao as a "pragmatist" (*shijizhuyizhe*) who subscribed to the unity of theory and practice as contrasted with bourgeois "pragmatism" that presumes theory, or ideology, must be sacrificed to expediency in the process of modernization. Western critics began in the 1980s to associate new emphasis on the "four modernizations" and the economic reform and open door policies of Deng Xiaoping with the gutting of socialist ideology. See, for example, Maurice Meisner, "The Chinese Rediscovery of Karl Marx: Some

Reflects on Post-Maoist Chinese Marxism," *Bulletin of Concerned Asian Scholars*, vol. 17, no. 3, July–Sept., 1985, p. 5; and also Arif Dirlik, "Postsocialism? Reflections on Socialism with Chinese Characteristics," *Bulletin of Concerned Asian Scholars*, vol. 231, no. 1, 1989, p. 35.

11. R. C. Keith, "Mao Zedong and his Political Thought," Anthony Parel and Ronald C. Keith, eds., *Comparative Political Philosophy: Studies under the Upas Tree*. New Delhi: Sage, 1992, p. 103.

12. Jiang Zemin, "Hold High the Great Banner of Deng Xiaoping Theory for an All-Round Advancement of the Cause of Building Socialism with Chinese Characteristics into the 21st Century," 12 September 1997, *Beijing Review*, October 6–12, 1997, p. 14.

13. Jiang Zemin, "Constantly Making Innovations in Accordance with Practice," *On the "Three Represents,"* p. 59.

14. The newer emphasis on the "liberation" (*jiefang*) as distinct from the technological "development" (*fazhan*) of productive forces legitimized the Party focus on the social conditions that were seen as hampering the productive forces and on the related changes to social structure in the new era. See "Dialectics of Liberating, Developing Productive Forces," *Renmin ribao*, 18 September, 1992, p. 5 in FBIS-CHI-92–191, 1 October 1992, pp. 38–39. The distinction was incorporated into the Party's revised constitution of 18 October 1992. A key example of such structural change related to the 14 November 1992 CCP Central Committee Decision on Some Issues Concerning the Establishment of a Socialist Market Structure. For the first time the Party endorsed the principle that the market is "to play the fundamental role in resource allocations under macro-economic control by the state" (the text of the decision in the special insert of *Beijing Review*, November 22–28, 1993).

15. Jiang Zemin, "Hold High the Great Banner of Deng Xiaoping Theory for an All-Round Advancement of the Cause of Building Socialism with Chinese Characteristics into the 21st Century," pp. 19–20.

16. For further analysis of these formulations see R. C. Keith and Zhiqiu Lin, *Law and Justice in China's New Marketplace*. London: Palgrave/Macmillan, 2001, pp. 50–51.

17. For theory on "rights and interests" (*quanyi*) see Ronald C. Keith, "The New Relevance of 'Rights and Interests': China's Changing Human Rights Theories," *China Information*, Leiden, vol. 10, no. 2, Autumn, 1995, pp. 38–61, and Keith and Lin, *Law and Justice in China's New Marketplace*.

18. Jiang Zemin, "On the Three Represents Is the Essence of the Existence of Our Party . . . ," *On "The Three Represents,"* p. 18.

19. R. C. Keith, "Legislating Women and Children's Rights in the PRC," *The China Quarterly*, no. 149, March 1997, pp. 29–55.

20. Jonathan Hecht, "Can Legal Reform Foster Respect for Human Rights in China?" testimony before the Congressional Executive Commission on China, 11 April 2002, p. 2.

21. Jiang Zemin, "On the Three Represents Is the Essence of the Existence of Our Party . . . ," *On "The Three Represents,"* pp. 22–23.

22. On the anti-Hindu origins of Mawdudi's fundamentalism, see Seyyed Vali Reza Nasr, *Mawdudi and the Making of Islamic Revivalism*. New York: Oxford University Press, 1996; also his *The Vanguard of the Islamic Revolution: The Jamaat*

I Islami of Pakistan. Berkeley and Los Angeles: University of California Press, 1994.

23. On Nadvi's involvement in the *tablighi* movement, see Barbara D. Metcalf, "The Tablighi Jamaat in America and Europe," in Barbara D. Metcalf, *Making Muslim Space in North America and Europe.* Berkeley and Los Angeles: University of California Press, 1996, pp.110–27; and John King, "Tablighi Jamaat and the Deohandi Mosques in Britain," in Peter B. Clarke, ed., *New Trends and Developments in the World of Islam.* London: Luzac, 1994, pp. 75–91.

24. Nadvi, *Islam and the World.* Lucknow: Academy of Islamic Research and Publications, 1982 (1950), 7th edition.

25. Nadvi, *Islam and the World*, p. 85.

26. *Ibid.*, p. 75.

27. *Ibid.*, p. 83.

28. *Ibid.*, p. 1.

29. *Ibid.*, p. 158.

30. *Ibid.*, pp. 91–94.

31. *Ibid.*, pp. 92–93.

32. *Ibid.*, p. 137.

33. *Ibid.*, p. 150 ff.

34. *Ibid.*, p. 196.

35. *Ibid.*, p. 49, n 1.

36. Machiavelli, *The Prince*, ch. 6.

37. Qutb, *Milestones.* Beirut: The Holy Koran Publishing House, 1978 (1965); *The Religion of Islam.* Damascus: The Holy Koran Publishing House, 1977 (1962); Islam, *The Religion of the Future.* Damascus: The Holy Koran Publishing House, 1978 (1962); Roxanne L. Euben, *Enemy in the Mirror.* Princeton, NJ: Princeton University Press, 1999.

38. Qutb, *Milestones*, pp. 14–16.

39. *Ibid.*, p. 82.

40. *Ibid.*, p. 207.

41. *Ibid.*, pp. 207, 220, 230.

42. *Ibid.*, p. 148.

43. *Ibid.*, pp. 148–54.

44. Qutb, *Islam the Religion of the Future*, pp. 78–116.

45. Leonard Binder, *Islamic Liberalism.* Chicago: University of Chicago Press, 1988, "The Religious Aesthetic of Sayyid Qutb: A Non-Scriptural Fundamentalism," pp. 170–205, and Malise Ruthven, *A Fury for God: The Islamic Attack on America.* London: Granta, 2002, "The Aesthetics of Martyrdom," pp. 72–98, give very interesting, if somewhat overstated, accounts of this aspect of Qutb's thought.

46. Qutb, *Milestones*, p. 245.

47. *Ibid.*, p. 243.

48. *Ibid.*, p. 263.

49. For the importance of Mawdudi in reviving jihad for our times, see Gilles Kepel, *Jihad.* Cambridge, MA: 2002, pp. 32–36, passim; John L. Esposito, *Unholy War: Terror in the Name of Islam.* Oxford: Oxford University Press, 2002, pp. 54–56.

50. Mawdudi, *Jihad in Islam.* Damascus: The Holy Koran Publishing House, 1977 (Lahore, India, 1939), p. 5.

51. *Ibid.*
52. *Ibid.*, p. 6
53. *Ibid.*, p. 7.
54. *Ibid.*, p. 17.
55. *Ibid.*, p. 26.
56. Mawdudi, *Towards Understanding Islam*. Lahore: Idara Tarjuman-ul-Qurabm 1977, 17th ed., p. 120. This was first published in 1932, in Urdu, in India, and translated into practically all the Indian languages and English.
57. Esposito, *Unholy War*, p. 54.
58. Mawdudi, *Political Theory of Islam*. Lahore: Islamic Publications, 1976 (1939).
59. *Ibid.*, p. 23.
60. *Ibid.*, 24.
61. *Ibid.*, pp. 46–47.
62. *Ibid.*, pp. 28–31.
63. V. D. Savarkar, *Hindutva, Who Is a Hindu?* New Delhi: Bharti Sahitya Sadan, 6th ed., 1989 (1923).
64. Savarkar, *The Indian War of Independence 1857*. New Delhi: Rajdhani Granthagar, 1987 (1909).
65. *V. D. Savarkar: Historical Statements*. S. S. Savarkar and G. Joshi, eds. Bombay: Popular Prakashan, 1967, p. 1.
66. Savarkar, *Hindutva, Who Is a Hindu?*, p. 17.
67. *Ibid.*, p. 24.
68. *Ibid.*, 42.
69. *Ibid.*, pp. 52–70.
70. *Ibid.*, pp. 83–102.
71. *Ibid.*, p. 113.
72. *Ibid.*, 136.
73. *Ibid.*, p. 139.
74. *Ibid.*, p. 140.
75. *Ibid.*, p. 92.
76. *Ibid.*, p. 141.
77. Golwalkar, *We or Our Nationhood Defined*. Nagpur: Bharat Prakashan, 4th ed., 1947, (1939), p. 2
78. Golwalkar, *Bunch of Thoughts*, Bangalore: Jagarna Prakashan, 2nd ed., 1980, (1966), p. 156.
79. Golwalkar, *We or Our Nationhood Determined*, p. 56.
80. Golwalkar, *Bunch of Thoughts*, p. 145.
81. Golwalkar, *Bunch of Thoughts*, p. 145.
82. Ibid., pp. 197–98.
83. Golwalkar, *We or Our Nationhood Defined*, p. 43. On Golwalkar's German sources, see Christophe Jaffrelot, *The Hindu Nationalist Movement and Indian Politics*. New Delhi: Viking (and New York: Columbia University Press), 1996, pp. 53–55.
84. Cited in Jaffrelot, *The Hindu Nationalist Movement*, p. 87.

Preface

The study of substantive equivalence or parallelism in the development of different traditions of political philosophy is obviously a taxing intellectual exercise. Given the highly specialized training involved, few master one let alone several traditions. Also, university curriculum and scholarly research are in many cases rigidly compartmentalized along disciplinary and area study lines. If we put aside the Eurocentric tendency of contemporary philosophical inquiry, and look at non-European curriculum and research, there is no common understanding of the limits of 'Asia' or the 'Orient'. 'Area studies' focusing on tradition and modernity lack a strict international consistency as to which countries and cultures should be included in 'Asia' as opposed to 'Asia Minor', 'South Asia', 'East Asia', 'Northeast Asia', 'Southeast Asia'. Can we even agree on what the available traditions are?

Then there is a veritable mine of disciplinary and methodological biases which stands in the way of any scholar who rises to the challenge of comparison. Historians may protest that events are inevitably discrete. Social scientists will counsel caution as in the study of politics there are no dependable empirical experiments to be repeated at will in the great laboratory of society. And, of course, there are the great debates over the nature of the disciplines themselves; for example, we need only recall how Anthropology was convulsed by the issue of 'cultural relativism'.

The seminar on comparative political philosophy held by the University of Calgary once again raised the issue of 'cultural relativism'. Realizing our own limitations and fully cognizant of the inevitable reservations of the scholarly community, we, nevertheless, consciously decided to focus on equivalences rather than differences. We did so with the sense of caution suggested in the Chinese proverb, 'feeling for rocks on the bottom so as to cross the river', *mozhe shitou guo he*. In an elementary sense we are only just balancing ourselves on the first rock.

Parallel seminal concepts between traditions are indeed hard to establish but seminar participants often find that there are very inviting and suggestive comparisons to be made particularly in the light of the perilous transition between 'tradition' and 'modernity' and the commonality of human distress which characterizes such a transition.

The sub-title of this volume of essays focuses the reader's attention on the historical dilemma of cross-cultural understanding in the threatening context of modernity as conveyed in the legend of the Upas tree. Native Malaysians concocted an arrow poison which co-mingled strychnine and Upas latex. For a long time they withheld knowledge of this poisonous mix from the Europeans, and then they widely cultivated the myth that the tree was so toxic that it killed all that came near. The tree later underwent further metamorphosis as Gandhi took it as a symbol of the ruinous impact of modernity on the moral dimensions of social life.

Acknowledgements

We wish to thank Dr. Roger Gibbins, Head of the Department of Political Science, the University of Calgary, for meeting the cost of preparing this volume for publication; and Judi Powell of the same department for her expert editorial and typing assistance.

For permission to include K.J. Shah's article, 'Of *Artha* and the *Arthasastra*', in this volume, we thank the Indian Institute of Economic Growth and the Editor, *Contributions to Indian Sociology*, Vol. 15 (1–2), (1981).

Anthony J. Parel
Ronald C. Keith

1 The Comparative Study of Political Philosophy

Anthony J. Parel

Scholarship in the area of political philosophy has necessarily come to mean the study of modern western political philosophy, especially liberalism/utilitarianism and socialism. It is as if these are not just products of the *modern West*, but that they are products of universal reason itself. But no one can seriously doubt that these, in their origin and content, are products of modernity, which, in turn, is a product of modern western civilization. Comprising of studies of discrete political philosophies, this volume aims at stimulating interest in the comparative study of political philosophy.

There is mounting evidence which suggests that the claims of universality made by modern western political philosophy are being questioned by other cultures, or at least by the significant representatives of these cultures. Indeed, in the West itself the claims of modern western philosophy are being questioned by those who challenge the assumptions underlying modernity. Such critical inquiry makes the comparative study of political philosophies both opportune and intellectually satisfying.

But what is comparative political philosophy? Political philosophy, as Leo Strauss states, is the quest for 'knowledge' of the political phenomena—'knowledge' as distinct from 'opinion', or mere ideology or social science theory. Such 'knowledge' is the product, ultimately, of rational reflection on the data of *insight* and *experience*. Each culture has its own basic insights about what constitutes the good life and the good regime; it has its own peculiar experiences which give institutional and intellectual expression to these insights. A political philosophy emerges as a result of the interaction between such insights and experiences.

But the emergence of political philosophy is conditioned by the cultural and linguistic traditions within which it occurs. And these traditions tend to produce, among other things, texts which are recognizably political, that is, texts which consciously attempt to develop a philosophic understanding of the theory and practice of governance. A proper study of such texts, taken in their historical and intellectual contexts, would reveal that they contain differences as well as similarities with respect to their key ideas and assumptions. Further reflection and analysis would reveal that the similarities are more significant than the differences and as such would reveal the presence of what Eric Voegelin has called the phenomenon of 'equivalences'. Thus, to take just a few examples from a lengthy list, the Aristotelian *politikos* and the Confucian *junzi*, Indian *dharma* and the pre-modern western notion of 'natural justice', the Islamic prophet-legislator and the Platonic philosopher-king, may usefully be considered as instances of 'equivalences'. Producing a long list is not our aim here; rather it is to suggest that it is the presence of such 'equivalences' that makes the comparative study of political philosophy possible. It follows that such a study is nothing other than the process, first, of identifying the 'equivalences', and second, of understanding their significance. Such 'equivalences', if and when they are found, would both deepen one's understanding of one's own tradition and engender understanding and respect for the traditions of others.

In the present volume we have selected four such traditions—western, Chinese, Indian, and the Islamic. The list is by no means exhaustive. We focus on these four political cultures as, in our opinion, they hold the key to the task of identifying points of equivalences. We limited ourselves to these for reasons of space and expertise available to us. Knowledge of the languages, histories, theologies, philosophies, and jurisprudences of more than one tradition is needed if one is to engage fruitfully in the comparative study of political philosophies. The task is formidable and we are conscious that our effort here is more pioneering than conclusive.

The strategy we have followed is to select significant representatives from each tradition, representatives who express their *insights* in the context of their own *experiences*. Thus from the pre-modern West we have taken Plato and Aristotle, Augustine and Aquinas; from pre-modern China, Confucius; from India, Kautilya; and from Islam, Farabi. This is followed by a consideration of the philosophies of those who attempted either to update or subvert the tradition of their political philosophy. Thus from the West we have taken Hegel and Marx, who are of course subverters of the classical and medieval traditions of political thought in the West. The exclusion of other great political thinkers from the modern West, Machiavelli, Hobbes, Locke, Rousseau, Bentham, and Mill for example, may seem arbitrary and unfair. However their omission, in our present context (and only in that context), may be excused for the reason that Hegel and Marx bring to culmination an important strand in modern political thought, namely, the flowering of modernity, a process which these others had set in motion. For it is modernity that divides western political philosophy into the classical and medieval on the one hand, and the modern on the other. Internal differences within modern western political philosophy, however sharp they may be, are less significant than differences between modern western political philosophy and classical-medieval political philosophy taken as a whole.

But here a problem presents itself. We have noted that modernity has subverted the classical and medieval traditions of western political philosophy. If this is the case, surely it invites a further comment. For modernity challenges and attempts to subvert the political philosophies of other cultures as well. The reason is that modernity is opposed to tradition as such, not just the western tradition. For modernity is at home only in the present: it is a philosophy of the present—a moving target no doubt. Not only does modernity consider tradition as 'oppressive', 'authoritarian', and/or 'aristocratic', but it considers all tradition as devoid of *present* relevance. This conclusion is reached thanks to the philosophies of history, which are embraced as the pseudo metaphysics of modern western political thought. Thus modern political philosophy leads to the notion that philosophical thought regarding political phenomena should result in the creation of the universal homogeneous state or the universal classless society. Given this, no comparative study of political philosophy is possible within the framework of modern western political philosophy. Comparisons are possible only between mutually recognized philosophical traditions. Comparative political philosophy, as we have already stressed, assumes the validity of cultural pluralism, and philosophical pluralism. Modern western political philosophy, on the other hand, is unable to recognize the validity of the pre-modern philosophical traditions, eastern as well as western.

Now it is the anti-traditional and universalistic pretensions or assumptions of modern western philosophy that a Gandhi or a Khomeini questions. Mao attempted to domesticate Marxism within the Chinese tradition, but the outcome is still rather in doubt.

Not that within the modern West itself modernity has gone unchallenged. Two significant tendencies can be noticed in contemporary western political philosophy: One attempts to criticize certain elements of modernity—domination for example—without seriously questioning the epistemological and ontological foundations of modernity itself. The philosophies of Habermas and Foucault belong to this category. They attempt to cure the patient, but their ministrations seem only to prolong the agony. In the meantime, modernity has begotten post-modernity, and only the future can tell what post-modernity is going to beget.

The other tendency is to criticize modernity where it is vulnerable, viz., in its inability to constitute itself into a tradition and its unwillingness or disinterest or arrogance to pay attention to non-western traditions in political philosophy. The philosophies, for example, of Alasdair MacIntyre and Charles Taylor, not to mention Eric Voegelin, may fall within this category. They attempt to look outside modernity itself, for at least some of the available insights. In other words, in the West too there is at present a school of thought that is attempting to update western political philosohy with reference to a tradition.

Though there is criticism of modernity in the West itself, it is not this element of western political philosophy that has had an impact on the Chinese, Indian, and Islamic political philosophies. What has influenced them is western modernity, mostly in the form of liberalism or socialism. Accordingly we see India, China, and Islam responding to modernity either in the manner of accepting it or, conversely, challenging it. We believe Gandhi, Mao, and Khomeini are the most significant political thinkers of their respective cultures.

Their basic focus was to update their particular political traditions in the light of the challenge from modernity—outcomes of such efforts were of course quite different from one another.

THE EXPERIENCES AND THE INSIGHTS OF THE WEST

As Barry Cooper argues in chapter 2, classical European political philosophy rests on the twin foundations of 'nature' and 'virtue'. Their rationale was established as a result of debates between the Sophists and the Socratics. The Socratic insight has been that humans have a nature which endures unchanged despite all the empirical changes humans undergo both as individuals and as members of a political community. And it is this nature which defines the permanent and important issues of political life. This insight led Aristotle to state that man is by nature a political animal and that it is through life in the polis that he can attain one of the essential purposes of living, namely, the attainment of social peace and happiness. This insight about human nature leads to the further insight that social peace and happiness are the outcome of virtue rather than the life dedicated to the production and consumption of goods and services. Thus a philosophy of human nature and a philosophy of virtue remain the permanent concerns of the original western political philosophy.

According to Aristotle a philosophy of human nature without the complement of an adequate political philosophy would remain incomplete.[1] Accordingly, Greek political philosophy focused on two fundamental points: on the regime and citizenship on the one hand, and on the civic virtues necessary for the realization of the aims of the regime and citizenship on the other. Thus the search for the meaning of justice, prudence, etc., became as important a part of political philosophy as the discussion of the nature of the constitution, and the causes of its rise and fall. In Plato's thought such enquiries gave rise to two basic theses. The first being that all actual regimes can be properly understood only in the light of the ideal regime. And second, that there is a parallelism between the order in the soul and the order in the city and that unless moral virtues find their complement in civic virtues, and vice versa, politics would not be able to make its humanizing contribution. Or as

Aristotle would put it, the student of politics must know somehow the facts of the soul: he must study the soul.[2] The overall aim of political philosophy is to enable the citizens 'to be of a certain character, viz., good and capable of noble acts'.[3] However highly Plato and Aristotle prized the value of political life, they did not prize it as the highest perfection attainable by human beings. There was something higher still than political philosophy, political virtues, and social peace and happiness obtained through politics. Thus, *phronesis* (political wisdom), was different from *sophia* (theoretical wisdom), and more so inferior to it. Saying this, however, did not amount to undervaluing the significance of politics for them. It only gave the original European vision of politics its peculiar, intermediary position in the final scheme of things. That is to say, in the original European vision, politics was thought to elevate man from a mere brutish existence to a fully human condition; by the same token, politics was never thought to be capable of raising man to the highest perfection open to him. Aristotle expressed this idea when he wrote that man is neither a beast nor a god, but one who realizes his humanity in and through the polis.[4]

True, the grafting of the Biblical vision of man, particularly that expressed in the New Testament, to the original Hellenic vision, introduced a further modification in the European conception of political philosophy. If *sophia* was superior to *phronesis,* an Augustine or an Aquinas would add that both *sophia* and *phronesis* were inferior to divine wisdom as revealed in the incarnate Logos. But they would also add at once that this did not mean any essential undervaluing of the place of political philosophy in the general scheme of things. As Aquinas would put it, 'The city is, in fact, the most important thing constituted by human reason. For it is the object and final aim of all lesser communities. It is necessary therefore for the completeness of philosophy to institute a discipline which will study the city: and such a discipline is political philosophy.'[5]

If Plato, Aristotle, and Aquinas articulated original insights of western political philosophy, and spoke of human nature, of virtue, and of grace, the innovators of this philosophy from the sixteenth century onwards articulated a different point of view. As Barry Cooper argues in chapter 3, they called into question the three concepts so central to the founders. Thus the concern for nature in humans was replaced by concern for history in and through which humans created themselves. Given this shift, it appeared to the innovators that there were no permanent characteristics to human nature; that human nature evolved according to the needs and circumstances of history. These ideas find mature expression in the philosophies of Hegel and Marx. As for virtue, this was now perceived to be too utopian a task for humans to undertake. If traditional European political philosophy argued that virtue consisted in the orderly pursuit of human passions of wants and desires (orderly in the sense that the order was discovered in the soul and recommended by reason), modern European political philosophy asserted the priority of passions over reason, of the body over the soul. In this view, politics became an organized attempt to satisfy the need for security and consumption. Accordingly, politics is taken to be the exercise of reason of state, which then enters into an alliance with modern natural science and modern technology. The place of virtue is now taken by human practice rooted in faith in political engineering, science, and technology.[6] As for grace, modern western political philosophy has banished all interests in what transcends the empirical and the historical as either methodologically irrelevant or as utopian or illusory. In place of the recognition of the need for grace, modernity has introduced the historicist idea of history: humans create their history and in so doing they are their own makers. As individuals they may be limited, but as a species they can create their own world, either through thought or through labour (depending on whether one is a Hegelian or a Marxist). In other words, as has been said, modern political philosophy attempts to immanentize the transcendent. The historicist conception of history joins hands with reason of state, science, and technology. Modernity creates and justifies political systems in which the individuals are either lulled into a state of conspicuous consumption or they are subject to a thorough-going control of their behaviour by external means of coercion. As Cooper points out, the dialogue in western political philosophy concerns the promises and dangers of a philosophy of history; it brings into the dialogue the cases for and against a permanent sub-stratum in human nature, for virtue and for grace. No one can read the writing of a Voegelin or a Toynbee or a Maritain or a Leo Strauss without being reminded of these important issues.

THE EXPERIENCES AND INSIGHTS OF CHINA

Everyone has watched China's experiment with Marxism with great interest. Nothing could be considered more alien to traditional Chinese political thought than historical materialism, the notion of a vanguard party, and the notion of the primacy of economics over all spheres of human existence. Even though these ideologies have been imposed from above, Mao's revolution for all that is factually real. At least it has been so up to now. But how are we to understand the significance of what is happening in China under the Marxist regime? Is it comparable, say, to what happened in Europe in the fifth century AD, when Christianity was imposed on the Roman Empire as its official civil religion? Or is it to be compared to what happened in Europe in the thirteenth century when Thomas Aquinas successfully integrated the essence of Aristotelian political philosophy onto an antecedent Christian political philosophy? Questions such as these spring from a curiosity to know whether the millennial political traditions of China have suddenly vanished, or whether they have instead continued to be active in an unobtrusive but real way.

The question of the continued relevance of the tradition for the functioning of contemporary China has been a source of controversy among experts. The famous thesis of Joseph Levenson spoke of the 'modern fate' of Confucianism: but his prognostication of a total collapse of the Confucian tradition has been found to be somewhat premature.[7] As Ronald Keith and Robert Ware argue in chapters 4–6, the Chinese have become increasingly aware of the degree in which their past is entrenched in their present. No doubt, the phenomenon of the dictatorship of the proletariat would have been unintelligible to a Confucian scholar, but the imposition of such a system has not eliminated from Chinese Marxist practice the Confucian tradition of thought and action. The very virulence of the radical reaction against the 'four olds', *sijiu* (old ideas, old culture, old customs and old habits) during the Cultural Revolution of the 1960s suggested a very serious element of continuity in social and intellectual terms. There has been criticizm of persisting 'patriarchal ways' and 'one man rule'. The Chinese Communist Party's focus on 'socialist spiritual civilization' revealed a central paradox whereby the Party, without identifying 'traditional Chinese values', attempted to revive these very values in order to reconstitute the social order, which had gone through the trauma of the Cultural Revolution. Many critics tend to describe the contemporary scene in China in terms of 'patriarchal socialism' and 'Communist neo-traditionalism'.[8]

From the perspective of this volume, three notions from the Chinese tradition seem to be of special interest: the notion of *junzi* (the morally superior gentleman), the idea that virtue is more important for politics than mere mastery of techniques, and the ancient debate between Confucian ethics and traditional Legalism. As Ronald Keith suggests, Mao, in this respect, presents a paradox. As a Marxist-Leninist he challenged the Confucian emphasis on social harmony, but in presenting the alternative of a Marxian vision he had adopted a Confucian style, stressing internal consciousness as the normative basis for political action. Though he accepted the materialist view of history, he also focused on a subjective element of consciousness. He could not accept what he called 'the man eating' doctrine of *li*, and the notion of the *junzi*, and the social inequality it stood for. At the same time he found no intellectual difficulty in assigning to the Chinese Communist Party the role of a collective *junzi*. Party members would have to be good examples for the mere non-party members of Chinese society; they would need to develop a new vision of self-cultivation. This reminds one of the intellectual feat performed by Antonio Gramsci in Europe by means of which he assimilated the modern Communist Party, a collective entity, to what Machiavelli in the sixteenth century had called the prince. According to Gramsci, the Machiavellian prince was no longer to be an individual person, but a collective agency, i.e., the Communist Party.

Again, as a Marxist-Leninist Mao valued modern European notions of science and technology; yet as a Chinese he would not give technology priority over politics and the imperatives of subjective consciousness. While he was positive about the productive forces released by modern technology, he had trouble with the tendency to hand over technology to experts and bureaucrats. In other words, he would have preferred technology to remain within the bounds of what he called a dedication to 'essence'. Similarly, there was ambiguity regarding the question of whether Mao was a representative of the ancient Legalist tradition, with its claim that government by positive law was superior to government by the morally superior Confucian scholar or whether he was a ruler in the typical Confucian tradition. As a revolutionary he could not accept the aristocratic values associated with Confucianism, but as a Chinese political leader, he himself could not completely transcend the Confucian past.

Robert Ware's discussion of the existence of democracy in contemporary China also highlights the interplay of tradition and innovation. Ware grants that the notion of politics put into practice by the Chinese Communist Party (with its espousal of historical materialism, and all that flows from it concerning politics) is European in origin and content and as such alien to the Confucian tradition of politics. At the same time it appears that the notion of democracy has a natural affinity to certain traditional Chinese social and political values. Ware identifies several such values: the priority of the notions of 'goods' and 'benefits' over those of 'rights' and 'voting'; of collectivism over individualism; of objective interests over subjective interests; of substantive practice over formal procedures. The question remains, however, as to whether these traditional predispositions are likely to undermine or strengthen the claims of historical materialism. If, in order to survive and succeed in China the institutions of historical materialism need the props of Confucian political values, what does it say of the revolutionary elan of Marxism-Leninism in contemporary China?

THE EXPERIENCES AND INSIGHTS OF INDIA

One of the unresolved questions facing political philosophy in India today is that of the relationship which should exist between traditional Indian political philosophy and western modernity. Indian classical political philosophy emerges from an original insight. It is that the pursuit of *artha* (power and prosperity) should be conducted within a framework of *dharma* (the moral principle or principles that hold society together), such that human beings can attain the final end of their existence—*moksha*, liberation. Indian political philosophy did not see any incompatibility between the material aims of life (*artha* and *kama*) and its moral and spiritual aims (*dharma* and *moksha*). Indeed, the criterion of a good regime was that it recognized this overall harmony, and encouraged individuals towards its attainment. Conversely, the sign of an evil regime was that these basic ends of life became disordered, so that *artha* and *kama* were pursued as if they were ends in themselves. The aim of the basic texts of the tradition—the *Vedas*, the *Upanishads*, the *Gita*, the *Dharmasastras*, and the *Arthasastras*—was to inculcate the idea of harmony of the four ends in the minds of the people.

In his essay K.J. Shah argues that contrary to what is generally believed, Kautilya's *Arthasastra* upheld this tradition even in the context of India's experiences of empire and prosperity. It is his claim, a claim supported by his methodology, that Kautilya ramains faithful to the Indian classical tradition, and that Kautilya is no Indian Machiavelli. Shah's explanation of the relationship between the *Dharmasastra* tradition and the *Arthasastra* tradition is worthy of careful attention. To put it simply, Kautilya's *Arthasastra* attempts to formalize and specify what are often stated in general terms in the *Dharmasastras*. The *Arthasastra* develops concrete rules for day-to-day administration. But the stress on concreteness does not mean that it invalidates the basic requirements of the dharmic code. Insofar as this is true, the *Arthasastra* does not assert any pretended autonomy of *artha* over *dharma*.

Details of administrative needs abound in Kautilya. The stern necessities of statecraft, particularly in war and diplomacy, are frankly recognized. There is a proper 'science' or *sastra* of administration and statesmanship, but such a 'science' should operate in harmony with the basic requirements of moral philosophy. Shah, in other words, explains how the basic insights of the Indian tradition established its modus vivendi in the experiences of the actual life of a great state.

In contrast to the traditional insight, what can one say of the insight that guides modern Indian politics from about the middle of the nineteenth century, but especially from about the middle of the twentieth century? It is safe to say that, except for Gandhi and to some extent Dayanand Saraswati and Aurobindo Ghosh, the import of ancient insight has been largely neglected. Modern Indian political philosophy has been preoccupied with modern western political philosophy, with liberalism, and especially with socialism. Marxist socialism, in many instances, has become the opium of the Indian intellectual. The theory of planning has attained the status of a modern *sruti* (revelation).

The one significant effort to challenge modern western political philosophy and to adopt the original insight of tradition to modern experiences is no doubt reflected in Gandhi's classic text *Hind Swaraj*. Though Gandhi pays no attention to Kautilya, the *Hind Swaraj* is a subtle attempt to restate the traditional view that *artha* should be pursued within the bounds of *dharma*. The worst effect of modernity has been the separation of *artha* from *dharma*, and ultimately, from *moksha*. Gandhi's term for modernity is 'modern western civilization'. Modern western civilization has introduced the modern state, modern technology and science, modern legal system, modern education, and the modern notion of rights. What is wrong with all this, in Gandhi's view, is that modernity has no room for virtue and duty in public life. To make things worse, modernity relies too much on force and fear; it is unable to develop a vision of politics based on love, *daya* (compassion), moderation, and self-control. The main aim of *Hind Swaraj*, then, is to argue that Indian politics should seek a foundation more in harmony with India's original insight about politics. That foundation is supplied by what he called 'Indian civilization' or 'true civilization'. Such a civilization is defined 'as that mode of conduct which points out to men the path of duty. The performance of duty and observance of morality are convertible terms.'[9]

Swaraj or self-rule is possible only if the inner self is purified and firmness of virtue is attained. Outer *swaraj*, political freedom, becomes meaningful and conducive to the attainment of the overall aim of life (which is liberation), only when the inner foundations are recognized. There is an inseparable relationship between inner *swaraj* and outer *swaraj*, between freedom of the soul and the freedom of the city. Justice in the economic sphere follows if the soul is free— free from greed (*lobh*), self-interest (*swarth*), attitude of arrogance towards fellow citizens (*abhiman*).

Such in brief is the form that the Gandhian restatement of the original insight of India takes. It has nothing to do with revivalism, sectarianism, nostalgia, or *hindutva*.

Satyagraha, one of the means of making the original insight currently practical, is an eminently adaptable technique of action. *Sarvodaya* is equally practical: it is an economic philosophy that seeks the *good* of all in the community, even the very last and the least of its members. All this and more are discussed in chapter 8.

THE EXPERIENCES AND INSIGHTS OF ISLAM

What gives Islamic political philosophy its specific character is the way it approaches the issues of the relationship between reason and revelation. The original Islamic theory of politics was formulated wholly under the influence of revelation as contained in the Quran and as lived in tribal civilizations of the desert. God was the supreme legislator. Muhammad was His final messenger. The Muslim *umma* was considered to be simultaneously a political community and a religious community, the *Shari'a* was to be the basis for legislation and government, and the legitimate ruler had to be a recognized successor of the Prophet. The theory that the political community and the community of believers had to be identical created a problem for the minorities: What if non-Muslim minorities lived in a predominently Muslim state? What if a Muslim minority lived in a predominantly non-Muslim state? Were the concepts of the *faithful* and the *citizen* to be identically the same? These questions posed little difficulty so long as Islam did not come into any serious contact with alien cultures with different philosophies of politics. But these questions became intellectually problematic when Islam entered into serious dialogue with Greek philosophy, especially the philosophies of Plato and Aristotle.

As Yusuf Umar points out in his article, the Islamic philosopher chiefly responsible for initiating this dialogue was Farabi. He became the founder of a tradition which sought to bring both the religious and the political phenomena under the scrutiny of philosophy. He attempted to make *Greek* political philosophy compatible with Islamic theology, and in so doing, introduced a new way of looking at religion and revelation, and their relationship to philosophy and politics.

The key concepts here are those of imagination and intellect. Religion, according to Farabi, belonged to the sphere of imagination, and philosophy to that of intellect. God reveals religious truths through the imagination of prophets, while philosophic truths are discovered by human intellect. The most perfect human being would be one in whom both imagination and intellect work in harmony. Such a perfect human being would be both prophet and philosopher. He would also be the rightful ruler of any human community. He would combine religious and political sciences, and would know how to harmonize statecraft, prophecy and philosophy.

Admittedly, Farabi places religion and prophecy at a lower level of excellence compared to philosophy and intellection. This is not to be interpreted, in Farabi's mind, as a slight of religion and Islam. On the contrary, he readily recognized that religion had an indispensable role to play in the formation of ethical character, and that it was necessary for the education of the masses. For the latter were neither interested in nor capable of intellectual pursuits, and therefore, not concerned with philosophy. For such individuals (and according to Farabi, the vast majority of mankind belonged to the non-philosophic multitude), religion was an indispensable means of ethical life. The works of imagination were suited for their lives. Imagination adapted the eternal verities to the capabilities of the non-philosophic multitudes of the political community. So long as religion made individuals virtuous, there could be no harm arising from religion.

Farabi believed that such a philosophic attitude towards religion, far from undermining the value of religion, would rather enhance it, and would make religion a means of moderating, if not eliminating, sectarian and confessional quarrels. Insofar as religion was thought to belong to the sphere of imagination, and insofar as imagination could represent eternal verities in different but still valid ways, all religions could be considered valid. Such a philosophic understanding of religion could create a climate of toleration and mutual respect. Since all religions had some representational validity, there was no point in being intolerant or fanatic about religious symbols and beliefs.

But such an attitude towards religion, including the religion of Islam, entailed a recognition of the higher status of philosophy. Philosophy, properly cultivated, could become an antidote to sectarian strifes, as well as a means of attaining the final end of human existence, namely, happiness. Philosophy therefore should enter into an alliance with divine jurisprudence and statecraft. There was no question of statecraft becoming tyrannical, because philosophy would always be there to guide the statesman and deter him from temptations of tyranny. In fact, the best ruler for Farabi is a philosopher-prophet, the person in whom imagination and intellect function at their best, and who understands the relative place of religion and philosophy in society.

Farabi was realistic enough to recognize that the creation of a virtuous city where the philosopher-prophet would rule, and whose rule would be accepted by the multitude, was an almost impossible task to achieve. He is, therefore, prepared to describe the various political alternatives open to humanity. Opposed to the virtuous regime were alternate regimes—the regime of necessity (looking after bare necessities of life), the vile regime (oligarchy), the base regime of the pleasure seekers, the regime of honour seekers, the tyrannical regime, and the democratic regime. Whatever be the basis of these regimes, whether it be love of pleasure, or wealth, or honour or domination, they were all opposed to the principle of philosophic wisdom. Given these limitations in human desires, the task of political philosophy was to contribute towards their proper education. Philosophy, accordingly, should work in tandem with religion, but religion relativistically understood. Such, very briefly, has been the impact of Greek political philosophy of Farabi's thinking, and through him, on Islamic political theory. Farabi's works were influential on such subsequent Islamic philosophers as Avicenna and Averroes. They also gave strong support to Sufism. But, in the final analysis, Farabi did not influence Islamic political philosophy in the decisive manner in which Aquinas influenced European political philosophy, and the subsequent development of Christian political philosophy. A political philosophy independent of revelation, and complementing Islamic theology never gained open acceptance in Islam. As far as permanent transformation of thought affecting the whole Islamic tradition was concerned, the first contact with Greek political philosophy appears to have been unfruitful.

Islam's intellectual contact with Europe was renewed many times throughout history, but none was more significant than that which occurred in the nineteenth century. This is the background against which Majid Tehranian analyses, in chapter 10, the significance of the political theory of Ayatollah Khomeini. If Farabi had put Islam in contact with the classical political philosophy of Europe, the nineteenth century Islamic political thinkers, and their contemporary successors had put Islam in contact with the main currents of modern European political philosophies: popular sovereignty, nationalism, liberalism, socialism, technology, individual rights, secularism, in short, European modernity. And what Khomeini has demonstrated is that European modernity has had even worse luck with Islam than had European classical political philosophy.

The wellspring of Khomeini's political theory is the notion of Islamic legitimacy. Who may legislate for an Islamic community? And who is entitled to rule such a community? The answer to the first question, according to Khomeini, as Tehranian points out, is that God is the true legislator of Islam. Insofar as this can be true, all human legislating bodies would have to be looked upon more as planning bodies than as legislative bodies in the strict sense. As for the second question, the jurists of the *Shari'a* (who, according to Khomeini, are the rightful representatives of the Hidden Imam), should be the rulers both in temporal as well as spiritual matters. The supreme Imam has the right to interpret and to apply Islamic law in particular cases, especially in cases where, in the Imam's view, the integrity of Islam is being threatened. This, as everyone now knows, was the theoretical basis for Khomeini's issuing the famous *fatwah* condemning the author Salman Rushdie.

It followed that a government that was not in conformity with the *Shari'a* as interpreted by the jurists, was not only heretical but also unconstitutional in the Islamic sense of jurisprudence. Such a fundamentalist approach to Islamic political theory cuts at the very root of those approaches in Islam which were influenced by the western idea of modernity. Thus, in Khomeini's eyes the ideas of nationalism and the nation-state, both European in origin, were inconsistent with Islamic theory of politics. Muslim identity likewise had to be defined in terms of the *umma* rather than in terms of any secular political community. The theory of modern European individual rights was also incompatible with Islam and the *Shari'a* because that theory had its origin in an agnostic if not an atheistic conception of man. It ignored the right of God to legislate and to constitute a political community, a right that had to have precedence over any humanly devised set of rights. The civic rights and civic freedoms that western modernity prides itself in are nothing more than licence to indulge in any and every human appetite without regard for the higher law promulgated by the *Shari'a*. Khomeini's rejection of the western notion of modernity was complete and uncompromising. If Gandhi's rejection of it was qualified, and if Mao's attitude towards it was ambivalent, there was no doubt at all about Khomeini's attitude. In this connection we must bear in mind that his fundamentalist interpretation of Islamic political theory was made infinitely easier by the spectacle of the Shah's miserable attempts at adapting modernity to an Islamic society. In Khomeini's view the regime of the Shah represented all that was corrupt in modernity. The Shah was no Cyrus, and his Iran not a successor to the ancient Persian empire. In fact the Shah's efforts to revive the memories of a glorious pre-Islamic Iran failed miserably, Islamic consciousness being totally opposed to any pre-Islamic tradition of politics.

Whatever the success of Khomeini in mobilizing latent Islamic consciousness, his political theory, as Tehranian argues, places contemporary Iran and Islam generally, in a difficult philosophical situation. It has not enabled Iran to combine three things Iran needs if it is to continue as a vital political force, namely, an Islam open to internal development, a view of science and technology compatible with the teachings of Islam, and an economic theory that Islam can approve. As far as Khomeini is concerned, the rest of the world would have to see things in the Islamic way. The opportunity for a dialogue with non-Islamic political philosophy for him does not exist.

UNDER THE UPAS TREE

We have used the metaphor of the Upas tree in the title of this volume. *The Shorter Oxford English Dictionary* describes the Upas tree, *antiaris toxicaria*, as 'a fabulous Javanese tree so poisonous as to destroy life for many miles round'. Metaphorically, it stands for an entity which has 'a baleful power or influence'.

In using this metaphor in our title we were inspired by the use Mahatma Gandhi made of it in the *Hind Swaraj*.[10] There he used it to describe the impact of modernity or 'modern civilization' on humanity. Gandhi's point is that modernity, with it consumerism, its technology, its disregard for the eco-structure of nature, its inequality, its violence and its atheism, exerts 'a baleful power and influence' not just on India but on the humankind as a whole.

The use of this metaphor, we hope, would make us realize the difficulty of neutralizing the 'baleful' effect of modernity in thought and action. It is a sad state of affairs that in doing political philosophy, we have to depend solely on modern or post-modern political philosophy. We need a valid term of comparison, one that can at least tell us that the field of political philosophy need not be preempted by modern western political philosophy. A comparative study of political philosophies of the four traditions, and of course the traditions we have not included here—the Buddhist tradition for example—can give us such valid terms of comparison. Modern experiences can be integrated, to the extent they are worth integrating, from the perspective of the insights of tradition.

The association of the metaphor of the tree with the idea of human well-being is not something unknown in the history of ideas. Buddha is said to have received enlightenment under the Bodhi tree. Plato is supposed to have taught under an Olive tree.[11] And Bentham spoke of 'Tree of Utility'. And so, if we want to stay with the tree metaphor, under which tree are we to seek enlightenment today? Under the Bodhi, or the Olive, or the tree of Utility or the Upas tree? Comparative political philosophy can give us a neutralizing antidote to the 'baleful power or influence' of uncontested modern western political philosophy.

NOTES

1. *Nicomachean Ethics*, Bk X, ch. 9. 1181b 15.
2. *Ibid.*, Bk. 1, ch. 13, 1102a 15–25.
3. *Ibid.*, Bk. 1, ch. 9, 1099b 25–30.
4. *Politics*, Bk. 1, ch. 2, 1253a– 14–16.
5. *Commentary on the Politics of Aristotle*, the Spiazzi edition, Rome: 1966, p. 2.
6. In this context see the excellent collection of essays, *Science, Hegemony and Violence: A Requiem for Modernity*, Ashis Nandy, ed., Delhi: Oxford University Press, 1988.
7. Joseph Levenson, *Confucian China and Its Modern Fate: A Triology*, Berkeley: University of California Press, 1968.
8. See for example, Andrew G. Walder, *Communist Neo-Traditionalism, Work and Authority in Chinese Industry*. Berkeley: University of California Press, 1986.
9. *Hind Swaraj*, Ahmedabad: Navajivan Press, 1939 (1958), p. 61.
10. See *Hind Swaraj*, p. 58.
11. According to Associated Press reports, in 1976 the Olive tree under which Plato was supposed to have taught was struck by a bus and severely damaged—a good example of tradition meeting modernity! 'Plato's tree, in whose shade the ancient Greek is said to have taught his philosophy 2,300 years ago, lay uprooted and torn, the victim of a modern-day traffic accident. The 15-foot-tall tree, judged by scientists to be 3,000 years old, stood alongside the Sacred Way, the highway between Athens and the nearyby port of Piraeus, until it was struck by a bus'. The Greek Government immediately gave 'top priority aimed at saving an irreplaceable part of an ancient culture whose teachings are followed even today'. 'It said parts of the tree were quickly replanted in the same location and surrounded by a protective steel fence in an effort to save it'. The tree was one of the several in an olive grove but was identified as 'Plato's tree' in 1931 when remains of Plato's Academy were found in nearby excavations.

    On the first anniversary of the accident the supervising archeologist, Elizabeth Spathari, said: 'After careful daily treatment over the year, we have at last got the desired result. Plato's tree has taken root again'. As reported in *The Calgary Herald*, 9 October 1976, and 11 October 1977.

2 Classical Western Political Philosophy

Barry Cooper

It was a contemporary western political philosopher, Leo Strauss, who most clearly described the distinctive characteristics of classical western political philosophy.[1] One reason he was able to do so was because he could contemplate the ruin of modern western political philosophy. Living in the midst of what he and many others have called 'the crisis of the West', Strauss and a few others have turned to Plato, Aristotle and Xenophon, to the Bible, St. Augustine and St. Thomas, in order to recover a sense of balance, in order to learn from the great thinkers of the past, and in that way begin to understand the modern world. One may summarize modern western political philosophy as a doctrine in service to the view or opinion that the best possible political regime is one of ecumenic affluence. It is because of the widespread affluence in the western world and the equally widespread recognition, however reluctant, that affluence does not mean justice, that some western political philosophers have returned to the ancient thinkers. We will consider modern western political philosophy in the following chapter. Here we shall provide a summary account of the origins in the thought of the philosophers and in Christianity. One would like to have included the Israelite political speculation, the Stoics, the medieval Christian scholastics as well but within the space available not even a summary of these topics is possible.

Classical political philosophy did not exist as a distinct area of study until the existence of modern political philosophy made it possible to draw a contrast between the two. One cannot even say without qualification that there ever was an original, classical western political philosophy because those thinkers whom *we* so designate understood their reflections to apply to all political regimes and not merely to those that we nowadays identify as western. Of course, westerners like to think of the Greek philosophers as their own, as in a qualified sense they are. But are the Persians or Egyptians also western? And if not, what is one to make of Xenophon's opinion that the Great King, Cyrus, was the perfect ruler? Or of Socrates' remark that the perfect polis might exist 'in some barbaric place'? Or of Herodotus' report that practically all the names of the gods came to Greece from Egypt?[2] Thus, classical western political philosophy was neither understood as classical nor western but simply as political philosophy. Still less was it understood as 'traditional'. A tradition is literally something that is handed down. Classical western political philosophy may be handed down to us, but for that same reason cannot of itself be traditional. For these reasons we will use the unmodified term, political philosophy, to refer to those thinkers whom we today qualify classical and western as well.

Political philosophy may be characterized by two distinctive features. First, its subject-matter is related directly to political life and is indicated by the commonsense questions that concern all citizens and probably all humans: what is justice? What is virtue? What is the best kind of education? What is the best form of government?

Second, its method of analysis proceeds directly from the experience of politics even though it aims to transcend politics. Answers to the aforementioned commonsense questions do not always agree. For the political philosopher they then become topics suitable for analysis. As we shall discuss subsequently, the political philosopher aims at moving from opinion to 'science', *episteme*, and he does so by means of philosophic analysis in the sense developed by Aristotle in the *Posterior Analytics*. In commonsense language, political statements are cut up into pre-analytic opinions and philosophically justified propositions. Terms such as 'national unity', 'peaceful coexistence', or 'third world' can be analyzed by political philosophers so as to enable one to make a reasonable statement about the truth of the premises implied by these linguistic formulae. Such a procedure involves a series of presuppositions regarding the nature of man or the truth of existence or more generally still, the order of being. 'Political philosophy', wrote Strauss, 'is the attempt truly to know both the nature of political things and the right, or the good, political order'.[3] In order to succeed as political philosophy, the analysis of commonsense questions must not only be formally logical but must proceed on the assumption that the truth of the order of being can be apprehended. Otherwise, analysis can show only that opinions contradict one another or that a single opinion may contradict itself or that conclusions do not follow from premises. Philosophical, as distinct from formal analysis seeks to adjudge the truth of the premises.

The substance of the first point has been indicated already in the observation that political philosophy was not traditional. Indeed, if one could render the essentially Roman notion of tradition into the Greek, one would use the term convention. And political philosophy was in certain crucial respects opposed to convention or to conventional political practices. But to say that political philosophy was opposed to conventional political practices is to say that it was related directly to such practices. There is no more direct a relationship than opposition. The chief concern of political philosophy, a concern that directly expressed the opposition of political philosophy to conventional political practice, was the topic: what is the best regime?

One knows from everyday experience that republican citizens are of the view that republican self-government constitutes the best regime, and one can imagine that loyal subjects might hold a similar opinion about monarchy. In the eighteenth century, British North American colonists killed one another in defence of their divergent views on this question. The political philosopher, however, is impressed neither with the heat of such exchanges nor with the seriousness with which the antagonists clash. The political philosopher's chief and sometimes sole concern is with the truth of conflicting opinions and not with the strength of the convictions that sustain those opinions.

This aspect of political philosophy may lead directly to the conflict of the political philosopher with political opinion as such, even when political opinion is divided against itself. For example, during the American Revolutionary War of Independence opponents were unlikely to be concerned with the question of the best regime. Their convictions directed them to more immediate practical matters. They were, accordingly, likely to view with suspicion the person who raised the question. The political philosopher, unlike the enemy, does not take political disputes entirely seriously. Or rather, he understands politics in a way that made the understanding of partisans questionable. And no one likes being questioned, especially during the heat of conflict, about his understanding of the nature of the conflict.

This observation introduces the second characteristic of political philosophy. Granted that political philosophy arises from the clash of conventions or traditions or opinions about the best political regime. However, it is also true that it is opposed to them categorically, as conventions, and not necessarily in terms of what they (conventionally or traditionally) hold dear. Political philosophy is opposed to political conventions because the latter are unreflective or thoughtless. It is from this formal or categorical but nevertheless direct opposition that the method of analysis of political philosophy proceeds.

Specifically, political philosophy begins but does not end with opinions as they occur in political life. In the *Ethics* and the *Politics*, for example, Aristotle did not make up his concepts of the polis, the regime, the citizen, the forms of justice and happiness, but began with what he found around him, namely, opinions. Though opinions were primarily developed in political assemblies, there were numerous other areas of discussion, such as, clubs and gymnasiums; hunting and hiking expeditions; and even groups of soldiers and sailors as they prepared for war. Opinions were familiar, ordinary, and related to one another in an intelligible hierarchy: some questions were generally understood to be more important than others.

Political life, we know, is often characterized by conflict based on conflicting claims that nevertheless use similar language—the language of justice. If opponents argue, they advance claims regarding the justice of their cause, and if the claims are to be judged, an intelligent arbitrator will be required to render a decision. Such a decision would be just when the conflicting parties get what they deserve. One can make such a decision only by considering the arguments offered by the partisans. Aristotle stated this explicitly in Book III, chapter 9 of the *Politics* (1280a7 *ff*). The political philosopher surveys common opinions and orders and clarifies the meaning of these opinions. The obvious question is: how? This is a complex question, and another, tributary to it, is even more complex: once the meanings of opinions have been clarified, what then?

Let us approach these questions indirectly. At the very beginning of the *Politics* Aristotle made the point that all partnerships and hence all action aimed at some good, be either to preserve what is already good or to change what exists into something better. We have seen that an awareness of what is good or of what could be improved appears in the world as opinion. At first, opinions seem true and are unquestioned, but if we think about them they soon enough turn out to be questionable. No one is content to remain in such a state of uncertainty for long. Thus do we begin to search for and are drawn towards a good that is not questionable. We search for and are drawn towards knowledge that is no longer opinion. Accordingly, as Strauss remarked, 'political philosophy will then be the attempt to replace opinion about the nature of political things by knowledge of the nature of political things.'[4]

Now, the nature of a thing is what makes it one thing and not another and it is in the nature of political things to appear as opinions expressing approval or disapproval, praise and blame of men, of policies, of regimes. Political things, therefore, are essentially or by nature not neutral.[5] If this is so, the argument requires for its conclusion an elaboration of a standard of justice and injustice in light of which sound judgement of the nature of political things may be made. In other words, if political philosophy is the attempt to replace opinion by knowledge of political things, the political philosopher must strive to know the true standards by which justice, happiness, courage and so on are to be measured.

The first book of Plato's *Republic* raised and then dismissed the possibility of formulating an explicit doctrine taking the form: justice means paying one's debts, or, justice means helping friends and harming enemies. Earlier we raised the question: how does the political philosopher order and clarify the meaning of conventional opinions? We may reformulate it in light of the foregoing remarks. If the political philosopher simply clarified the meaning of opinions such as, 'justice means paying one's debts', then anyone who followed the procedure of such formal analysis would be a political philosopher. It would seem, however, that something more is involved. Socrates did not simply clarify the opinion of Cephalus in Book I of the *Republic*, he indicated that it was an untenable opinion and he indicated why Cephalus clung to it even after he was made aware that it was untenable. The conclusion would seem to be that the political philosopher possesses standards, true standards, of interpretation by which he measures the opinions, conventions or self-interpretation of political practice. If that is so, clarification means more even than critical analysis; it means an interpretation of political reality superior in quality to the conventional or self-interpretation. Once again we are brought back to the possibility of a conflict between the political philosopher and political life. Moreover, the dramatic outcome of Book I of the *Republic* and of other equally dramatic encounters, means that intellectual defeat through critical analysis of defective opinion need not be followed by a change of heart.[6]

The conventions of political life are meant to be true. If the political philosopher questions those conventions, he must do so on the basis of a different truth regarding political life. But what is this truth of the political philosopher? Where does it come from? Why does it oppose the truth of political life by characterizing that truth as convention? And if the truth of the political philosopher is indeed different from the conventions of political life, how can the one be developed from the other?

Before indicating the response to this complex of questions that was made by political philosophy, one should make the observation that much the same process occurred outside the Hellenic civilizational area. One thinks, for example, of Confucius, of the Buddha, of Zoroaster, of the Israelite prophets, of Muslim *failasauf* and the difficulties these individuals encountered with their respective social orders. Accordingly, the responses of the political philosophers of Hellas are to be understood as part of this more general process.

Analysis of opinion, therefore, proceeds upon the assumption that there is an order of being, that political philosophy has access to it, and that it is beyond opinion. It is insufficient, however, merely to make an assumption and proceed with analysis: the insight concerning the order of being must also really be present in the mind of the analyst. That is, political philosophy does not begin, and never has begun, with speculation on its own conditions of possibility but rather proceeds concretely with an actual insight. And that particular and concrete experience is what initiates the analysis in the first place. So far as political philosophy is concerned, the crucial experience may be expressed in the proposition that, beyond the realities of the world, the lasting and passing of things, there is the world-transcendent source or ground of those things or of their being. This statement receives its experiential validity from the real movement of the psyche that is expressed as being drawn towards or seeking the being that is beyond the world. Plato, for instance, expressed these experiences as variations of eros: toward the *sophon*, the *agathon*, the *kalon*. On the basis of such experiences the image of the order of being was made, and beyond that order lay the *epekeina*, the beyond that is beyond all images.

On the basis of the experiences of the order of being as a whole, which included the world-transcendent ground, the analyses of political philosophy were undertaken. When Plato indicated that Themistocles and Pericles should be blamed for filling Athens with junk (*Gorg.*, 519a) rather than praised for making the Athenians powerful, he was not undertaking a piece of cheap moralizing but was analyzing the truth of existence. The important can *really* be contrasted with the thoughtful.

The particular form of this general response, which found expression in equivalent symbols in other cultures, gained succinct formulation in Plato's famous phrase that the polis is man written in large letters (*Rep.*, 368c–d). This is a diagnostic aphorism of great importance: it enabled Plato, for instance, to describe his own polis as a Sophist writ large, which then enabled him further to explain the peculiarities of Athenian politics by reference to defective sophistic opinion. He used the principle to construct his paradigmatic polis of speech as the expression of the philosophical man, and he used it again towards the end of the *Republic* when he interpreted the changes in political regime as the expression of corresponding changes in the predominant type of humans in those regimes (*Rep.*, 492b, 435e, 544d–e).

We mentioned earlier that the basis for such an analysis was the experience of reality that Plato symbolized as variations in eros. The logic of the argument is clear enough: in order for Plato to order different types of humans and the corresponding regimes in an intelligible hierarchy, he must have discovered a true order in his own soul and have had a desire to express the discovery. Negatively, this discovery was expressed in the critique of existing opinion, and more fundamentally in the analysis of the desires of the philosopher and his opponents (*Rep.*, 480). In the analysis of the experience of conflicting desires is found the elusive criteria of truth and untruth, *pseudos* (*Rep.*, 382a). The truth of the soul, we said, was experienced as an orientation towards and by the *sophon*; in opposition, was the experience of an orientation towards and by the opinions, the *doxai*, of political life. One or another such experience predominates and forms the souls of human beings in such a way that various empirical characters appear in the world: the philosophic character, the thymotic or honour-seeking character, the appetitive character, the philodoxic or opinion-loving character, and so on.

Political philosophy, by this account, is to be explicitly contrasted with opining about justice or about the meaning of human existence or about God. It is the explication, analysis and interpretation of a specific class of experiences. This understanding of the experiential basis of political philosophy was by no means confined to Plato. For example, in the *Ethics*, Aristotle identified the character of an individual whose soul had been exposed to these experiences and had been formed by them as the *spoudaios*, the man who had actualized as fully as possible the potentials of his nature. In his daily life, the 'mature man' habitually exercised the dianoetic and the ethical virtues (*EN*, 1113a29–35).

Not all human beings can become *spoudaioi* and, among those who have the talent and the leisure, even fewer have the inclination or desire. What this meant historically is that the political philosopher was not accepted into political life. The result was, pragmatically speaking, an impasse. The two-fold connection of political philosophy with pre-philosophical political life, on the one hand, and philosophical existence in loving tension toward the divine *sophon* meant that all was not lost. The philosophical experiences were, indeed, handed over or handed down, and the philosophers were able to transmit their experiences of reality in a way that the non-philosophers could understand. But certain compromises were necessary.

These compromises are usually discussed under the heading, 'rhetoric', or speaking the truth to an audience in such a way that the audience can understand it. Closely related to rhetoric is the question of 'political science', *episteme politike*, as a practical science devoted to the actual founding of the best regime in light of existing circumstances. Indirectly, such political science is devoted to the instruction of legislators and statesmen. However understood, such political science must be a compromise between what is simply best and what is permitted by local circumstances: traditions, education, size of territory, ethnic composition, economic conditions and so on.

The question of compromise or of the practical implications of political philosophy was discussed by Aristotle in Book I:13 of the *Ethics*. There he makes the following observations:

1. 'The true *politikos* seems to be one who has concerned himself especially with virtue, *arete*, because his aim is to make citizens good and law-abiding.' He goes on to say that, since the *arete* involved is human, and since human *arete* involves the human good and the human happiness, and since those things involve the psyche, the soul, rather than the body, therefore:

2. 'The *politikos* must know something about the psyche, just as the one who is to heal the eyes or the body must know something about the eyes or the body. All the more so, since political science is higher and more honourable than medicine. And even among physicians, the better ones devote much attention to the body.' So,

3. 'The *politikos*, therefore, must study the psyche; and he must do so with these objects [of the human good and happiness] in view and to the extent sufficient for the purposes of his inquiry' (*EN*, 1102a).

This passage summarizes the principal aspects of political philosophy, in the distinct meanings of the term *politikos*.

The first occurrence is exemplified by the lawgivers, the *nomothetes* of the Cretans and the Spartans. Here the *politikos* is a statesman whose office is to draft the fundamental laws of the regime. In the second occurrence the *politikos* is likened to a physician who is understood as a craftsman with knowledge of the body. There is no implication of office, but it is not excluded. We may notice as well that the comparison with medicine carried with it the implication that there was nothing particularly Greek about political philosophy. The best regime is no more Greek than health is Greek. By the same token as some nations are more healthy than others, so too some nations may be more politically excellent than others. In the third occurrence of the term, the *politikos* is one who studies so as to be a good craftsman. As student, this *politikos* is without office. Concretely, Aristotle was a *politikos* in the third sense who never became a *politikos* in the first sense and so we can have no idea whether he would have been any good as a *politikos* in the second sense.

The multiple meanings indicate that private citizens had become politically visible and were capable of expressing the results of their investigations in the literary form of the dialogue or treatise. No longer were nomothetics the monopoly of office holders. Aristotle himself indicated in the *Politics* that Hippodamus of Miletus was the first to inquire about the best regime (*Pol.*, II, 8). Before him the mystic philosophers, especially Heraclitus, and before them, Hesiod, put themselves forward as authorities critical of public affairs.

As was indicated earlier, the resistance of a specific individual and after him, of a school, to the corruption of political order or of the political regime, is by no means confined to Hellas. Indeed, at approximately the same time in China the same development took place, but the implications were much more clearly expressed. According to the Chinese political practice, the son of Heaven was, by reason of his virtue, *teh*, the mediator of the cosmic order, *tao*, to society. The prince, the *ch'un*, was the sole mediator. Similar structures and practices existed in Egypt, Mesopotamia, the Hittite kingdoms and so on. Under the pressure of the disintegration of the Chou dynasty the Chinese *politikos* appeared: Confucius claimed the authority to offer counsel with regard to public order. He was not, to be sure, a *ch'un*, but he was a *ch'un-tse*, a princely man who by his own *teh* could mediate the cosmic *tao* when the *ch'un* was unable to do so. In Greece there was no symbol developed to express the transfer of authority, but there is no doubt that it took place. In the *Gorgias* Socrates says that he is perhaps the only one who practices the true art of politics (*alethos politike techne*) and practices politics in accord with it (*prattein ta politika*) (Gorg., 521d).

Both the Hellenic and the Chinese political philosophers undertook the transfer of authority under conditions of political disorder. Indeed, one of the few empirical generalizations that seems obvious to pre-analytic commonsense is that in times of crisis the basic problems of political existence in history appear to everybody and so afford the political philosopher an opportunity to reflect on the principles of order that he experiences within his own psyche but that clearly do not exist in society at large. The break between public disorder and the order of the psyche of the philosopher has often been expressed in medical metaphors or comparisons, as was evident in the passage from Aristotle. In fact, much of the vocabulary of classical political science was borrowed from the medical vocabulary of physicians. The term 'crisis', for example, is used today with the same medical-political connotations as is found in the use of the term *kinesis* by Thucydides.

The attempt to move from the third meaning of *politikos*, which we may call that of political philosopher, to the second, or political physician, may well be pointless. Even if the diagnosis is correct and the remedy prescribed on the sound basis of a knowledge of right order, the disease, the *nosos*, of the body politic may be incurable. Under such circumstances, the knowledge of health and disease of the political physician is retained by the political philosopher but is transfigured by his analytic attitude.

These reflections underscore the observation made earlier regarding Plato's aphorism, that the *polis* is a man written in large letters, namely that political philosophy has two topics, the one expressed by the science of order of psyche and society, and the other expressed by the analysis of disorder. The matter was recast by St. Thomas Aquinas in the opening chapter of the *Summa Contra Gentiles*. Because, he said, it is 'incumbent upon the philosopher, the *sapiens*, to meditate on the truth of the first principle, and to communicate it to others, so it is incumbent upon him to refute the opposing falsehood.'

The two topics of political philosophy are in tension with one another both in its Greek and its Christian form. In both instances, this tension exists concretely in the psyche of the political philosopher. Both the disorder of society and the order of the philosopher's psyche are real; the one continues to exist as a disease even if nothing can be done about it, and the political scientist's insight is not invalidated merely because it cannot be operationalized. This observation leads to another empirical generalization: the distinction between the two topics of political philosophy makes sense only when the analysis of disorder is undertaken with an awareness that it is indeed disorder. Such an awareness can be lost either through an atrophy of the experiences of order or through what might be called spiritual impatience. In the first case the basis for understanding the surrounding disorder as pathological is lost; in the second, remedies are applied with insufficient attention to the nature of the disorder in the hopes of effecting a quick cure.

In this context I would like to indicate one of the 'complications' introduced to political philosophy by Christian experience and by the symbolization of those experiences in the Bible stories. Perhaps the easiest way to do so is to make the observation that the political philosophy of Plato and Aristotle did not lead to political therapy but to the Academy and the Lyceum. These institutions were, perhaps, more like research facilities or think-tanks than monasteries; at the same time, however, they sheltered members from the immediate distractions of politics and permitted political philosophers to cultivate the theoretical life, the *bios theoretikos*. A fulfilling mode of existence could be found separate from politics in the rational analysis of the position of human beings in the divine cosmos and in society. The cultivation of philosophy did not appeal to everyone: so far as the non-philosophers were concerned, it was clear to the philosophers that the *nosos* of the psyche could be cured neither by politics nor by philosophy. Politics and philosophy grew apart as did the philosophers and the non-philosophers.

At this point the decisive solution to the split between philosophers and non-philosophers was provided by Christianity. In his letter to the Colossians, St. Paul expressed the basis of the new community formed by faith, 'where there is neither Greek nor Jew, circumcision nor uncircumcision, Barbarian, Scythian, bond nor free: but Christ is all, and in all' (*Colossians* 3:11; see also *Romans* 10:12–13). The contrast with the classical Greek substance of community may be specified as follows: for Aristotle friendship consists in *homonoia*, in a likemindedness that, for the philosopher, meant the desire to actualize the most divine part of the psyche, the *nous*. Insofar as humans are equal in the erotic actualization of their noetic self is friendship possible; insofar as they are unequal in this will friendship be difficult. Indeed, in one of his most notoriously misunderstood passages, Aristotle even spoke of slaves by nature. It is difficult for philosophers and non-philosophers to be friends just as it is difficult for the servile to be friends with the noble. More to the point, it is impossible for humans, even if they are philosophers, to be friends with the god. The reason lies in their radical inequality (*EN*, 1158b–59a). There is, therefore, a continuity in the inequality of philosophers and non-philosophers, which is expressed by their varying degrees of participation in the divine *nous*, with the inequality of divine and human being. There can, therefore, be no *homonoia* between the god and humans, and therefore no friendship.

This gap between the divine and the human, along with the divisions between Greek and Jew, circumcised and uncircumcised, and, one assumes, between philosopher and non-philosopher, may be overcome by Christian faith. On the one hand, such faith constitutes the likemindedness or *homonoia* of the Christian community, but it is made possible because of the friendship of God, which

Christians call grace. In I *Timothy* 6, for example, the author admonishes slaves to respect their Christian masters because they were brethren in Christ and not in spite of that fact. Such a sentiment is unlikely to have been developed by Aristotle. One finds a systematic formulation of the difference between Greek and Christian experiences in the passage of St. Thomas where he spoke of the *amicitia*, the friendliness, of God made evident in the experiences of mutuality between the divine and human.[7] Commonsense would at least assent to the elegance of the solution: if Aristotle is right in emphasizing the inequality of divine and human being, and if friendship demands a kind of equality or *homonoia*, and if philosophical experience only leads to a separation of philosophers and non-philosophers and of humans from the god, then if these several separations are to be overcome, it can only be by a divine act and not a human one. In the language used by Thomas, divine grace imposes a supernatural form on the nature of man.

In conventional Christian language one speaks of the revelation of grace through the incarnation of the divine logos in Christ. Revelation, however, is far from a specifically Christian experience. In Thales' formula, when all things are filled with gods, revelations are commonplace.[8] More precisely, revelation is a 'special occasion' (Whitehead) that provides 'an image by means of which all the occasions of personal and common life become intelligible.'[9] It is for this reason that, for example, Eric Voegelin could write that the Christian revelation 'intelligibly fulfilled the adventitious movement of the spirit in the mystic philosophers.'[10] The specific intelligibility that is our present concern is that Christianity provided a kind of relief to political philosophy that was not available to Plato and Aristotle, namely relief from the burden of care for, and cure of the diseased psyche of human being. Henceforth that burden in the West would be borne by the Church. There remained to political philosophy the not inconsiderable burden of rational analysis of the problems of order in society and in history. One may speak, therefore, of a balance not only between the Church and the political order, which constituted the great drama of the Christian middle ages, but of a balance of Church, the political order and political philosophy. Such, it seems to me, is the methodological complication introduced by Christianity to the foundation of political philosophy as laid by Plato and Aristotle.

One may summarize the argument in this chapter as follows. Political philosophy arose from the fact that political life was characterized by verbal controversy and struggles for power. The task of the political philosopher was to settle those controversies on the basis of analysis, not partisanship, and in accord with his noetic apprehension of human excellence, *arete*. By raising the question, what is *arete?* one is led to reflect on the virtue the possession of which makes a person fit to rule. One begins to answer that question by examining common political opinions and the several desires expressed in them—for honour, for wealth, for recognition, for comfort. Analysis of these desires establishes a hierarchy of the objects of desire and reflection on the experience of analysis itself points the political philosopher beyond opinion as such and thereby beyond politics. One may say, therefore, that the analysis of politics by the political philosopher tends to separate him from the political community. Political order exists, as it were, to enable the philosopher lead a life of contemplation. In this way the life of the political philosopher changes into the life of the philosopher.

The directness of the relation between pre-philosophical political life and political philosophy was established by political philosophers after generations of reflection. Aristotle summarized the achievement of political philosophy as being the analysis *peri ta anthropina*, about the things pertaining to man's humanity. Those 'things' constitute a comprehensive field, from the divine things above mere humanity to the natural things of organic life and matter below. The place of philosophical desire or of *nous* in this field is at the centre. It appears in the world as questioning and as wonder.[11] The experience itself may be described abstractly as one of tension between what is above and what is below human being but in a state of openness to the whole of reality.

Here one feels the decisive impact of Christianity on the symbolism developed by the political philosophers. The ascent of the philosophers was, to be sure, towards the divine ground of being but the god remained 'beyond being' in a kind of immovable transcendence. The Christian experience of a wholly divine and wholly other who nevertheless draws near to the soul is outside the experience of the philosophers. To use a common enough historical account, the search of the philosophers was adventitiously concluded by the incarnation of the *logos* in Christ. To use a more theoretical or philosophical language, the notion that the experiences of the mystic philosophers of Greece were fulfilled through Christianity assumes that the substance of history consists in the experiences by which human beings understand their own humanity. It also means that there exists a strict relationship between the several experiences of reality, which following tradition we have identified as classical western political philosophy and as Christianity, and political self-understanding. In turning to modern western political philosophy, therefore, one turns to a distinctive experience of reality and so to a distinctive symbolization of it.

NOTES

1. The briefest statement, which is followed in this chapter, is 'On Classical Political Philosophy', in *What is Political Philosophy? and Other Studies*. Glencoe: Free Press, 1959, pp 78–94.
2. Xenophon, *Cyropaedia*, I, 1–2; Plato, *Republic*, 499c–d; Herodotus, II, 50.
3. Strauss, 'What is Political Philosophy?' in *What is Political Philosophy? op. cit.*, p. 12.
4. Strauss, 'What is Political Philosophy?' *op. cit.*, pp. 11–12.
5. If one happens to be of a contrary opinion, one would have to defend an argument that maintained political things are neutral or are unrelated to justice and injustice or have no nature. Something like this is, in fact, maintained by certain modern western political thinkers, but no classical political philosopher could do so.
6. See *Rep.* 354a; *Gorgias*, 471e.
7. *Summa Contra Gentiles* III, 91.
8. Aristotle, *De Anima*, 411a 7.
9. H. Richard Niebuhr, *The Meaning of Revelation*. New York: Macmillan, 1941, p. 109; cf. p. 93.
10. Voegelin, *The New Science of Politics*. Chicago: University of Chicago Press, 1952, p. 78.
11. Plato, *Theaetetus*, 155d; Aristotle, *Metaphysics*, 982b18.

3 Modern Western Political Philosophy

Barry Cooper

Classical or ancient western political philosophers were in fundamental agreement regarding the goal of political life, namely, virtue. They also agreed that the regime most likely to promote virtue, or at least the regime least likely to prevent people from cultivating virtue, was either aristocracy, the rule of the best, or a mixed regime. An equivalent compromise was obtained, after many generations, within Christian political philosophy. Saint Augustine, for example, continued the Platonic emphasis on *eros*, desire. In his most famous book, *On the City of God Against the Pagans*, he made the following formulation of the problem: 'These two cities [namely the City of God and the Earthly City] were made from two loves: the Earthly City by love of self even unto the contempt of God, and the Heavenly City by the love of God even unto the contempt of self' (*DCD*, XIV: 28). The two cities, accordingly, were intertwined from the beginning and would co-exist until the end.

In institutional terms, the moderation of political philosophy was continued as well. At its origin, moderation was derived from its direct connection with political life. In the medieval Christian era it was sustained by the on-going relations between Church and Empire. Such relations were, in this respect, equivalent to the direct connection between philosophy and political life in the ancient *polis*. In the late fifth century AD, Church–Empire relations received doctrinal formulation in the teachings of Pope Gelasius; Christendom was a single community, but it existed for two different ends, one spiritual and the other temporal. Accordingly, God had given two sacred swords to two interdependent authorities, one sacerdotal, the other

imperial. The consequence of this teaching, like that of the philosophers, was to diminish the tendency of human beings to divide
themselves against one another and to justify their divisions in terms
of strident fanaticism. The symbolism of the Christian middle ages
differed greatly from that of classical antiquity, but it maintained the
earlier teaching that evil cannot be eradicated. The result was to
encourage moderate expectations regarding what can be achieved in
political life.

Notwithstanding the similarities and equivalences in the meaning
of classical and medieval western political philosophy there remained several significant elemental or external differences. These
differences became more pronounced in modern political philosophy.
Indeed, contrasts outweighed similarities. Where the ancient was
directly related to politics, the modern. has become mediated by
texts and traditions. Where the ancient was concerned with certain
practical questions centred on rhetoric and prudence, the modern is
reckless and enlightened. Where the ancient was concerned almost
exclusively with the internal order of the regime, the modern is
more concerned with relations among regimes. Where *the* question
for ancient political philosophy was concerned with virtue or
human excellence, that quesion seems to have been superseded by
the moderns. Where the ancients were concerned with the full range
of human experience and symbolization, the moderns have a more
restricted understanding of reality experienced.

Other comparisons are no doubt possible. We will simplify the
range of topics by focusing upon a central and, indeed, categorical
change between ancient and modern political philosophy, the change
from an understanding based on nature to one based on history. In
antiquity the distinction was clear: the question of the best regime, a
philosophical question, is of a different sort than any historical
account of events. During the Christian middle ages, a philosopher
did not study Aristotle's *Politics* in order to find out about 'Greek
civilization' but to apprehend the principles regarding right political
order. Naturally, such a philosopher would deviate in detail from
Aristotle when it came to the application of Aristotle's political
principles to a situation or to circumstances that Aristotle could not
possibly have foreseen.

Modern philosophers do not read Aristotle this way chiefly
because, in one way or another, they adhere to the doctrine or the
religion of progress. Progress means, among other things, that

certain elementary questions have been settled absolutely so that hereafter they need not even be raised. In its most systematic form, the doctrine of progress has been called philosophy of history. It shares with all other modern doctrines of political philosophy the opinion that the understanding of classical political philosophy, namely that politics aims at virtue, was unrealistic. The one thing needful in politics, by this modern view, was not a good character formed by a specific class of experiences, but a reformation of political institutions. The most radical or most irresponsible version of this opinion asserted that history was moving in a direction towards the sought-for reforms.

This book is concerned to explore the topic of comparative political philosophy. For the founders of western political philosophy such a topic would seem strange, not to say unintelligible. For Plato and Aristotle and Xenophon, the *polis*, the city, was the preferred unit of analysis not simply because it was familiar but because it was essentially superior to other forms of political association. In particular, the city combined desirable features of association in a way that could not be duplicated in any other form of association. The two common forms with which the city was often compared were the tribe and the oriental kingdom. The tribe was characterized by liberty and spiritedness, but not by education or civilization. The oriental kingdom had plenty of education and perhaps even more civilization than the city, but it lacked spiritedness and liberty. In light of the intrinsic or natural desirability of civilization and liberty, it was entirely reasonable for the classical political philosophers to consider the city to be the most perfect form of political association. Of course, this did not prevent them from admiring or even preferring oriental kingdoms of their own.

The topic, comparative political philosophy, is novel because it is connected to a focal concern for the historical differentiation of cultures or societies or civilizations rathar than to a focal concern for the nature of political things or regimes. Against this assertion it may be objected that all political philosophy is comparative and that Herodotus, for example, should be admitted to the status of founder along with Plato and Aristotle and Xenophon. There is something appealing in this suggestion: it is always edifying to consider the ways of Nubians and Scythians. But it is evasive not to reflect upon the philosophical question of the virtue of those ways and of their justice and civility, to say nothing of the spiritual and intellectual power of the account of them. Concretely in the case of Herodotus, it seems clear that his own inquiries were governed by the pre-Socratic understanding of cosmic balance. *The Histories* is philosophical without becoming a work of philosophy because the stories it relates are not about speeches but are about deeds. And as Bernadete observed, 'in attempting to discover a *logos* in *erga* [deeds], a disproportion arises that cannot be explained.'[1] All that can be done is describe proportions and necessities, not their reasonableness. Herodotus might best be described as the father of comparative politics, which is surely an indispensable prelude to Aristotelean political science, and also to the philosophical study of political thought.

A more compelling case can be made that the class of arguments topically identified as philosophy of history are in fact comparative and philosophical analyses of political thought. After all, the subject matter of philosophy of history is the systematic presentation of the pragmatic history of mankind and of its interpretation and self-interpretation. The term owes its origin to polemic, however, and must be used with caution. It was 'invented', as Karl Loewith observed, in the middle of the eighteenth century by Voltaire under circumstances that deserve recollection because they reveal clearly the issues involved.

Voltaire's quondam hostess and patron, the Marquise du Châtelet-Lorraine, had turned her attention from the arts and sciences to the field of history and undertook the study of Bossuet's *Discours sur l'histoire universelle* (1681). Bossuet's book began with the creation of the world and concluded with an account of the empire of Charlemagne. Part II was an account of the diffusion of religion that culminated in Christianity; Part III discussed the rise and fall of empires. In plan and execution it was patterned on St. Augustine's *City of God*, Part III being parallel to Orosius' continuation of Augustine in the *Seven Books of History Against the Pagans*. Voltaire reported that the Marquise found fault with Bossuet on two points: while the Jews were rightly important so far as theology was concerned, they 'merit little space in history'. Second, she asked, 'why does the author say that Rome engulfed all the empires of the universe? Russia alone is bigger than all the Roman Empire'.[2] The Marquise did not initiate a historiographic revolution; rather, her shrewd naivete was evidence that the 'crisis of European conscious-ness', as Paul Hazard called the phenomenon, had already taken place. That it had penetrated society to a significant degree was apparent by the remarks of the Marquise.[3] Since Bossuet's account followed from his Christianity, the illustrious lady was in fact objecting to his Augustinian conception of history as being guided by divine providence.

Augustine's treatise began as a kind of political pamphlet directed against the popular misconception that Christianity was an elaborate insurance policy against political disaster. The formal construction was evidently Platonic, the first ten books corresponding to the ten books of the *Republic*, the last twelve to the corresponding books of the *Laws*. The main topic treated, however, was the construction of world history focused on the birth of Christ. Pre-Christian politics, including the Platonic, were concerned with the myths of the several peoples whose story they expressed, but not with man-kind. The specific Christian supplement, in this context, was the new question: where does this people stand with respect to all human history? In attenuated form this question lay behind the queries of the Marquise.

St. Augustine's repsonse to this question was to rework a variegated complex of materials into a symbolic periodization of world history. He divided the history of the world into the traditional six periods, corresponding to the six days it took God to create the world, and connected these symbolic divisions to the generations from Adam to Noah, to Abraham, to David, to the exile, to Christ and from Christ on. Finally, the entire complex was integrated to the six phases of an individual's life: infancy, childhood, adole-scence, youth, maturity and old age. The present age is the *saeculum senescens*, the senescence of the world, existing in anticipation of the second coming of Christ, but without additional purpose.

History ran on a double course, the sacred history of mankind expressed in the six symbolic ages, and the history of good and bad souls, which is expressed in membership in the Heavenly or Earthly City. The theory was complex because it combined a transcendental spiritual history of souls with an empirical spiritual history of man-kind over six ages. The Church had the purpose of representing the transcendental spiritual realm but did not constitute it. Neither line of speculation, however, considered the significance of the non-spiritual community. Augustine did argue that the nations, the *gentes*, had a right to individual existence because they retained their own civilizational personalities that might be raised spiritually to the level of Christianity.

But what of the history of those outside the Israelitic-Christian symbolic and ethnic horizon for whom the generations after Adam were unknown? Augustine's pupil, Orosius, attempted to establish the parallel periodization between the symbolic ages and those of profane history. The model was found in the periodization of the Danielic monarchies, which he extended from Macedon to Rome. The fit was not particularly good because the disintegration of the Macedonian diadochean empires did not coincide with the establishment of the Roman. In addition, there was the embarrassment of the contemporaneous Parthian and Sassanian empires. The pressure to align these profane imperial developments on a single line of time, however, remained strong.[4]

Orosius followed the general pattern of profane Danielic chronology. The four empires were the Babylonian, the Macedonean, the African (Orosius was himself from North Africa), and the Roman. These four imperial organizations corresponded to the four cardinal points of the Mediterranean cosmos, with the two greatest· occupying the longer east-west axis and the two minor ones the shorter north-south axis. More important than this revival of cosmological symbolism was the integration of profane with sacred history. In particular, Rome became the final empire. This is why the concluding chapter on Orosius' *Seven Books of History* reported with considerable satisfaction that Ataulf, King of the Visisoths, had assumed the role, of restorer of Rome. In fact he would have been described by commonsense as one of its destroyers. The Romancentric pathos, however, overrode mere events and continued to do so through the integration of the migration-empires into the medieval Sacred Empire, which was understood as existing in symbolic continuity with the Roman Empire of antiquity. The Renaissance broke the spell of a single western civilizational course but significantly did so by means of the symbol of rebirth. What was reborn was the same historically linear. construction; only the accents of approbation and disapprobation were shifted and the Christian middle ages became 'dark'. The Marquise du Châtelet therefore raised an important methodological issue when she questioned the significance of the Roman achievement in light of the Russian.

According to the Augustinian construction, Israelite history, the birth of Christ and the history of the Church were a meaningful *historia sacra* because they accounted for the spiritual drama of God with his creatures between the creation and the destruction of the world. That is, sacred history was the representative history of mankind. The same claim enabled Bossuet to employ the adjective 'universal'. The story of the rise and fall of empires carried with it the meaning of educational tribulation or preparation for the final apocalypse. Even in antiquity, however, Christian apologists had difficulty in demoting Hellas and Rome to the sideshow of profane history. By the high middle ages, the conflict of the doctrine with the contemporaneous existence of the Byzantine-Orthodox, the Arabic-Islamic and the western-Roman empires had made matters worse. By the eighteenth century, the conflict with reality had become unbearable.

Voltaire's response to the observations of the Marquise, which he described as 'philosophy of history' in contrast to Bossuet's Augustinian 'theology of history', was presented at length in his *Essai sur les Moeurs et l'Esprit des Nations* (1756). On the surface he continued Bossuet's account from Charlemagne to Louis XIII, but in fact it constituted a repudiation of the form and substance of Christian universality. The objections of the Marquise carried the implication that the presence of the Israelities, Christ and the Church was an event 'in' history, conceived as being meaningful on some other basis.

Like Bossuet, Voltaire had to organize his materials according to some kind of historiographic principle. It was a comparatively easy task to indicate that the Eurocentric, unilinear, Christian construction had to ignore or do interpretative violence to the phenomena of China, India and Islam. But neither China, India nor Islam could be understood as constituting mankind either. Or rather, each, along with Christianity, might well have understood its own existence as being representative of humanity. For Voltaire, however, this was evidence only of the untruth of them all. Voltaire proposed to replace the defective Augustinian construction with an account, as the title of his book indicated, of the human spirit. Specifically, he was concerned with the evolution of opinion from barbarian rusticity of earlier times to the *politesse* of Voltaire's present, which he called the softening of morals.

Voltaire's argument was not a model of analytic rigor. For

Augustine, sacred and profane history were distinguished, which meant that the universality of the one did not exist without the particularity of the other. Voltaire and his progressive successors attempted to combine the two as secularized history, an innerworldly chain of events that is in that respect akin to profane history, but one endowed with universal meaning and so in that respect akin to sacred history. For Voltaire, the universal-historiographic category was the aforementioned evolution of the human spirit from barbarism to *politesse*. In order to indicate the validity of his category, Voltaire undertook to write an encyclopaedically complete account of history. Not only did he finish the story from Charlemagne to Louis XIII, but he added supplements on the history of China, India, Persia and Islam.

The purpose was as clear as it was pointless. On the one hand, the Chinese would have to appear in the story of mankind, but on the other, encyclopaedic completeness must presume that history as a whole is known. In fact, only the past can be known, which meant that the secular meaning of history was derived from the author's present, which in turn would soon enough be itself a past. Voltaire's witticism, that history is a pack of tricks we play on the dead, cannot be extended to itself without contradiction, even though the claim of universality meant that it must be. The doctrine of a secular historicism is fallacious. In principle, the fallacy can be spelled out in detail: the secular historian selects a partial structure of meaning and proclaims it to be a total meaning; he then ransacks the past for suitable historical evidence that may be arranged around the selected centre of meaning, which is then dignified as proof of the truth of the initial choice.

Voltaire's choice was the softening of manners. One might expect that it would have an appeal to persons whose manners were already softened and who therefore embodied a spirit of *politesse*. A century or two later the choice of a hardening of manners would do equally well. Accordingly, we must understand the reconstruction of the Augustinian theology of history as the introduction of an intramundane apocalypse. The purpose of such apocalyptic speculation is to endow the author's perfectly genuine sense of epoch with a meaning that may radiate into the otherwise chaotic past and provide it with a structure. The structure may then be used to freeze the contemporary sentiments in a form that presumes to be final. For Voltaire, manners could never harden without destroying his intramundane apocalypse, which was the meaning of his universal history.

Reconstruction of the Augustinian theology of history in accord with Voltairian principles of philosophy of history must, in principle, be considered a dead-end. By itself, the popular success of progressive doctrines is evidence only of the spiritual and intellectual breakdown of the western tradition. And yet, Voltaire's approbation of the Marquise for her insight regarding the scandal of ignoring the Chinese because they had never heard of Christianity contained an obvious truth. The enlargement of the historical horizon has provided a genuine problem for the present topic. There are two distinct ways to respond to the problem, the first by an expansion of the Augustinian *historia sacra*, the second, to resolve in detail the internal incoherence of philosophy of history.

The expansion of the Judeo-Christian sacred history has as its objective the purpose of demonstrating the participation of the non-Biblical communities in the unfolding of the historical Logos. The most important effort along these lines was undoubtedly that of Hegel. Despite gaps in chronology regarding the relative positions of China and Egypt, despite the virtual non-existence of Biblical criticism, to say nothing of such recent exotica as Carbon 14 and Bristlecone pine dating, Hegel was able to construct a plausible account of the development of spiritual order from China, through India, to the Mediterranean basin. In order to create a single line of sacred history, an enormous amount of highly recalcitrant material had to be hammered into shape along a single timeline. Instead of Voltaire's softening of morals, Hegel proposed the dialectical unfolding of *Geist*, Spirit, from the East to the West over the whole course of history. The chronological position of Egypt and Mesopotamia had to be shifted away from the beginning in order that they be preceded by China and India, and demoted from being autonomous empires into 'phases' of the Persian empire that destroyed them. Persia owed its position to geography but was doomed by the even further western empire of Rome, which was followed by the Germanic World that attained complete self-consciousness in the aftermath of the French Revolution and Napoleonic Empire. The transfiguration of Mohammed into a character in the picture gallery of the Germanic World ought to give even the most enthusiastic Hegelian reason to pause.

What enabled Hegel to distort the historical record with a good conscience, so to speak, was that he omitted an essential factor in historical reality, namely its mysteriousness. In reality, history was no more known to Hegel than it had been to Voltaire because it is not now and never has been an object of cognition. Hegel, however, assumed that it was by means of a couple of additional, and seemingly innocuous assumptions. The first was that the appearance of Christ was the 'hinge' of world-history because God revealed in Christ the Logos of history; but God did so by means of the *Gestalt*, the form, of religion, not of 'reason'. The revelation, therefore, was incomplete because it was not self-conscious; only the labour, the absolute labour, of the Hegelian 'philosopher' could completely reveal the Logos by providing it with its proper *Gestalt*, namely, 'reason'. To use the (for Hegel) superseded religious vocabulary of Christianity, the revelation of God in history reached its perfection in him, Hegel, because Hegel had fully comprehended it. The Augustinian waiting for the apocalypse had ended in Hegel.

In fact, of course, history has not ended. It may appear that way owing to a second, equally innocuous looking remark made in the Preface to the *Phenomenology*. Philosophy, Hegel said, should abandon its name, love of knowledge, (*Liebe zum Wissen*) and become actual knowledge, (*wirkliches Wissen*).[5] If one translates Hegel's terminology back into the Greek, he appeared to be advancing a programme of moving from *philosophia* to *gnosis*. In this programme he resumed the eighteenth-century sense of progress so that philosophy can eventually become *gnosis* or wisdom, to use Hegel's preferred term. As with his 'completion' of Christianity, Hegel had likewise 'completed' philosophy. In the *Phaedrus* (278d) Socrates described the attributes of the true thinker. Phaedrus asked him how he should be called and Socrates replied that to call him *sophos*, wise, would be too much, for only the god is wise. One might, however, call him *philosophos*, Socrates said.

The passage is central to an understanding of what philosophy is. The god of the *Phenomenology* is the ego of the speculative gnostic expanded to an ersatz knowledge of the whole of history. In Platonic terms, the gnostic speculation proceeded from hatred of God, or at least from a desire to be or to replace God. In reality, as with the speculative end of history, no such thing is possible. The apparently innocuous changes to the meaning of the Christian revelation of the Logos in Chirst and to the meaning of philosophy, in fact imply the violent destruction of reality. But in fact, not even Hegel can destroy reality. The best he could do was to seem to do so through the construction of a system within which all questions appeared to be answered and outside of which no questions could be conceived. Whatever else may be said of Hegel, it is clear that he also violated the first criterion of classical political philosophy, the raising of commonsense questions about justice, law, the best regime, and so on.

Several years ago George Misch observed that Hegel's speculation was experientially close to the speculation of the *Upanishads*. In particular the identity of the *atman* or conscious self with the *brahma* or supra-personal reality was very similar to Hegel's identity of identity and non-identity, of substance and subject and of other equally paradoxical formulations.[6] Within the economy of the Indian speculations, the ahistoric nature of the experience has been widely acknowledged. What is less easy to accept is 'the apparent absurdity that the most comprehensive and penetrating philosophy of history should be motivated by an ahistorical experience of order.'[7] Gnostic speculation, however, moves within the form of the myth, even when its subject matter is a philosophic and historical tradition, and even when such otherwise central realities as God, philosophy and history are transformed into gnostic cyphers. With considerable confidence, therefore, we can conclude that the attempt to create an expanded sacred history is also a dead-end.

As a postscript one may consider the attitude of the greatest of Hegelian epigones, Karl Marx. In Marx we are confronted with a novel kind of thinker: he knew that the Hegelian enterprise was a dead-end but he, nevertheless, refused to abandon it. Instead he prohibited the asking of commonsense questions and developed a kind of doctrinal screen to hide what he was up to. The widespread allegiance commanded by Marx's teachings today must be seen, therefore, as further evidence of modern philosophical deculturation.

In the 'Economic and Philosophical Manuscripts' of 1844 Marx advanced the opinion that the process of nature constituted the whole of being. During the course of its development, natural being disgorged human being, but in such a fashion that human being was both 'directly a being of nature' and opposed to nature insofar as human being assists the development of nature by labour.[8] By recreating nature, a human being thereby also creates human history, which in turn 'is nothing but the production of man by human labour.'⁹ There is, accordingly, no ground of being transcendent to the self-creation of man-and-nature.

In this context Marx then introduced the question of the creation of the first man. The 'particular individual', he said, might find the account just offered unsatisfactory or even 'inconceivable' because, Marx said, 'it contradicts all the tangible aspects of practical life.' Indeed it does. Such a person might be concerned with the question of the origin of human being and he might arrive at perplexity regarding that question by meditating on the significance of the infinite regress of generations. Marx's answer was as brutal as it was simple. Such questions are 'a product of abstraction'. Anyone who inquires 'about the creation of nature and man' engages in abstract speculation. The appropriate response, therefore, was: 'give up your abstraction and you will give up your question along with it.'¹⁰

The questioning of the 'individual man' was, in reality, a means of thinking about and expressing the experience of not being ontologically self-sufficient. It is an expression of not existing of oneself, an expression of one's creatureliness. Marx knew this. For this reason he shut off any exploration of the issue with the dogmatic declaration that since 'for socialist man, the whole of what is called world history is nothing but the creation of man by human labour, and the emergence of nature for man, he, therefore, has the evident and irrefutable proof of his self-creation, of his own origins.'¹¹ To translate this elaborate piece of sophistry into the language of commonsense, one would say that Marx was of the opinion that, when 'socialist man' opens his mouth everyone else, including the political philosopher, must keep silent. Moreover, as Marx pointed out in the following sentence, once this opinion of socialist man 'has become evident in political life', the quest for 'a being above man and nature', which is to say, a quest for the ground of being, 'becomes impossible in practice.'¹² One may translate this remark into commonsense as follows: when socialist man takes power, political philosophers will be liquidated.

The path from Hegel to Marx takes us, within the revisions of Augustinian sacred history, from the arena of speculative mysticism to activist mysticism. Hegel was a speculative mystic because his attempt to transform the mystery of historical existence proceeded as 'thought', or as Hegel would say, 'within the ether of the concept.' Marx was an activist rather than a speculative mystic because he sought to transform reality directly by historical activity. Both men, and numerous others who have assimilated intellectual scraps from their table, posit the evolution of human being into a 'god', as with Hegel, or into 'socialist man' (Marx). Such a being, whatever else may be said of it, is no longer human. On their own terms, such people serve a higher historical cause; the rest of us, merely human and in search of our humanity, must view them as demoniaically deformed.

It is not necessary to renounce commonsense nor to renounce political philosophy even in the modern world, and join the ideologues. There is another line of reversion of the Augustinian synthesis that begins, as did Voltaire, from the side of profane history. This alternative, unlike the Hegelian or Marxist, does not engage in the prohibition of questions nor in the distortion of historical evidence in order to impose a meaning on events.

What one loosely refers to as the cycle theory of history began with the Augustinian-Orosian construction but removed both the cosmological context along with the context of sacred history. Parallel histories without any interconnection were methodologically isolated one from another and subject to sequential analysis designed to specify a series of phases valid for all instances or rising and falling empires. The unit of study was not mankind but the civilizational course of growth, flourishing and decay; all civilizations were said to conform to the type. Typical regularities, therefore, can be used as a guide to diagnose the present. Indeed, that appears to be the purpose of the enterprise. More particularly, the purpose seems to be one of diagnosing the state of western civilization as one of decline on the brink of collapse. Spengler provided a representative example. The title of his famous book should be translated as the Going-Down of the West. A somewhat less fatalistic version is found in the early volumes of Toynbee's great work, A Study of History.

Such doctrines are not really cyclical because there is no return to the beginning and no repetition. An original and genuine cyclical theory was the Babylonian cosmological speculation on the course of the Great Year, which in turn is to be understood as a speculative mythical response to the experience of certain celestial movements known since antiquity as the precession of the equinoxes.[13]

The mythic experience was subjected to hypostatic analysis by Aristotle in Problemata XVII, 3. There he developed the concept that the course of history was a 'thing' that had a beginning, middle, and end; like a tragic performance it could be staged again. And so, Aristotle wondered whether his times were closer to the Trojan War in the past when it last occurred or in the future when it next will occur. One finds similar speculation in the heretical doctrines of the Latin Averroist, Siger De Brabant,[14] in the *Defensor Pacis* of Marsilius of Padua in 1324, in the sixteenth-century commentary of the humanist Louis Le Roy on Plato's *Timaeus*, and of course in Nietzsche's doctrine of the eternal recurrence. Compared to Spengler, these genuine cycle theories are noticeable for their absence of gloom and foreboding. The reason seems to be that they are speculations from within the medium of cosmic myth, so that for purposes of the argument at least, human history is not differentiated from cosmic change.

The suppression of Siger's doctrines in the late medieval period, to say nothing of Nietzsche, indicates the incompatibility of a genuine cycle theory with the Christian or Jewish doctrine of the transcendent spiritual destiny of humanity. According to this teaching, mankind moves along a single line towards messianic or apocalyptic fulfilment. Nor will such doctrines be compatible with secular progressivism or various dialectical elaborations of the Hegelian or Marxian type.

Spengler's doctrine could more accurately be described as being one of parallel histories. Somewhat simplified it states: (*a*) there exist a plurality of civilizations; (*b*) they grow and decline; and (*c*) there is no reason to think of the West as an exception. The last component in Spengler's doctrine, which might be called civilizational pessimism, evokes a particularly strong complex of sentiments. One is reminded of Plato's myth in the *Statesman* where the divine helmsman lets go of the rudder of the world. Left to itself the world starts spinning backwards and things fall apart. A more obvious precursor is the Germanic national myth, the *Nibelungenlied*, a great song of disaster for the West at the hands of the Asiatic hordes. One thinks again of Nietzsche here.

Not all civilizations provide equal amounts of evidence for Spengler's theory. The model civilization is the Greco-Roman. One reason, of course, is that it was probably better known to him than any other. There is more to it than familiarity, however. You recall that the commonsense of Orosius was sufficiently anaesthetized that he identified Ataulf the Visigoth as the restorer of Rome. Rome, which is still called the eternal city, is the great symbol of western spiritual continuity. By the eighteenth century the sentiment of discontinuity had found expression in the famous debate between ancients and moderns and in a less well-known debate, begun by Vico and Montesquieu and continued by Gibbon, Niebuhr and Mommsen into our own century by Eduard Meyer and Michael Rostovtzeff, on the decline and fall of Rome. According to Spengler's preface, the decline of the West was a late phase of our civilization analogous to the decline of Rome. And likewise in 1926, upon completion of his monumental *Social and Economic History of the Roman Empire*, Rostovtzeff wondered: 'Is it possible to extend a higher civilization to the lower classes without debasing its standard and diluting its quality to the vanishing point? Is not every civilization bound to decay as soon as it begins to penetrate the masses?'[15] One, but only one, of the reasons why Allan Bloom's *Closing of the American Mind* has found so many readers is that it expressed anxieties over the moral and spiritual disintegration of the West, and added to a tradition three centuries old.

In order for an analysis of the decline and fall of Rome to serve as an instrument of critique for the decline of the West, there must have occurred a break with the Orosian myth of continuity between Rome, Christianity and the West. With the rise of national states, natural science and a plurality of religious sects, the connection was gone. At the same time, however, these events were accompanied by the enormous destruction of national and religious wars. The resulting sentiments were highly ambivalent, not to say schizoid. On the one hand the destructiveness gained by the modern West in opposition to Roman antiquity was considered optimistically as progress; on the other it was viewed pessimistically as spiritual disintegration for which the accompanying violence was the most impressive evidence. The shifting moods and sentiments have become a structural feature of modern western self-consciousness.

Let us return to Orosius. The scantiest biographical information indicates that Ataulf was a destroyer of Rome and in no way its restorer. He was the brother-in-law of Alaric who in 410 sacked Rome for three days and nights, and prompting Augustine to begin his great work of analysis and retheorization. Ataulf's overriding ambition was to destroy the very name of Rome, Orosius said, but he contended himself with pillaging Etruria and southern Gaul.[16] As indicated earlier, the sentiment of symbolic continuity of profane history was strong. A millennium later, commonsense also indicated that the disintegration of the medieval sacred empire was effectively complete. What was the meaning of these profane events? Vico's *New Science* of 1725 and the final edition of 1744 provided an answer that was not unlike that of Spengler and Toynbee, but he did so by leaving Augustine's sacred history alone. Let me mention only the major elements. The pattern of Roman history, its *corso*, was the model for the 'eternal ideal' history of all civilizations. Western history is the *ricorso*, the second course, distinguished from the Roman in virtue of its distinct spirituality.

Toynbee resumed Vico's theory of the profane *corso* and *ricorso* in his famous metaphor of the wheel and the chariot. The rhythms of growth and decay, he said, are in no way fatal. They resulted from the ordinary fact that civilization results from a successful response to an environmental challenge and will grow so long as a creative minority responds successfully. Likewise, civilizations decline when either a challenge is too great or a dominant minority is strong enough to suppress a creative minority, which might meet the challenge, but is not itself flexible or imaginative enough to do so. With disintegration comes rebirth, which Toynbee expressed by the Chinese symbol Yin-Yang: the tranquility of Yin gives rise to the creativity of Yang, followed by disintegration back to a new Yin. The rhythm continues without end, but rebirth is not repetition. Rather it means, for Toynbee, the establishment of a new society at a higher stage of spiritual consciousness. The civilizational course is the wheel; the advancement of mankind towards the realization of humanity is the chariot moved by the civilizational wheel. Toynbee's theory, whatever its defects in gross or in detail, has the tremendous advantage of acknowledging a meaning in history on the supra-civilizational level of mankind.

But who or what is mankind? The question first arose in the West with the reflections of nineteenth-century Orientalists who discovered that in the India of Buddha and the China of Laotse and Confucius were spiritual outbursts the significance of which was comparable to those of the prophets of Israel or the Greek philosophers. At the same time the phenomena were accounted for by unspecified mechanisms of cultural diffusion, which had the apparent advantage of maintaining a hypothetical but single sacred history. In the work of Karl Jaspers and of the later Toynbee one finds the construction of parallel sacred histories.

Jaspers began with 'an article of faith: that mankind has one single origin and one goal. Origin and goal are unknown to us, utterly unknown by any kind of knowledge. They can only be felt in the glimmer of ambiguous symbols.'[17] It is true that Christianity claims universality in virtue of the fact that, to use Hegel's phrase Christ is the axis of world history. The claim, however, 'suffers from the defect that it can only be valid for believing Christians.' Accordingly, if there exists an axis of world history, it 'would have to be discovered empirically, as a fact capable of being accepted as such by all men, Christians included.' During this axis-time would be found a frame of historical understanding common to East and West in its significance for the formation of humanity.

Jaspers found it 'in the spiritual process that occurred between 800 and 200 BC..It is there that we meet with the most deepcut dividing line in history. Man, as we know him today, came into being.'[18] To the Chinese and Indian spiritual insights Jaspers added Zoroaster, the Israelite prophets and the Hellenic poets and philosophers. 'What is new about this age,' Jaspers said, 'in all three areas of the world, is that man becomes conscious of Being as a whole of himself and his limitations. He experiences the awfulness of the world and his own impotence. He asks radical questions. On the edge of the abyss, he strives for liberation and salvation. Conscious of his limitations, he sets himself the highest goals. He experiences the absolute in the depth of himself and in the luminosity of transcendence.'[19] In both thought and religion, the symbols and categories by which men live were developed during this period. It was in all respects an age during which humanity advanced toward the Universal.

Jaspers added that there existed a 'sociological' parallel as well. Small states grew into empires; a sense of history developed by way of historiographic records; political catastrophe led directly to the spiritual responses just noted. Toynbee himself has objected to Jaspers' account because the spiritual personalities involved were only chronologically contemporaries and not 'philosophical contemporaries' because their speculations were conditioned by different phases in the disintegration of their respective civilizations. Second, Toynbee maintained it was methodologically proper to consider the full periods of civilizational disintegration of the Indic, Syriac, Sinic, and Hellenic civilizations. When this is done the 'axis' extends from the tenth century BC to the thirteenth century AD. Otherwise Christianity, Mahayana Buddhism, Hinduism and Islam would all be excluded.[20] One may therefore doubt whether the term 'axis-time' is entirely apt for an epoch of 2300 years.

Toynbee's objections were advanced in a section of his long book where he explained his revision of the classification of societies he had used in the first six volumes (3500 pages) of his *Study*. In the earlier volumes, history was the 'humane study' of 'the lives of societies in both their internal and external aspects.'[21] By the seventh volume, however, he made the following observation: 'Now that our operations on these lines have proved fruitless, let us try the effect of reversing our point of view. Let us open our minds to the possibility that the churches might be the protagonists and that vice versa the histories of the civilizations might have to be envisaged and interpreted in terms, not of their own destinies, but of their effect on the history of Religion.'[22] Civilizations, therefore, 'have forfeited their historical significance except insofar as they minister to the progress of Religion.'[23] Instead of merely resuming the impasse of Spengler, namely the unconnected and essentially meaningless account of parallel histories, Toynbee recovered a kind of Augustinian sacred history, but expanded it to include the four parallel 'higher religions', namely Hinduism, Buddhism, Christianity and Islam, each of which was given equal spiritual dignity.

Considered in light of the present topic, comparative political philosophy, the advantages of these modern developments are obvious enough. Spiritual insights may occur within any of the major civilizations, which in turn receive their meaning as the vehicles by which humanity, in various different ways, advances towards the truth. Both Jaspers and Toynbee accord respect to every order and its symbolization as truth. Accordingly, the Eurocentric and unilinear constructions, which exhausted the field of historical speculation from Augustine to Hegel, Marx, Comte and their intellectual epigones, must be rejected as being untenable. Moreover, by locating the meaning of civilizational change in the area of religious experience, both Jaspers and Toynbee have rid themselves of ideological fantasies of the progressivist type.

Theirs, however, is not the last word. Neither Jaspers nor Toynbee seems to mention Moses in the context of 'higher religions' and yet it would seem to be inconceivable that history as a symbolic form that expressed the experience of existence in the present under God could ever exist without the Mosaic revelation.[24] Moreover, the breadth of toleration that engenders respect for the experiences of order and symbolization in a plurality of civilizations may degenerate easily enough into the wisdom of Lessing's Nathan, which is to say: resigned indifference. Accordingly, an awareness of differences in rank with respect to the search for truth and with respect to the insight achieved in the search will have to be retained.

Eric Voegelin has proposed a solution to the apparent conflict of Eurocentrism with criteria for determining differences in rank. It is possible here to give only the barest hints, but they should be sufficient to deal with the methodological issue.

First, with regard 'to the great question of Eurocentrism it will be advisable, therefore, to distinguish between its phenomenal and its philosophical aspects.' With respect to historical phenomena, the geographical restriction of the older accounts to the ancient near eastern, Mediterranean and western evidence has obviously given way in response to wider historical knowledge. Moreover, the time horizon has been pushed back well into the paleolithicum so far as continuity of cosmological symbolism is concerned. On the other hand, 'The Eurocentrism of position and standards cannot be abandoned by the philosopher of history, because there is nothing he could put in its place. History is made wherever men live, but its philosophy is a western symbolism.'[25] One might say analogically that political thought is undertaken wherever human beings exist in society, but its philosophy is a western symbolism.

There is no implication of any pragmatic or even moral significance to the empirically evident fact that political philosophy is a western achievement. It has the same status as the fact that the order of existence under the cosmic *tao* is a Chinese achievement. To say that both symbolisms are an achievement implies that, in different ways, they attained a truth that previously had not been gained. Truths have to be about something; and the most general thing there is, is being or the whole. Voegelin has called this fundamental reality the 'primordial community of being'. The structure of this community is expressed by the symbols God and man, world and society. It is known not as a phenomenon in the external world but only in virtue of human participation in the mystery of its being. The mystery of being and the essential human ignorance that accompanies it can never be extinguished, even though essential ignorance is not complete ignorance.

We know we participate; we know some things last longer than others; we know we have created symbols to make this participation and our awareness of durability and transiency intelligible to our-selves. The community of being, for example, is a cosmos. In order to last, humans and human societies must attune themselves to cosmic changes. The symbolism of the cosmos is also an achievement, but it is one that is so fundamental and, chronologically speaking, was achieved so early in human time (approximately 50,000 years ago, according to some authorities) that so far as the present topic is con-cerned, we may view it as coeval with human beings. The attunement of human beings and society to cosmic rhythms, therefore, may be taken as the fundamentum from which all subsequent symbolisms grew.

The stability of this symbolic form is attested by its longevity. It does, however, break down on occasion, so that a search for order must then be undertaken; and both the search and the insight into the source of order must then be re-symbolized.

By this account, the cosmos is unstable as well as stable. The rains do not come; the earth quakes; the equinoxes precess; comets appear; eclipses occur; women are barren; foreigners invade. During what Toynbee characterized as the Time of Troubles, efforts to under-stand the meaning of cosmic disorder are especially likely to be undertaken. There are exceptions to this generalization, the most important of which is Babylonian society. To the creative spiritual response to the Time of Troubles Voegelin has given the name 'leap upward in being' or 'leap in being'. The leap is experienced, so far as the evidence allows generalization, 'not as the result of human action, but as a passion, as a response to a revelation of divine being, to an act of grace, to a selection for emphatic partnership with God.'[26]

The break with the cosmological form or the leap in being is, Voegelin said, an 'epochal' event. In the near eastern and Aegean civilizational areas the break with what he called the 'compactness' of the cosmological form occurred twice and produced two distinct symbolisms to express the experience of the break, namely philosophy and revelation. 'Moreover', he said, 'comparable breaks with the myth, again of widely different complexions, occur contemporaneously in the India of the Buddha and the China of Confucius and Laotse.'[27] The break with the myth of the cosmos is, indeed, a 'special occasion', because it changes the order of being. No longer, for example, are the things of the world, the institutions of society, for example, so important as compared to the emphatic partnership with the divine. Thus, as was observed with Confucius, his insight did not lead him to become *jun* but to express himself as a *junzi*. Plato's term for the experience was 'turning-around', *periagoge*, an inversion or conversion toward the true source of order. One may conclude, therefore, that a change in the order of being has really taken place. Voegelin's terminology for the process is that of a movement from compactness to differentiation of experience of reality and its symbolization. But, 'the leap upward in being is not a leap out of existence.'[28] In commonsense language, the achievement of insight regarding the order of being cannot be undertaken unless one is adjusted to the order of ordinary mundane existence. What develops instead are various kinds of compromise between the modes or levels of existence. In classical political philosophy one finds Aristotle indicating that the lover of myth, the *philomythos* is also a kind of *philosophos* (*Meta.*, 982b 18) and even Plato says that every myth has its truth (*Epinomis*, 989 c–d). These formulae do not mean that the insight is compromised but that its expression must be undertaken with caution. Caution is necessary in order to do justice to the experience of continuity as well as to the experience of differentiation. The structure of reality does not change any more than does 'human nature' despite differences in the individual manifestation as myth or philosophy or, indeed, as revelation.

In a similar way it is possible to compare Aristotle and Confucius. Both have made the leap upward in being, away from the compactness of the cosmological myth and towards a more differentiated experience and symbolization of reality. One may speak, therefore, of a search for order in society, in the individual, and in history that is common to both. We are, however, still in search of a language appropriate to discuss this common search. In comparative religion, a discipline that is at least textually and analytically close to comparative political philosophy, may find a certain amount of guidance.

Discussions of myths and rituals, of cults, ceremonies and stories of posthumous existence, all use the language of equivalence. The Confucian *junzi*, by analogy, would be equivalent to the Aristotelean *politikos*, in the third sense discussed earlier, or perhaps to the *spoudaois*, the 'mature man' (*EN.*, 1113a25). Such statements proceed upon the assumption that the similitude that justifies the language of equivalence lies not in the symbols but in the experiences that engendered them. In this instance, the experience was characterized as the leap in being. The language of equivalence, therefore, implies the theoretical insight that 'what is permanent in the history of mankind is not the symbols but man himself in search of his humanity and its order.'[29] To identify this equivalent activity we may use the Platonic term *zetema*, search (*Rep.*, 368c).

The *zetema* for right order, which is the substantive content to the present topic, cannot conclude with a catalogue of propositions concerning right order nor a list of 'permanent values' because existence does not have the form of order. It does not have the form of disorder either, no more than does the cosmos. The cosmos and existence are both ordered and disordered, the structure of the one being expressed in myth, the other in the *zetema*. If you prefer, the *zetema* is structured as a tension between truth and untruth, and not the relief of an arrival at one or another pole. Voegelin's preferred term is the Platonic *metaxy*, the in-between (*Symp.*, 202a). That is, the constants that appear to the *zetema* express the structure of existence as an in-between: the prepositional language indicates the tension between life and death, truth and untruth, order and disorder, perfection and imperfection, joy and despair.

An obvious theoretical conclusion is that if we hypostatize these terms into separate entities 'we destroy the reality of existence as expressed by the creators of the tensional symbolisms.'[30] If, nevertheless, the distinct symbolisms may be understood as equivalent, the reason must lie in the equivalence of the engendering experience. As an example of historically equivalent truths one could hardly improve on the formula of Clement of Alexandria: 'To the barbarians God has given the Law and the Prophets; to the Hellenes he has given Philosophy; so that the ears of both might be prepared to hear the Gospel.'[31] Clement's observation should not be seen as a literalist dogma but an expression of the process of differentiation, and therefore a warning against ending on a note of finality. The *zetema*, therefore, cannot conclude with a catalogue of equivalent experiences.

The reason is clear: if it did, then it would take the form of an account that accounts for all possible symbolizations. This was Hegel's solution and it must be rejected in principle because it was based on the untenable claim that it was more than a historically equivalent truth. Analytically, therefore, we must extend the equivalence to the engendering experiences of truth, but with the proviso that an account of experience beyond the symbolization that makes it articulate is impossible. All that can be said is that it is a beyond or a depth from which the symbols emerge. The depth (or the beyond) is therefore beyond articulate experience; the emergent symbols cannot furnish any substantive information or content beyond expressing the structure of reality experienced as God, man, world and society, which is to say, the primordial community of being.

And yet, that is itself a significant insight. It is, perhaps, the most important achievement of modern western political philosophy. Moreover, it directs political philosophers toward the questions initially raised during classical antiquity as well as outside the western civilizational area. At all times and places, the exploration of this community of being is concerned with establishing the true nature of man, God, world and society; the discursive establishment of that true nature constitutes the verities found in the historical field of equivalent experiences and symbols; the analysis of that historical field is both the task and the content of comparative political philosophy. The criteria by which more adequate symbolizations of truth can be distinguished from less adequate ones is therefore already present in the differentiation of consciousness that is present concretely in the analyst. Considered from the side of the evidence of phenomena rather than the consciousness of the analyst one would say: historical phenomena emerge as 'a newly differentiated truth recognizably equivalent to the more compact truth it is meant to replace.'[32] Either way, the literary form appropriate to comparative political philosophy is the meditative exegesis of experiences.

A summary of these concluding reflections requires but a brief statement.

First, there is no constant in history but only the constancy of the *zetema*. Second, by 'history' is meant the trail of equivalent symbols and experiences left by the *zetema* in time and space. Third, the historical field constituted by the experiences of the concrete individuals and the symbolization of those experiences—by a Plato, an Augustine, a Confucius, a Kautilya, a Farabi—is itself not the result of any one person's insight, and yet it does constitute an intelligible whole. Aristotle's opening words of the *Metaphysics*, 'all men by nature desire to know' is not an empirical generalization but expresses a faith in the premise that even though the truth concerning the reality of human being can only be found concretely by one person at a time, it is also true that, as a truth, it applies to all people. The one who experiences the truth and expresses it does so, therefore, as a representative human being. The search for truth, the *zetema*, which is the subject matter of comparative political philosophy, makes sense only if we assume that the articulation of a specific truth on a particular occasion by a distinct symbolic form has been brought up from the inarticulate depth. The symbolism, which is found in the great texts of western and non-western, of ancient and modern political philosophy, is not, therefore, the ultimate truth of reality but a representative of the depth, or of being.

Behind the field of equivalent experiences and symbolizations is the individual who undertook the *zetema* for a truth that was more than equivalent. Comparative political philosophy is likewise a *zetema* that renders equivalent truth, though it rests on the same faith that its truth will be the same for all human beings. This insight, which is expressed in the linguistic formulae of modern western political philosophy, is itself equivalent to ancient and non-western insights into the structure of reality experienced.

NOTES

1. Bernadete, *Herodotean Inquiries*. The Hague: Martinus Nijhoff, 1969, p. 209; cf., *Phaedrus*, 97b–100b.
2. Quoted in Eric Voegelin, *From Enlightenment to Revolution*. Durham: Duke University Press, 1975, p. 5.
3. Hazard, *La Crise de la Conscience Européen*. Paris: Boivin, 1935.
4. For an account of the theoretical issues involved, see Voegelin, *Order and History*, vol. IV, *The Ecumenic Age*. Baton Rougè: Louisiana State University Press, 1974, pp. 59–113; and Barry Cooper, *The Political Theory of Eric Voegelin*. Toronto: Edwin Mellen, 1986, pp. 125–60.
5. G.W.F. Hegel, *Phaenomenologie des Geistes*, ed. J. Hoffmeister. Hamburg: Meiner, 1952, p. 12. For a detailed account of the implications see Barry Cooper, *The End of History*. Toronto: University of Toronto Press, 1984.
6. Misch, *The Dawn of Philosophy*. Cambridge: Harvard University Press, 1951.
7. Eric Voegelin, *Order and History*, vol. II, *The World of Polis*. Baton Rouge: Lousiana State University Press, 1957, pp. 18–19.
8. Marx, 'Economic and Philosophical Manuscripts', in T.B. Bottomore, ed. & tr., *Early Writings*. London: Watts, 1963, pp. 206, 164.
9. *Early Writings, op. cit.*, p. 166.
10. *Early Writings, op. cit.*, pp. 165–66.
11. *Early Writings, op. cit.*, p. 166.
12. *Early Writings, op. cit.*, pp. 166–67.
13. A wealth of detail and analysis is in Geiorgio de Santillana and Hertha von

Dechend, *Hamlet's Mill: An Essay on Myth* and the *Frame of Time*. London: Macmillan, 1970.

14. See Eric Voegelin, 'Siger De Brabant', *Philosophy and Phenomenological Research*, 4 (1944), pp. 505–26.
15. Rostovtzeff, *Social and Economic History*. New Haven: Yale University Press, 1926, p. 487.
16. Orosius, *Seven Books of History*, VII, *op. cit.*, 43. See also Gibbon, *The Decline and Fall of the Roman Empire, op. cit.*, ch. 21.
17. Karl Jaspers, *The Origin and Goal of History*, tr. M. Bullock. London: Routledge and Kegan Paul, 1953, p. xv.
18. Jaspers, *Origin and Goal, op. cit.*, p. 1
19. Jaspers, *Origin and Goal, op. cit.*, p. 2. Slightly altered on the basis of the original German text.
20. Arnold Toynbee, *A Study of History*. London: Oxford University Press, 1954, Vol. VII, B, pp. 421–22, n. 2.
21. Toynbee, *A Study of History*. London: Oxford University Press, 1934, Vol. I, p. 46.
22. Toynbee, *Study*, Vol. VII B, *op. cit.*, p. 420.
23. Toynbee, *A Study of History*, Vol. VII B, *op. cit.*, p. 449.
24. See Eric Voegelin, *Order and History*, Vol. I, *Israel and Revelation*. Baton Rouge: Louisiana State University Press, 1956, Ch. 12.
25. Voegelin, *Order and History*, Vol. II, *The World of the Polis*. Baton Rouge: Louisiana State University Press, 1957, p. 23.
26. Voegelin, *Order and History*, Vol. I, *Israel and Revelation*. Baton Rouge: Louisiana State University Press, 1956, p. 10.
27. Voegelin, *The World of the Polis, op. cit.*, p. 1.
28. Voegelin, *Israel and Revelation, op. cit.*, p. 11.
29. Voegelin 'Equivalences of Experience and Symbolization in History'. *Philosophical Studies*, 28 (1981), p. 89.
30. Voegelin, 'Equivalences', *op. cit.*, p. 92.
31. Clement, *Stromateis, op. cit.*, VI.
32. Voegelin, 'Equivalences', *op. cit.*, p. 101.

4 Law and Society In Confucian Thought

Ronald C. Keith

CONFUCIUS AND CHINESE POLITICAL THOUGHT

Within the grand, syncretic Confucian tradition, successive generations of scholar literati engaged in the textual exegesis of Confucius' *Analects*, *Lunyu*. Down through dynastic history, each generation had to come to terms with the central theoretical issue of the relation of law and state to society. Chinese political theory and practice continuously sought to resolve the tension between the bureaucratic resort to law as a matter of reward and punishment and the commitment of the scholar literati to 'teaching by moral example.' Bureaucratic legalism strengthened the state's autonomy from society even while political theory regarded the state as the external reflection of the anterior moral ordering of human relationships within society. This debate has had profound implications for the development of modern Chinese political culture, and over the last several years Chinese Marxist-Leninist theorists have self-consciously examined these implications in terms of 'feudalism' which has survived the rigours of revolution.

The debate started with Confucius, who happened upon the stage of Chinese history at a critical juncture of social and institutional crisis. He lived in an era of anomie and military conflict. There was then only the myth of the sage kings and the declining prestige of

Acknowledgement: I wish to thank the Social Sciences and Humanities Research Council for its support of the project, 'China's "Lawful Society": Law in the Politics of Modernization'.

the Zhou dynasty's nominal imperium to sustain men of principle against the spiralling military conflict between feudal states. Confucius did not live to see the germination of the seeds which he planted, but his ideas became the single most powerful unifying force in the subsequent development of the Chinese empire.

His own antecedents were decidedly modest as was his political career. According to the *Shi Ji* (i.e., *Book of History*, which Confucius is said to have edited himself), he was born in 551 BC to an impoverished noble family in the state of Lu (part of contemporary Shandong province). His father died when he was three, and he was brought up by his mother. Confucius did not have sufficient noble status to acquire high position. The tradition which suggests he was a high judicial official in Lu is controversial.[1] As a young man he was employed as an accountant and as a field superintendent.[2]

In 497 BC he left the service of Lu to become an itinerant teacher. For 13 years he wandered between the various feudal courts offering sagely though at times unwelcome and blunt advice to princes. The *Analects*, which were posthumously compiled by his disciples, provide a rambling anecdotal account of such advice to the bellicose feudal lords.

Within his own temporal and social context, Confucius was a living paradox. His political conservatism had revolutionary implications. Confucius sought sanction for the prevailing moral ordering of society in the golden age of the western Zhou dynasty when apocryphal sage kings ruled. Access to political office in his own time was still largely, although not exclusively, a matter of heredity. The 'nobles', *shi*, who acted as state ministers, in contrast to the sons of rulers, acquired their state positions on the basis of ability as well as birth. The *shi* included scribes, warriors and stewards who were the scion of great aristocratic houses.[3]

Confucius, although he was himself a scribal member of the *shi* class, ignored hereditary credentials to choose his own disciples on the basis of their moral worth. The sage kings likewise were thought to have appointed their ministers and successors. In his self-professed modest role as a transmitter of the past, Confucius had an earnest Tory wish to reinstate a traditional moral order, but his advice persisted down through the centuries to challenge the hereditary claims of military aristocracy.

This great historical social dilemma was explicit in Confucius' usage of the term, *junzi*. Past connotations of *junzi* meaning 'son of the sovereign' were progressively dropped in favour of *junzi* as a morally superior gentleman.[4] All too often the avaricious, pugnacious feudal lords of his day were more likely to fall into the opposite category of *xiao ren*, or 'small man', i.e., man of base, materialistic instincts. Confucius' fearless admonitions to feudal lords to aspire to the moral and intellectual level of the *junzi* who seeks 'the root of knowledge' may well help explain his own difficulties in acquiring high office; however, his emphasis on moral qualification in government service eventually became the dominant ideal in Chinese imperial history.

Confucius did not live to witness the final repudiation of the Zhou imperial legacy and the full blown development of a feudal system of warfare in the era known as the Warring States Period, 463–222 BC, but his ideas were carried forward in the context of great debates over the nature of the state and its relation to an understanding of human nature.

Sharply veering towards a pessimistic view of human nature, Legalist rivals frontally challenged Confucius' disciples and their notion of government by virtue. Arguing that the future appearance of sage kings was extremely unlikely, they opposed government by law to government by moral example.

Law had previously been reserved for querelous, malodorous foreigners and commoners whereas the principle of *li* has applied in the application of ritual to the social relationships of the upper classes. Rather than treating the state as the moral extension of society, the Legalists sought to create an autonomous state which would mould society for its own purposes of 'wealth and power'. Law as an instrument of the state was designed to contain the evil nature of man through the systematic and efficacious application of punishment and reward. Legalism, however, achieved its own nemesis in its identification with the sheer brutality of the first imperial dyansty, the Qin dynasty, 221–206 BC. Thereafter, Legalism as a state philosophy was simply politically unacceptable.

Successive generations of Confucian scholars denounced the Legalists for their disparagement of virtue as the basis of government, and for their superficial focus on quantification and measurement. However, even though Legalism had discredited itself, some of its bureaucratic methods of rulership were later surreptitiously incorporated into the Confucian tradition by the Confucian *junzi* themselves. Confucian officials had to resort to law even though its very existence called into question the practicality of government by moral example.

Within the western democratic context, a certain dignity accrued to to the notion of law which may have originated with the influence of some of the more optimistic assumptions of the European natural law tradition. The latter as an exercise in human reason transcended the merely prudential requirements of man's ascent from the perilous state of nature. St. Thomas Aquinas, for example, viewed lowly human law, even with all its imperfections, as the ordinance of reason for the common good. Even so, comparative political thought has not stressed enough on the significance of the status of law as an element of modern political development. Perhaps this is because it is almost axiomatic that a healthy respect for law as the reflection of widely held moral principles in society is a mark of a sophisticated political culture.

Since 1978 and until very recently in China, there has been a strong emphasis on the 'dignity of law' as an essential element within 'socialist spiritual civilization' (*shehuizhuyi jingshen wenming*), and this essay will examine the interstices of classical and modern Chinese political thought in relation to the dignity accorded to law in Chinese society.

THE PLACE OF LAW IN THE CONFUCIAN TRADITION

The 'Confucian tradition' was a grand eclectic tradition culled from the different interpretative schools of Confucianism as well as from rival schools of Maoism, Daoism, and Buddhism. This tradition encompassed a great debate on the role of law in society, but within Confucian theory, law posed a political dilemma with respect to the legitimacy of 'government by virtue'.

Confucianism within the 'Confucian tradition' was interested in the cosmic immanence of virtue, and the Confucian imperial official was in theory primarily concerned with the moral demonstration of such virtue in society through the compelling example of his own conduct. The latter theoretically rendered the application of law as largely unnecessary as the exercise of government focused on teaching by moral example (*shenjiao*). The latter would flow faster than imperial writ. Even so, in the context of his governmental responsibilities, the Confucian as a moral but technically unaccomplished personality was called upon to make legal judgements and to participate in the making of law.

The Confucian official was, thereupon, locked in a resulting contradiction insofar as the use of law drew attention to the failure of his own moral example—a point which had been drawn out in the original arguments of Legalism.

Even so, in the Confucian tradition, there is at least some hint of a theoretical linkage between law in human society and the laws of nature. The *Book of Changes* says, for example, that law is derived from '...an understanding of ways of nature and from a study of the activities of men. It is modelled after the constant law of nature, and it is useful to guide the people.'[5] However, according to Joseph Needham, who laments the Daoist failure to move towards the systematic identification of the 'laws of nature', China did not have an equivalent differentiation between the twin ideas of a natural law tradition and a body of the laws of nature regarding the physical properties of the universe. The following explanation highlights the lack of a religious conception of God in the Chinese intellectual universe:

In order to believe that Nature was rational and intelligible the western mind found it congenial to suppose the existence of a Supreme Being, himself rational, who had put it there. The Chinese mind did not think in these terms at all. Imperial majesty corresponded not to a legislative creator but to a Pole Star, to the focal point of a universal ever-moving pattern and harmony not made with hands, even those of God.[6]

Like many others, Needham did recognise a rudimentary element of 'natural law' in the Chinese intellectual focus on *li*, implying the ritual manifestation of what is right in society, and he concludes: '...*li* was much more important for society than natural law was in Europe.'[7]

The secular dimensions of the Confucian tradition may have been overstressed in western comparative analysis. The highly respected research of Derk Bodde and Clarence Morris, for example, opines: 'The contrast of the Chinese attitude to the belief in a divine origin of the law is indeed striking, for in China no one at any time has ever hinted that any kind of written law...could have a divine origin.'[8] This general point, however, is qualified with reference to the phenomological tendencies within the Confucian tradition requiring the application of the full force of the law against any crime which disrupted the sense of order within the cosmos.

Both '*fa*', law, and '*li*', the ritual extension of the inner moral sense of 'benevolence' or 'humaneness' (*ren*) into social relationships, were theoretically entangled with 'filial piety' which focused on the perpetuation of the family through ancestor worship. *Li* was a central aspect of Confucian theory linking man, earth and heaven as is evident in Confucius' instruction to 'first cultivate the self, then regulate the family, then order the state and there will be peace under heaven' (*xiu shen, qi jia, zhi guo, hoping tianxia*).[9] The Legalists disparaged *li* as a specious Confucian justification for privilege and corruption. Alternatively, they offered *fa* as the ordering principle of society, which was to be imposed directly by the state, thus reversing the relation between society and state.[10]

Confucius transmitted the wisdom of the ancients, but he was not a lawgiver. His concern was the living out of moral principles in social life. He did not explicitly advise rulers on what to put in the law; he did advise rulers as to how they might avoid disharmonious litigation among the populace. *A priori* to government is 'knowing the root' (*zhi ben*). Moral self-cultivation by the 'superior man' would lead to the regulation of familiar relationships on the basis of *li* as the external social extension of internal benevolence, i.e., *ren*. The wider extension of such relationships became *a priori* to the ordering of the state. In the *Great Learning*, Confucius compared governing with teaching and he provided a brief internal gloss on the meaning of what subsequently became a famous instruction 'in order to rightly to govern the state, it is necessary first to regulate the family by saying "it is not possible for one to teach others, while he cannot teach his own family."'[11] In Chapter Four, Confucius highlighted the following question: 'In hearing litigations, I am like any other body. "What is necessary to cause the people to have no litigations?"'[12] Confucius' point was simple enough—if there are no 'depraved thoughts' there would be no need of litigation and legal pettifoggers or 'litigation sticks', *song gun*.

Confucius cast the 'Son of Heaven' as the 'north polar star' and he intended to use *li* as one means of standing on guard against 'depraved thoughts'. Within this specific regimen, ritualised moral example becomes an active moral position which goes beyond 'speeches', whereas law becomes an invitation to induce a passive moral condition on the populace resulting in a narrow, negative focus on 'avoidance of punishment'.

Confucius taught in the *Analects*: 'He who exercises government by means of his virtue [*yi de*] may be compared to the north polar star, which keeps its place and the stars turn towards it.' In the same passage Confucius noted: 'If the people be led by laws, and uniformity sought to be given them by punishments, they will try to avoid the punishments, but have no sense of shame [*wu chih*].'[13] Confucius disparaged any exclusive preoccupation with uniform standards, and he conceptualised the progression in stages of human moral development from the age of fifteen when the mind turns to learning to the age of seventy, when a 'superior man' could 'follow what [his] heart desired, without transgressing what was right.'[14]

The theoretical debate within early Confucianism posed a major problem for the scholar official working within the Confucian imperial tradition as codified law became a practical necessity. Even Mencius, with reference to the necessity of 'benevolent government' (*ren zheng*) conceded: 'Virtue [*de*] alone is not sufficient for government; laws cannot carry themselves into practice.'[15] Like Confucius, Mencius abhorred the unseemly emphasis on punishment, but he argued that men of 'virtue' would, nevertheless; have to make the penal laws clear to the people.

Bodde and Morris have maintained that the Chinese dynastic legal codes demonstrated '...a continuity and authoritativeness which make them unrivalled instruments for measuring precisely, dynasty by dynasty, the shifting configurations of Chinese social and political values as officially defined.'[16] Bodde and Morris concluded that there was over the centuries 'a gradual Confucianization of law', in terms of 'an incorporation into the law codes of the social values originally contained in the Confucian *li*.'[17] The penal quality of the 'positive law' of attenuated Legalism had to co-exist with Confucianism's practical attempts to fashion the law in relation to 'society as a hierarchy of unequal components, harmoniously functioning at different levels to form an ordered whole.'[18]

Legalist theory granted the state autonomy from society, and the law was viewed as a precise instrument providing for political stability in society through a clearly defined system of rewards and punishments. Law did not originate with principles derived from the 'regulation' of the family and the teachings of 'superior men', for as the preeminent exponent of Legalism, Han Feizi, noted: 'By common observation, the virtuous are few and the worthless are many.' The populace would have trouble understanding the niceties of virtue but could intuitively relate to the necessity of law as a matter of deterrence, hence Han argued that '...the prohibition of evil is a universal standard.'[19]

Legalism disputed the continuous existence of 'benevolence' in society as the durable basis for government. The Confucian reliance on past moral examples of sage kings was disparaged as was the Confucian preoccupation with feelings of morality which would allegedly serve to generate confusion in the law and political and social instability within the populace. The issue was not 'the avoidance of punishment'. Where the Confucians feared contentiousness among the people as the result of written law, the Legalists feared the lack of clarity in law which was necessary in terms of the political stability of the state. Han Feizi focused attention on the political necessity of clearly understood laws in society:

> the best rewards are those which are generous and predictable, so that the people may profit by them. The best penalties are those which are severe and inescapable so that the people will fear them. The best laws are those which are uniform and inflexible so that people can understand them.[20]

Under this regime law rather than the official becomes the inspirational source of instruction.

THE 'DIGNITY OF LAW' IN CONTEMPORARY CHINA

From the late 1970s through to the present the Chinese Communist Party strongly emphasized 'lawful society' (fazhi shehui) or the 'dignity of law' (faludi zunyan) for two related reasons. In the first place, there has recently been a great desire for political stability in reaction to the political devastation of the party during the Cultural Revolution. The party leaders, themselves, had experienced the arbitrary judgement of competing armed mass organizations which had dispersed rough justice in kangaroo courts and engaged in the 'three negations', or the institutional dismantling of the courts, procuratorates and public security organs. They had a personal stake in establishing institutional checks against the violence of 'one-man rule' or 'rule by the individual' (renzhi). The origins of the latter were theoretically traced to 'feudalism' (fengjianzhuyi) which had persisted into the present stage of socialism.

The repeated official condemnation of some party members for thinking that they were exempt from the law's authority has some parallel in the Legalist accusation against the Confucians who allegedly excluded themselves from the application of the law. The widespread illegal violence against party leaders during the Cultural Revolution has been attributed in part to the failure to consolidate the legal and democratic system since 1949. Writing in the Central Committee's journal, Li Buyun and Wang Hanqing drew the following conclusion:

> The main reason for the imperfect democratic and legal system was that the law did not have lofty dignity.... Our Constitution and laws were unable to stop the leaders from erroneously launching and developing the 'Great Cultural revolution'.... Therefore, in order to prevent a repeat of the historical tragedy like the 'Great Cultural Revolution'...we must make our party and government leaders...act in strict accordance with the Constitution and laws and we must never allow anyone privilege overriding the law....[21]

Secondly, with the change in the party line de-emphasizing class struggle and underlining the 'four modernizations', political stability has become a self-conscious priority which is linked to the success or failure of economic reform, hence the party slogan 'grasping construction and reform with one hand and grasping the legal system with the other' featured a positive correlation between the development of the legal system and the interrelated goals of political stability and national economic construction.[22]

While Mao Zedong's theory of contradictions has been retained as a vehicle for understanding social and institutional reality, his focus on the merits of disequilibrium as the motor of human progress has been utterly rejected. Law in the early 1980s became the 'regularization of policy' in that it is more deliberately thought out, and it has the advantage of 'standardization'. This view was underwritten in Deng Xiaoping's objection to the 'two-line struggle' of the Cultural Revolution as the basis for interpreting leadership and policy disputes. This polemical struggle was an aspect of 'the rule of man' rather than the 'rule of law'. Mao's own personality cult had brought the Chinese legal system crashing down during the Cultural Revolution. A leading theorist, Zhang Yongming spelt out the following political implications:

> In the past our work was often guided by our leaders' spirit, which

might show inclination toward one orientation one day but the opposite orientation the next. Very often, some kind of intrinsically good 'spirit' could be freely interpreted by some people according to their own likes and dislikes or other own different ideas. In contrast, laws have the advantage of stability. They cannot be changed at will.[23]

In reacting to the need for economic reform and political stability, Deng Xiaoping lamented: 'Our country has no tradition of observing and enforcing laws.'[24] Why? Since the late 1970s, the party has traced the problem to a persisting feudalism in China's modern society.

'FEUDALISM' AND CHINA'S LEGAL TRADITION

Current events certainly suggest that the Chinese have yet to resolve the tension between '*quanli*', the power which legally derives from formal official position, and '*shili*', the power derived from political prestige and related patronage. However, since the late 1970s a new party consciousness has developed on this question as it relates to 'feudalism', defined in terms of the patriarchal absolutism associated with 'one-man rule'. The Chinese concept of 'feudalism' has to be rigorously distinguished from its European counterpart.

In the great span of Chinese history, the term has only a superficial relevance to European notions of 'enfeoffment', military obligation and property ownership. In fact its connotation of 'one-man rule' as it reflects imperial absolutism would seem to have little to do with the fragmentation of political authority implied in the European phenomenon. Derk Bodde has argued that from 'a strictly political point of view' 'feudalism' in its European connotations may have only occurred in the Zhou period, 1122–256 BC and in AD 221–589.[25] However, while western historiography assumed the supersession of feudalism in the making of the Confucian imperial tradition, Chinese Communist Party applied feudalism to the entire period from the Warring States Period up to 1949. And more recently, under Deng Xiaoping's influence, the term has acquired significance in the party interpretation of the Cultural Revolution.

Marx actually did try to iron out the conceptual wrinkles of Chinese social history by dropping feudalism and resorting to 'Asiatic' society as a *sui generis* which juxtaposed a highly bureaucratic state, capable of organizing large-scale agrarian projects as against the 'dispersed' condition of the 'Oriental' people who combined small agriculture and handicrafts in their essentially self-supporting villages. This theory was overcome by politics. Stalin's characterisation of the Chinese agrarian social order as 'feudal' was endorsed by the Sixth Congress of the CCP which had met under his watchful eye in Moscow in 1928. Chinese Communist theory, however, embraced this characterisation as it brought the Chinese revolution within the mainstream of world revolutionary development.

Professor Stuart Schram, who is well-known for his explanation of the Chinese Communist impulse towards the 'sinification' of Marxism-Leninism, has described the paradox in the Chinese theoretical subscription to 'feudalism' in the following way:

> But the determination of Mao and other non-Western Leninists to fit themselves at all costs in Western patterns may also be explained by the prestige of the West even among those who are politically most hostile to it, and their rejection of certain ideas on the inherent inferiority of their own societies.[26]

Important to the Weberian discussion of feudalism is the legal definition of the rights of lords and vassals in relation to the prevailing normative conception of honour and loyalty. In contrast, Chinese theory has spent little time on the question of enfeoffment. The focus is shifted to the connotations of absolute patriarchal authority implied in the emperor's role as 'Son of Heaven'. The Confucian feudal tradition only admitted of one singular source of 'truth'.

Deng Xiaoping used Mao's theory of contradictions and particularly his conception of 'seeking the truth from the facts' to debunk the 'whateverist' position in the party which emulated feudalism in its fervent conviction that Mao was absolutely and forever correct. In an important resolution, the party's Central Committee formally described 'feudal ideology' as including 'patriarchal clannishness, autocratic ways, the tendency to seek privileges and to form factions for selfish purpose....'[27] The issue of feudalism was the key to the trial proceedings of the 'gang of four'. One judge, Fei Xiaodong, depicted the proceedings, themselves, as a vivid lesson in the 'rule of law' which countered the tendency during the Cultural Revolution to favour 'rule by the individual.'[28]

In some respects the contemporary focus on feudalism is reminiscent of the liberal view of the Confucian tradition prevalent in the 1920s. Legalism had, according to Liang Qichao; addressed the failure of the latter, and it had even anticipated the 'modern theory of sociology' in its description of three stages of Chinese social development from the 'tribal stage' in which authority rests in the Confucian obsession with familial ties through a complex second stage marked by a division of labour favouring the incipient autonomy of the state from society to a final stage wherein the laws became 'fixed' thus providing impersonal standards for all time.[29] In the end, however, Liang could not abide Legalism, for, while it claimed that all were equal before the law, it gave the ruler an unqualified legislative authority. Legalism's interest in the autonomous state did not in the end serve Liang's interest in liberal democracy.

CONCLUSION

The contemporary party focus on feudalism relates to the outstanding problems of twentieth century political leadership as much as it relates to the lack of a legal tradition. While Deng may appear to share the Legalist concern for 'fixed standards' so as to achieve the political stability necessary for modernization, he has used 'Mao Zedong Thought' as the vehicle with which to assert 'seeking the truth from the facts' against 'personality cult' or 'one-man rule'. By the 'scientific' standards of Mao's own thought, Mao's leadership has been fairly accurately assessed although the party's political-sociological explanation, as it is premised in 'feudalism', is a cause for some theoretical confusion.

The frank admission of continuing 'partriarchal ways' in the context of modern China may turn out to be very important. Deng raised the issue, only to follow in Mao Zedong's footsteps. In assuming supreme power as 'helmsman' (*duoshuo*) he did not personally follow through in his own commitment to the 'rule of law'.

Deng's attribution of the lack of laws and law-abidingness in society to the lack of 'tradition' is somehow uninformative. It may distract from the underlying practical issues of political power and leadership in a Marxist-Leninist state and may also distract from an effective theoretical understanding of the complexity and contemporary influence of 'tradition'.

Within senior political circles, the discussion of Legalism has been conspicuous by its absence. The Chinese leadership in the mid-1980s was in a great rush to create law, and there is the possibility that in the absence of a solid social consensus too much of the responsibility for coping with the infrastructural problems of the newly emerging political regime was placed on the inadequate shoulders of the legal system. The party, even if it was inclined to do so, cannot will into existence a new social consensus underwriting the 'lofty dignity of the law'.

The Confucian tradition does not offer a direct equivalence to the natural law tradition in Europe in terms of the development of law as an extension of moral principles in society. Chinese political theory needs to move beyond the narrow interpretation of Confucianism as 'feudalism' to treat the totality of the 'Confucian tradition'. Within the Confucian tradition the scholar official feared too much law would discredit both the social requirements of *li* and the political imperium, and there was no systematic justification for the incorporation of human reason into law. However, Legalism within the same tradition sought to place law on a pedestal for reasons which had little to do with the cultivation of moral standards of behaviour within society. In the latter case the law could have an 'educative' moral effect in terms of the purposes of the state, but these purposes were at bottom genuinely authoritarian and inconsistent even with Mao's mass line and the on-going theoretical attempts to define 'socialist democracy'.

Ironically, it was Deng Xiaoping who identified law and democracy as necessary to the accomplishment of modernisation, but even given the ideological commitment to 'seeking the truth from the facts' a comprehensive theory has yet to be evolved whereby the 'rule of law' and 'socialist democracy' can be entwined in the party process of 'political restructuring' without seriously challenging the contemporary Marxist-Leninist structures of political leadership and the genuine development of 'socialism with Chinese characteristics'.

NOTES

1. H.G. Creel challenged official Chinese history on this point. See his *Confucius:*

The Man and the Myth. London: Routledge, 1951; and also Vitaly Rubin, *Individual and State in Ancient China*. New York: Columbia University Press, 1976, pp. 6–7.

2. On Confucius' rank and occupational experience see Cho-yun Hsu, *Ancient China in Transition*. Stanford: Stanford University Press, 1965, p. 35.

3. For sociological analysis of the *shi* see Benjamin Schwartz, *The World of Thought in Ancient China*. Cambridge, Mass.: Harvard University Press, 1985, pp. 58–59; and Hsu, *Ancient China in Transition*, *ibid.*, p. 34.

4. For the changing connotations of *junzi* see Rubin, *Individual and State in Ancient China*, *op. cit.*, pp. 20–21; and H.G. Creel, *Chinese Thought from Confucius to Mao Tse-tung*. Chicago: University of Chicago Press, 1975, p. 27.

5. Liang Ch'i-chao, *History of Chinese Political Thought*. New York: AMS Press, Inc., 1930, 1960, p. 113.

6. Joseph Needham, *The Shorter Science and Civilisation in China: 1*. London: Cambridge Press, 1978, p. 305

7. *Ibid.*, p. 304.

8. Derk Bodde and Clarence Morris, *Law in Imperial China*. Philadelphia: University of Pennsylvania Press, 1978, p. 305.

9. See 'Daxue' (Great Learning) in *Sishu* (The four books). Macao: Juwendangshu, 1962, p. 7.

10. Originally, '*fa*' related generally to 'standards', but under Legalism's influence it increasingly related to penal law and punishment. Roger Ames provides an extensive commentary on the connotations of '*fa*' in his *The Art of Rulership*. Honolulu: University of Hawaii Press, 1983, p. 109.

11. Confucius, '*Daxue*', *op. cit.*, p. 23.

12. *Ibid.*, p. 15.

13. Confucius, '*Lunyu*' (The analects), in *Sishu*, 1962, *op. cit.*, p. 13.

14. *Ibid.*, pp. 13–14.

15. Mencius, '*Mengzi*' (Mencius) in *Sishu*, 1962, *op. cit.*, p. 260.

16. Bodde and Morris, *Law in Imperial China*, *op. cit.*, p. 7.

17. *Ibid.*, p. 50.

18. As cited in Liang, *History of Chinese Political Thought*, *op. cit.*, pp. 134–35.

19. Burton Watson, trans., *Han Fei Tzu*. New York: Columbia University Press, 1964, p. 105.

20. Liang, *History of Chinese Political Thought*, pp. 134–35.

21. Li Buyan, Wang Hanqing, 'Adhere to the Principle that All Men are Equal Before the Law, Safeguard the Authority and Dignity of the Law', *Hongqi*, No. 12, 16 June 1986, JPRS-CRF–86–015, 7 August 1986, p. 45.

22. See, for example, Yang Yichen, 'Report on the Work of the Supreme People's Procuratorate,' *Renmin ribao*, 18 April 1988, in FBIS-CHI–88–017, p. 70.

23. Zhang Yongmin, 'Strengthening the Legal System is a Pressing Need in the Reform of the Economic System', *Hongqi*, No. 14, 16 July 1986, in JPRS-CRF–86–017, p. 70.

24. Deng Xiaoping, 'Reform the Political Structure and Strengthen the People's Sense of Legality', *Fundamental Issues in Present-Day China*. Beijing: Foreign Languages Press, 1987, p. 146.

25. Derk Bodde, 'Feudalism in China', in Ruston Coulborn, ed., *Feudalism in History*. Hamden, Conn.: Archon Books, 1965, p. 52.

26. Stuart R. Schram, ed., *The Political Thought of Mao Tse-tung*. New York: Praeger, 1969, p. 115. fn. 1.

27. For the 12th CCPCC Resolution of 28 September 1986 see *Beijing Review*, No. 40, 6 October 1986, Documents, p. v.
28. See the preface to Fei Xiaodong, *A Great Trial in Chinese History*. Beijing: New World Press, 1981, p. 7: In 1985 the party leadership officially endorsed the 'rule of law' concept. See Ronald C. Keith, 'Chinese Politics and the New Theory of the "Rule of Law"', *China Quarterly*, No. 125, March 1991, pp. 109–18.
29. Liang, *History of Chinese Political Thought*, *op. cit.*, p. 125.

5 Mao Zedong and his Political Thought

Ronald C. Keith

Gai guan lun ding—'only when the coffin lid is down can a man's reputation be fixed'. Mao has been considered by most as the greatest Marxist-Leninist theoretician from the Third World during the present century. However, despite the Chinese saying quoted above his reputation is still not fixed either in the West or in China. In a lighter moment, Mao once said that in a thousand years he, Marx and Engels would all appear as equally ridiculous.[1] He also had premonitions that the Chinese people would soon forget him; however, his spirit, as the spirit of the past in China's present and future, still roams the Chinese countryside.

Mao's brand of Marxism-Leninism and his own career self-consciously reflected the relationship between Chinese tradition and modernity. Mao preferred to describe his thought as 'Marxism-Leninism Mao Zedong Thought' rather than 'Maoism' which conveyed a negative connotation of dogmatism.[2] The former militated against the supposedly unscientific rigidity of a tradition of emperor-worship or 'one-man rule' (*renzhi*), the legitimacy of which was grounded in the dogmatic assertion of absolute moral standards. In his theoretical thinking at least, Mao reacted against tradition stressing the importance of recognizing mistakes on the part of everyone. He also warned his party against an 'upstage attitude' vis-a-vis the outside world. China would have to learn from the outside, and in this way China would learn more about herself.

However, Mao, as a modern Chinese nationalist, was also keen to achieve what he sometimes called the 'sinification of Marxism-Leninism'.[3] Marxism-Leninism, as a foreign doctrine, would have to achieve a Chinese essence. On this score, Mao pointedly reminded his allegedly dogmatic opponents who copied Soviet experience that they were 'foreign philosophers' while he was a 'native philosopher'.[4]

Mao insisted on retaining Chinese historical distinctiveness and yet he wished to transcend tradition in his search for a new modern culture. He thought of the Chinese people as a blank sheet of paper on which very fine characters would be written.[5] Seeing that China was so backward, he dialectically postulated that once the latent, pent-up energies of the Chinese people were released, the country would be catapulted into the modern world. His blank sheet of paper, however, was in reality more like a pamlipsest wherein many characters had been superimposed over one another. Despite the party's rhetoric concerning revolutionary change, tradition survived at multiple and sometimes conflicting levels of consciousness throughout Chinese society.

In the 1950s, Mao emphasized that the Chinese people were consciously lined up behind the party's socialist objectives. However, with the argument over leadership succession during the Cultural Revolution he became increasingly apprehensive regarding the extent to which the revolution had actually generated a new consciousness throughout society. The spectre of Soviet revisionism haunted him, and Mao theorized that the formal dimensions of the ·public ownership of the means of production would not guarantee the survival of his own socialist revolution.

In the mid-1960s, Mao was more keenly aware of the Chinese people's yearning for the certainty of a final moral authority. In explaining his own Marxist-Leninist mass-line opposition to 'genius theory', he told Edgar Snow that the ecstatic adulation of himself in part sprung from the Chinese people's desire for an emperor.[6] Mao argued that the major issue at work during the Cultural Revolution was 'for whom' the personality cult was to be utilised. He preferred to use it himself against the party elite which was promoting 'capitalist restoration'.[7]

As for his own place in history, he rejected the 'formalism' of the slogans of the Cultural Revolution hailing him as 'Great Teacher, Great Leader, Supreme Commander and Great Helmsman'. Mao told Snow that all of these would be eliminated sooner or later with the sole exception of the appellation of 'teacher'.[8] Though Mao was proud of the fact that he started out in life as just an ordinary primary school teacher, he was aware of the authoritarian role of the teacher in tradition, and no doubt he wished to be remembered as 'teacher' in the more modern and positive sense of innovative thinking.

Mao's theory was built on contradictions as was his own character. He had many Chinese personalities. During the Cultural Revolution he was like the quixotic, metamorphic 'Monkey King', Sun Wukong, mischievously encouraging chaos, revelling in contradiction and smashing cherished institutions with his golden cudgel.[9] Mao's enemies could hardly forgive him for his own simple self-depiction as the traditional figure of a 'lone monk walking the world with a leaky umbrella'.[10] Mao also projected himself as the great strong willed unifier of the Chinese nation and as the great party leader who had brought about social revolution in the early to mid-1950s.

He turned the tables on Taiwan and Hong Kong 'propagandists' by alleging that indeed he was just as ruthless as Qin Shihuang. As a revolutionary he had buried a lot more 'enemies of the people' than the 460 scholars allegedly buried by the First Emperor of the Qin dynasty. Mao was hardly a traditionalist subscribing to the reinstatement of Legalism; on the contrary he was a Marxist-Leninist who supported the First Emperor in his 'feudal' revolution against the slave-owning aristocracy.[11] Most importantly, Mao was for the Chinese people the 'Great Helmsman' (*da duoshuo*) who in the struggle between absolute right and wrong took the helm of the Chinese ship of state.

Mao's discussion of the people's need for authority in the light of 3,000 years of emperor-worship conflicted with his enthusiasm for the party's mass line and his optimistic view of the people as the motive force of history. The fact that the Chinese people were not a *tabula rasa* has been increasingly stressed in the attacks on 'feudalism' since Mao's death in 1976. Herein lies the central paradox of modern China. Mao wished to make China 'modern' in an indigenous Marxist-Leninist sense. This implied not only the accelerated development of productive forces, but also a new way of thinking and new culture which, on the basis of his theory of contradictions, would allow for greater levels of political participation in policymaking and a more complex view of political reality moving beyond the allegedly 'metaphysical' extremes of moral absolutes.

Mao, however, was himself largely responsible for the creation of the personality cult or 'one-man rule' during the Cultural

Revolution. He placed Marxism-Leninism in jeopardy by overturning the party's organizational traditions. Following in his footsteps Deng Xiaoping attempted to employ elements of 'Marxism-Leninism Mao Zedong Thought' selectively to serve the modernization process which he believed required a more responsive reading of reality through 'seeking the truth from the facts' and the greater reliance on praxis rather than the *ex cathedra* statements of a leader as an exclusive moral authority. Deng proposed to substitute socialist democracy and socialist legality for 'one-man rule'.

In the anthropological sense of the distinction between 'great tradition' and 'little tradition' (especially the distinction between the scholar-official view of history and society and the popular ideas which circulated among the rural masses of China), Mao hailed from the 'little tradition'. He was born into this tradition on 26 December 1893. From the perspective of the mass of poverty-stricken peasantry his family was comparatively well off. In the party's terms, his family background was that of rich peasantry.

Often in Chinese history, peasant leaders emerged to create new dynasties and in doing so demonstrated a great affinity for the 'great tradition'. In later life, Mao discoursed on the *Book of History* and aspired to the writing of classical-style poetry, but he condemned the hierarchical features of traditional society which had been justified by Confucian thought, and he morally admonished his people to 'scale the heights' of modernity. Confucian talk of *'ren'* ('benevolence') was, to him, a hypocritical humanism, which, despite its claim to universality, supported the inequalities associated with slave-owning society.[12]

Mao, like Confucius, was largely self-taught. His formal education was reasonably good for a peasant from the countryside, though quite limited on the whole. Mao, in his native place of Shaoshan, spent the obligatory six years' learning by rote the Confucian canon of the *Four Books* and *Five Classics*. He eventually understood such recitation to be contradictory to education and independent thought. In retrospect, Mao complained that the classics provided no basis for understanding the impact of 'imperialism' on China: 'None of the stuff I had learned in thirteen years was any good for making revolution.'[13]

His initial middle school education was interrupted by a six month stint in the army during the 1911 Revolution. Shortly after returning to school, he rejected the imperial-based Confucian curriculum of the First Provincial Middle School, and for six months he esconced himself in the Hunan Provincial Library where he devoured world history and geography. In this period of self-education, he read bits of Adam Smith, Charles Darwin, John Stuart Mill, Rousseau, Spencer, Montesquieu and tales from ancient Greece. Mao subsequently completed regular school, and began teaching at a primary school. In 1920, Mao became the director of the primary school attached to Changsha's First Normal School, and it was at this time that he ʰegan to identify himself as a 'Marxist'.[14]

While the Selected Works of Mao Tse-tung begin with a specific class analysis of rural society, dated March 1926,[15] Mao's real debut as a theoretician came during a lull in the fighting with the Japanese during 1936–37. He composed two lectures for use at Kangda, the Resist-Japan University in Yan'an, North China. These were entitled 'On Contradictions' (August 1937) and 'On Practice' (July 1937).[16] His thought directly flowed from his own revolutionary experience and his insistent nationalist adaptation of Marxism-Leninism to Chinese conditions. Often his unity of theory and practice specifically addressed problems of 'people's war' and political alignment within the united front against a class enemy which was also the national enemy. Drawing on Lenin's theory of imperialism, Mao theoretically entwined the class struggle and the national struggle. He did so without jettisoning the proletarian leadership of the revolution, but he did make the peasantry the 'main force' of the revolutionary forces. The latter were led by the party in the name of China's embryonic proletariat.

Mao's subsequent writings during the Yan'an period, 1936–45, have become increasingly important since his death. 'Reform Our Study' (May 1941) and 'Rectify the Party's Style of Work' (1 February 1942) provided the basis for what was later eulogised as the party's 'fine tradition' of leadership and organisation.[17] The same material outlined his epistemology as it was derived from his understanding of objective reality in terms of on-going synthesis and antithesis. Mao's formulation, 'seeking the truth from the facts' (shishi qiu shi), became the leitmotiv of the Deng Xiaoping regime which cites this formulation as the 'quintessence of [Mao's] philosophical thinking'.[18]

In the early 1950s, Mao's chief theoretical claim to fame rested with his elaboration of a 'colonial theory of revolution', suited to the rural backwardness of Asia; however, by the mid-1950s, Mao began to apply the unity of theory and practice in terms of a distinctive

Chinese road to development which was self-consciously different from Stalin's road. The latter's stress on 'primitive accumulation' and his tolerance for a 'scissors crisis' whereby the price of urban manufactures climbed while rural commodities declined was thought inappropriate for China's largely rural condition. Mao said that Stalin was only 30 per cent wrong, and yet he claimed that Stalin had 'a fair amount of mataphysics in him'. Mao was harshly critical of Stalin's failure to make 'the connection between the struggle of opposites and the unity of opposites'.[19]

Mao's speech of 25 April 1956, 'On the Ten Major Relationships' (which later became the theoretical reference point for Deng Xiaoping's post-1978 economic and political reform) was penned for the specific purpose of educating his own party on the differences between Soviet and Chinese economic development. He believed that Soviet 'mistakes of principle', (yuanzexing cuowu) were replicated in Eastern Europe as a result of Stalin's erroneous dictations.[20]

Mao's theories evolved in response to his own political practice, and this was also the case with his theoretical conception of democracy. In part he was responding to events in Hungary and Poland in 1956 when he made his famous 27 February 1957 speech 'On the Correct Handling of Contradictions Among the People'. Then reaffirming his commitment to materialism he said that democracy is a 'means' rather than an 'end' which belongs to the 'superstructure'.[21]

While the latter served the 'economic base', ideological virtue was neither self-inherent nor self-perpetuating. The development of a socialist consciousness would require continuous exertion and self-examination. Mao stressed that under socialism even the working class would still need 'remoulding': 'The working class remoulds the whole of society in class struggle and in the struggle against nature, and at the same time remoulds itself.'[22] While Mao sounded conciliatory, he was critical of comrades who had failed to concede that contradictions still existed in socialist society. In his view the latter could only be consolidated 'through the ceaseless process of correctly handling and resolving contradictions'.[23]

Mao's subsequent speech (30 January 1962) became a major reference point for post-1978 political reform and democratization. He recapitulated his Yan'an writings on praxis as the basis of epistemology. He frankly conceded his own infallibility in his personal contention with the complexity of contradictions in reality:

If anyone were to claim that...I, myself, completely understood the laws of the Chinese revolution right from the beginning, then that comrade would be talking through his hat.... When I explain how our Chinese Communist Party...came to understand the laws of the Chinese revolution, my aim in bringing up these historical facts is to help our comrades to appreciate one thing: that understanding the laws of socialist construction must pass through a process. It must take practice as its starting-point, passing from having no experience to having some experience; from having little experience to having more experience; from the construction of socialism, which is in the realm of necessity as yet not understood, to gradual overcoming of our blindness and the understanding of objective laws, thereby attaining freedom, achieving a flying leap in our knowledge and reaching the realm of freedom.[24]

Despite such philosophical detachment concerning the difficult epistemological reading of social reality, Mao was really quite rigid in his own political practice. By late 1962 he ominously served notice that a 'new bourgeoisie' was forming within the Party and the state. He was convinced that a corrupt political power was creating such a class even though the means of production had formally been brought under public ownership. This area of treacherous theoretical speculation has since been excluded by the party from the accepted canon, or 'collective wisdom' of 'Marxism-Leninism Mao Zedong Thought'.

Mao, in the Cultural Revolution, allegedly failed in his theoretical leadership as he distorted the distinction between 'antagonistic contradictions' with class enemies and 'non-antagonistic contradictions among the people'. As a result there was a general failure to 'seek the truth from the facts', and China's prospects for modernization were drastically set back.

MODERNITY AND CHINESE HISTORY IN MAO ZEDONG THOUGHT

Mao Zedong's view of modernity and the relation of China's modernization to the West was quite complicated and is still not especially well understood in the West. Mao rejected 'westernisation', as it implied the 'blind worship' of western cultural values rather than a critical evaluation. He was especially interested in the acquisition of natural science and technology from the West, but he also wanted a formal understanding of the comparative features of western as opposed to Chinese culture. In a broad ranging discussion of cross-cultural comparison in 1956, Mao stated: 'We learn foreign things because we want to study and develop Chinese things.'[25]

As a nationalist, Mao rejected iconoclasm, but in his Marxist-Leninist focus on class struggle, he fundamentally challenged the Confucian emphasis on social harmony. In the western conception of class struggle Mao saw a vehicle for a universal change of consciousness throughout Chinese society. Oddly enough, even while he challenged the social doctrine of Confucianism, Mao approached the question of revolutionary change in a manner which was stylistically suggestive of Confucianism, particularly as he stressed internal consciousness as the normative basis for morally informed political action towards social ends. Perhaps Mao's central notion in this regard was his conception of 'self-reliance' (*zili gengsheng*) meaning 'stand on one's own to turn over to a new life'. This notion theoretically encompassed the underlying theme of Mao's own revolutionary experience, and it brought together both the nationalist and socialist content of China's distinctive revolutionary process. Through an *a priori* change in Chinese consciousness, Mao had hoped to create a relatively independent and comprehensive industrial base within China.

This orientation basically informed his theoretical conception of the relation between technology and modernity. Politics would detail just how technology would be created and would also subordinate technology to the politically determined needs of the Chinese people. China's specific pattern of technological development and its applications in the economy required a breakthrough in terms of a higher level of creative thinking within society as a whole. In this aspiration, Mao may have placed an intolerable burden on the general application of his own difficult 'science' of dialectics.

Western comparative political theory casts 'modernity' not only in terms of the qualitative development of inanimate energy and technology, but also in terms of the unleashing of human creativity, the greater participation in decision-making, the redivision of labour in society, and the active consideration of innovative alternatives in the ordering of individual energies within differentiated and flexible social structures. In the Chinese revolutionary context, Mao more specifically related the mass-line creation of new, flexible social structures to the creation of new social attitudes and patterns of dialectical thinking.

In building a specifically Chinese modern culture, Mao had to come to terms with Chinese history. In 1956, Mao reiterated that he was against the rejection of history; he stated: 'It is no good cutting ourselves off from history and abandoning our heritage. The common people would not approve.'[26] Focusing on the 'benefits' of learning, he outlined his own particular concept of utilitarianism: 'We learn from the ancients in order to benefit the people of today, and we learn from foreigners in order to benefit the people of China.'[27]

Mao had rather consistently upheld these views since his own student days. During the May Fourth intellectual ferment and student radicalism of the 1920s, he was enthusiastic about 'Mr. Science' and 'Mr. Democracy' and he called out for the 'Overthrow of the Confucian Family Shop' (dadao Kongjia puzi). Perhaps, because the western democracies were admired so much, there was a profound sense of disappointment when they failed to support the Chinese youth in their struggle against 'imperialism' and 'feudalism'. Moreover, they were seen as participating in the privileges of extraterritoriality, hence Mao referred to 'the teacher [i.e., the West] aggressing upon the student'—a very politically powerful image given the traditional deference towards the authority of the teacher in society.[28]

As the senior Communist leader in 1940, Mao discussed the building of 'a new Chinese national culture'.[29] While stating that this would require the assimilation of 'a good deal of foreign progressive culture', Mao added the following caveat: 'To advocate "wholesale westernization" is wrong.'[30] As for the Chinese past, he held on to it in a deliberately critical way, comparing the necessarily critical exercise of absorbing the past to the passage of food through the human alimentary canal. The 'progressive' elements of the past would be retained as nutrient, while the negative elements would simply be excreted as waste. Mao, however, was not 'virulently iconoclastic' as suggested in the essays of Maurice Meisner.[31] In January 1940, for example, Mao opined:

China's present new politics and new economy have developed out of her old politics and old economy, and her present new culture, too, has developed out of her old culture; therefore, we must respect our own history and must not lop it off.[32]

Mao, however, would only consider the past in immediate relation to the present. Politically, he distinguished between 'making the past serve the present', (*gu wei jin yong*) and the 'reactionary' scheme of 'disparaging the present by extolling the past' (*yi gu fei jin*). Mao was not always consistent, and especially in later life he was attracted to Daoist notions of eternal flux; but in 1956 he clearly emphasized a linear notion of progress when he stated: 'I consider that human history advances. One generation is not as good as another—people who went before are not as good as those who follow later....'[33]

Mao, in 1958, was eerily prophetic when he observed: 'One should not negate everything. The result of negating all is self-destruction.'[34] Mao's version of 'history' was thought necessary for the survival of the revolution, itself, but it became stereotypical in 'speak bitterness' (*su ku*) sessions which often mechanically recited the virtues of China's socialist present over the 'feudal' inequities of pre-1949 China. In the context of successive post-1949 'rectifications' (*zhengfeng*) Mao urged all to 'learn from past mistakes to avoid future ones'. For Mao, 'history' was at bottom a 'science' by which the observer would understand 'dialectical development'.

Mao saw in Confucianism a major obstacle to the development of creative thinking and the triumph of modern dialectics. He claimed: 'Feudalism propagandized obedience to Confucianism making us feel inferior.'[35] Tradition seemingly had set China back in the related terms of its failure to allow for the unleashing of human creativity and its rigid social hierarchy. Mao also observed that the same tradition had created an unacceptable sense of superiority in relation to the outside world which was inappropriate to the investigation and study of modernity. Mao attacked this arrogance, but he also urged his party members not to feel inferior in relation to either foreign science or professionalism. With respect to cross-cultural 'study and investigation', Mao extolled the familiar virtue of modesty. He particularly wanted 'modesty compatible with reality'.

As a Marxist-Leninist, Mao claimed to promote the materialist conception of history, but he, nevertheless, focused on the subjective element of human consciousness in Chinese history, pointing to the popular tradition of revolt against social oppression. As a nationalist, Mao proudly referred to the fact that peasant uprisings such as those witnessed by Chinese history had no parallel elsewhere.[36] It is hard to tell whether it was the nationalist or the Marxist-Leninist talking when Mao indicated that because China's feudal society had a commodity economy: 'China would of herself have developed slowly into a capitalist society even without the impact of foreign capitalism'?[37]

As a Marxist-Leninist, and perhaps as a nationalist, Mao could not accept the Confucian 'man-eating doctrine of *li' chi rendi lijiao*. The 'superior man', in his perpetuation of ritualised social inequality, was cast as an elitist given to polite cannibalism. Also, the Confucian tradition, itself, allegedly engendered a sense of superstitious belief in the past. At the heart of Mao's strategy for modernization was his commitment to change existing social attitudes. Mao praised Confucius' villainous nemesis, Qin Shihuang, for the burning of the classics and the burying of the scholars. Qin Shihuang as China's 'First Emperor' (206 BC) was 'an expert in respecting the modern and belittling the ancient'.[38]

Confucian reverence of the past apparently stood in the way of creative, independent thinking. In answer to his own critics, who accused him of 'inconstant feelings' and who promoted 'the present is inferior to the past' (*jin bu ru gu*) Mao retorted: 'One cannot help being found of antiques, but one also cannot be too fond of them. When the memorial arches were dismantled in Peking and tunnels were driven through the city walls, Chang Hsi-jo wept. This is politics.'[39]

MAO AS THE CENTRAL PARADOX OF CHINESE MODERNITY

Mao was himself the central paradox of Chinese modernity. He rejected the content of the Confucian tradition, but his approach to modernity is very familiar in terms of style and perspective. His acceptance of 'materialism', did not modify his focus on the intellectual change necessary to achieve modernity. He focused on the subjective more than the objective aspects of social change. Stuart Schram has, for example, briefly discussed Mao's early interest in 'the realization of the self', and the overlap of 'Mao Zedong Thought' and Confucianism in terms of emphases on moral self-cultivation (*xiushen*) and virtue as a necessary element of knowledge.[40]

This focus helps explain Mao's view of the revolutionary process as based on 'self-reliance' (*zili gengsheng*). These four characters, connoting 'standing on one's own and turning over to a new life', captured China's relation with the outside world as well as the thrust of China's unique revolutionary experience. 'Self-reliance', for example, encompassed the release of China's peasantry from the weight of past 'feudal' authority. The peasants were urged to look beyond the village gate towards a new conception of the whole of society, hence they engaged in *fanshen* or 'turning over the body'. On this critical point, regardless of Mao's self-proclaimed personal comparison with Qin Shihuang and the largely specious content of the anti-Lin Biao, anti-Confucius campaign of the last years of his life, Mao had more in common with the Confucians than the Legalists.

The *junzi* or 'superior man', rejected Legalist measurement and technique as the basis of government, hence the principle, *junzi bu qi*, ('the superior man is not a utensil').[41] He released his human compassion (*ren*) into society, and this was the only legitimate basis of government. Virtue was to be reinforced in social relationships through *li*, or the social decorum or rites which governed the 'five relationships', namely, ruler and subject, father and son, husband and wife, older and ·younger brother and friend and friend. The Confucian scholar was interested in closing the gap in social reality between the aspiration to virtue and the actual achievement of virtuous behaviour, hence the focus on *zhengming* or the rectification of names.

Mao, in his attempt to ensure the closing of yet another gap, relied on the psychological rigours of criticism and self-criticism within 'rectification' (*zhengfeng*). For Mao, as a Marxist-Leninist, this Confucian 'rectification of names' was ruling class artifice designed to establish a rigid social hierarchy, but he, himself, insisted that party cadres had to continuously purge themselves of the corrupt practices of old society. In his discussion of anti-rightists in April 1958, Mao indicated that after 'rectification', the 'political root' is established and both cadres and masses will then have a clearer view of the contradictions in society.[42] In his discussion of the mass line, Mao assigned the role of collective *junzi* to the party. The party had to provide through its 'workstyle' (*gongzuo zuofang*), a shining example of socialist behaviour which would move the population at large. Deng Xiaoping made the power of such example the thematic basis for political restructuring in the late 1970s and early 1980s. Deng then called for the 'selecting of the virtuous and the appointing of the able' (*xuan xian ren neng*). He cited Mao's 'Rectify the Party's Style of Work' as follows:

Once our Party's style of work is put completely right, the people all over the country will learn from our example. Those outside the Party who have the same kind of bad style will, if they are good and honest people, learn from our example and correct their mistakes, and thus the whole nation will be influenced.[43]

Mao's concept of man, however, was not as positive as the Mencean mainstream Confucian concept. Mao insisted that man's thinking '...consists of concepts formed through the reflection of external matters', and he indicated that man's thinking is 'not endowed by nature'.[44] Man was capable of both 'scaling the heights' and descending to the depths of 'bourgeois' depravity. The party cadres could repetitively cite how they would 'serve the people', and yet they could still fall to the 'sugar bullets' of the bourgeoisie. They continuously had to reveal their intent by genuine deeds.

Mao feared that many of his cadres were too intimidated by returning students and 'big professors' who disparaged their rusticity and lack of education. In his view, these professors were hardly fit to judge given their 'confused personal relationships' and 'complicated psychology'. On the other hand, Mao believed that his cadres were capable of 'seeking the truth from the facts' (*shishi qiu shi*). This was not only a matter of science, but also a matter of 'honesty'. Mao praised their natural 'intelligence and honesty' saying: '...intelligence means asking many questions and thinking a lot; honesty entails seeking the truth from the facts.'[45] The latter implied real, honest practice in society.

Confucius might well have approved of this. Rhetorical long-windedness was a vice insofar as it was not derivative of genuinely internalised moral value. Confucius described the 'superior man' in the following simple terms: 'He acts before he speaks, and afterwards speaks according to his actions.'[46]

Both Confucius and Mao focused intensively on 'investigation and study', but neither could tolerate the veneration of books. Mao once remarked: 'If one believes everything in books, it is better not to read books at all. When King Wu [i.e., the sage king of 1121–1116 BC?] chastised Chou, blood flowed so profusely that it floated pestles. Mencius refused to believe it.'[47] Mao dismissed 'bookishness', but he attached great significance to strong writing skills so as to clarify the internal relations of any given argument.

Mao was impatient with those who would make bombastic speeches and not act. The modern cadre has to set an example through his humble, honest 'workstyle'. He had to 'eat, work and sleep' with the masses so as to help set policy predicated in social reality. Mao constituted in his own self a great contradiction. He had, himself, cast Marxism as a 'science' which in modern times contested with superstition in China's vast hinterland. He wanted conscious mass action based on 'self-reliance', and yet this eventually resulted in the absurd 'feudal' excesses of the Great Leap Forward and Cultural Revolution.

The frenzied repetition of snippets from his own works opposed Mao against his own thought. Mao's own concept of party organization presumed that all of the masses could *consciously* participate in modern scientific and democratic culture, but he recognized a certain 'psychological condition of long standing' in Chinese society.

Mao noted that the Central Committee had to have a first secretary just as there was a 'nucleus' in the atom, but he dropped any pretence to rhetorical subtlety when he said: 'After a while, an "idol" [*ouxiang*] emerges, and it becomes relatively difficult to eliminate [him].'[48] On another occasion, Mao explicitly discussed himself:

Yesterday a comrade said that one couldn't go wrong if one followed a certain individual. By a 'certain individual' he meant me. This statement needs modification. ... One must not follow without discrimination. ... We follow whomever has truth in his hands. ... It is dangerous to follow an individual without discrimination. One must have independent thinking.[49]

In dealing with the Stalinist 'personality cult' in the mid-1950s, Mao resigned as Chairman of the People's Republic commenting on the tendency in Chinese politics to look for an 'idol'. For his own political reasons in the mid-1960s, he allowed the Red Guards to celebrate himself as the 'Red Sun' at the centre of the universe, and then, in the 1970s, he rejected such unthinking adulation as unsightly 'feudalism' which had contradicted his own thought and had almost destroyed his own 'mass line'.

The issue of 'idols' in Chinese politics was highlighted in formal ideological terms in Mao's 1971 repudiation of the 'genius theory' as an explanation of history and as 'feudal' obstacle to the modern development of a Marxist-Leninist conception of 'science'.[50] The polemical labelling of innate genius as a 'Confucian' concept did serious violence to the complexity of Confucian discussion on this point.

'SCIENCE' AND TECHNOLOGY IN MODERN GOVERNMENT

At the mundane level of state business, Mao was always uncomfortable. Leaders adopted undesirable techniques to escape real policy debate. They presented documents as if they were 'perfect' and could not be questioned. The finance and economic departments were culpable of technocratic subterfuge. Mao decried their lack of analysis. They did not look for 'essence'. In January 1958 Mao stated:

> The finance and economics departments do not keep the Political Bureau informed. Generally, the reports, too, do not lend themselves to discussion as they do not mention textual research, phraseology, and essence [i.e, argumentation, yili]. The former is a question of rhetoric and the latter are questions of concepts and reasoning.[51]

These departments had adopted Stalin's bad habit of 'blockade' where they would introduce their documents ten minutes before a conference was due to convene. Mao also warned: 'Don't treat everything that has been issued as an "imperial edict"....' Mao even upbraided his own peers on the Politbureau for their lack of real discussion:

> the Political Bureau has become a voting machine. You give it a perfect document and it has to be passed. Like the opera, you have to go on stage and perform since the show has been announced. The document itself does not go into textual research and essence, and it also has foreign words.[52]

Stalin came in for great criticism for his substitution of 'metaphysics' (xing er shang xue) for dialectics (bianzhengfa). Perhaps, Mao was stating the obvious, but Stalin, he claimed, lacked a 'democratic workstyle' and had a 'slight overlord flavour'. His weak sense of dialectics was uncharitably ascribed to his education in a missionary school.[53] In Mao's vocabulary, the latter had acquired specific negative connotations relating to 'idealism'. With specific reference to his own party's debate over the failure of policy, Mao gave an incidental explanation of 'metaphysics':

Is it metaphysics or dialectics? Metaphysics has several characteristics. First, looking at problems in an isolated and one-sided manner: instead of regarding the world as a single entity and with the parts mutually linked, it regards it as disconnected, like sand. Second, looking at problems superficially: instead of looking at problems from their development, failing to see the contents through the forms, or the essence [i.e. *benzhi*] through the superficial.[54]

Stalin lacked a sophisticated, dialectical understanding of reality. He distrusted the masses and would allow technology to triumph over politics. Mao did not have to repeat that 'the superior man is not a utensil'. He wanted science and technology. He envisaged a socialist future for China which required the development of large-scale socialized production, but he insisted that technology had to be combined with politics. He deplored the failure of bureaucrats and vested professional interests to speak in easily understood language concerning 'essence'. Aside from the 'feudal' beliefs in the countryside, this was indicative of yet another form of 'superstition'. The abdication of political and intellectual responsibility for the choosing of a course of action in the face of professional expertise was additionally a form of 'bureaucratism'.

Mao insisted that the 'non-professional leads the professional' (*wai hang lingdao neihang*). This was more than a reflection of the fact that it is impossible for one individual in government to master all professions. Non-professionals had to lead through seeking the 'truth', and Mao emphasised: 'Politicians handle the mutual relations among men; they promote the mass line.'[55]

Mao advised the cadres, therefore, to pay no attention to the snickerings of backbiting engineers and scientists. His alternative view of history stressed that youth and members in the community of low station had made great contributions to science. Mao's mass line required the 'combining of leading with learning', and 'learning' required a fearless attitude with respect to existing authority. Mao stoutly claimed that it was everybody's duty to learn, and he resisted any exclusive association of wisdom with the aged. He did note accept Confucius' discussion of progressive stages of moral development according to age. Confucius had said: '...at seventy, I could follow what my heart desires without transgressing what is right.'[56] Mao, however, claimed: '...even when one is 70 or 80, there is much that one doesn't know.'[57]

Mao described Confucius' experience and station as very modest:

> Confucius had no position in his youth. He worked as a bugler and drummer and served as the master of ceremony at funerals. Later on he taught. ... Confucius' position as chief of the judicial department [of the small state of Lu] was only equivalent to a section chief in our country government.[58]

In 1964, Mao claimed that Confucius actually had relatively good class credentials as a poor peasant. He had hardly any formal education, and thus he came 'from the masses'. Unfortunately, Confucius' bodyguards overly protected him from the masses once he assumed office. While he, himself, had had a reputation for frankness, '...unpleasant sounds no longer entered his ears.'[59]

Mao indicted Confucius for not staying the course. His propagation of 'benevolence' was misguided. The concept only served the interests of part of the exploiting class.[60] Mao insisted that the pupil had to excel the teacher otherwise the latter was indeed a failure. He stated: 'Do not be intimidated by famous people and scholars. We must be courageous in thinking, speaking and doing.'[61]

Mao attacked those in his party who had said that industrialization would be difficult. This was yet another 'big superstition'. Through 'seeking the truth from the facts', he wanted the party members to achieve a 'modesty compatible with reality'. The complexity of reality could be unlocked through dialectics, and despite the material difficulties ahead, modernization could be achieved. Mao thought 'make the high mountain bow its head; make the river yield the way' was 'an excellent sentence'. He declared: 'No, we are not insane; we are pragmatists [shijizhuyizhe]; we are Marxists seeking truth from the facts.'[62] In Mao's mind, there was a difference between 'pragmatism', implying the 'unity of theory and practice', and 'bourgeois' 'pragmatism', (shiyongzhuyi) implying the end of ideology.

Deng Xiaoping's contemporary gloss for the singularly important concept, 'seeking the truth from the facts', lies in a speech Mao made in 1941 in which he described Marxisim-Leninism as an 'arrow' which could be used to hit the 'target' of the Chinese revolution:

> We Chinese Communists have been seeking the arrow because we want to hit the target of the Chinese revolution. To take such an attitude is to seek the truth from the facts. 'Facts' are all things which exist objectively, 'truth' means their internal relations, that is the laws governing them and 'to seek' means to study.[63]

Mao then contrasted 'seeking the truth from the facts' with 'dogmatism' and 'subjectivism' and pointed to the continuing relevance of the May Fourth movement of the early 1920s which had two 'main streams', one negative, the other positive. The revolution, or 'target' had benefited from the May Fourth movement's emphasis on science; it had not benefited from the dogmatic insistence on indiscriminate foreign learning. In particular, Mao had targeted Stalin's views as foreign dogma. In the course of the 'rectification' in 1941, Mao told his party enemies that 'without investigation there is no right to speak', and he suggested that their 'bombastic twaddle' and mere 'listing of 1,2,3,4' was no substitute for argument based on practical scientific investigation.

Even by the late 1950s, Mao had not changed his mind. He would not follow Stalin's example and leave industrialization to the technical experts. While the Confucian gentleman sometimes dabbled in agrarian technology on the side, he was formally opposed to any emphasis on the technical aspect of government. As a Chinese Marxist-Leninist, Mao was not burdened by such an exclusive reservation. The Great Leap Forward, for example, was billed as a 'technical' and 'cultural revolution'. Mao, however, was adamant that technology was to be guided politically towards purposeful ends on the basis of 'scientific' dialectics.

Part of Mao's own 'independence' related to the rejection of the Soviet ideological preference for the 'negation of the negation'. In the intense political context of Cultural Revolution and the dramatic public break with the Soviets, Mao rejected two of Engel's three categories of dialectical thinking: 'The unity of opposites is the most basic law, the transformation of quality and quantity into one another is the unity of the opposites quality and quantity, and the negation of the negation does not exist at all.'[64] Mao also took issue with Stalin who counted four instead of three laws of dialectics.[65] Incensed Soviet theoreticians retorted that Mao's own dialectics were vulgar reconstitutions of the Daoist *yinyang*. In his fascination with 'permanent revolution', Mao was cast as a dangerous 'Trotskyite', but Soviet analysis also likened Mao to a Confucian emperor who attempted 'to rectify the minds of the people'.[66]

There is an analytically significant, but, from the western point of view, somewhat confused conception of 'science' in Mao's discussion. He had decried the 'bourgeois' view of 'Mr. Science' in the May Fourth era. The latter was not so much a question of discrete, technical expertise, as a matter of a rigorous understanding of complex reality through investigation and study on the basis of Mao's own understanding of dialectics. The 're-evaluation of values' of modern China's most prominent liberal thinker, Hu Shi, was inspired by a specious, bourgeois 'pragmatism' as distinguished from praxis. Within his own party, Mao also attacked 'rightist empiricism' which delayed social change with a hidden agenda favouring the status quo. Mao always had ends in mind when he promoted praxis, but these were unachievable without 'seeking the truth from the facts'.

Mao urged party cadres to master social science, literature and natural science,[67] but in their 'workstyle' they were to combine 'revolutionary spirit' with 'science'. They were to be both 'hot' and 'cold'. They were to retain their enthusiasm and at the same time they had to scientifically read reality. Enthusiasm was necessary if the cadres were not going to be afraid to ask questions and to take up real responsibilities. On 19 December 1958, Mao indicated in the course of remarks concerning the dialectical study necessary to the formulation of policy:

> The Wu-ch'ang conference resolved that we must 'seek the truth from the facts.' We must be hot and cold at the same time when we do our planning. We must not only proceed with determination, but also earnestly engaged in scientific analysis.[68]

THE DIALECTICAL RELATION OF OUTSIDE AND INSIDE IN CHINA'S MODERNIZATION

In the context of US containment and the Sino-Soviet conflict, Mao emphasized 'self-reliance' and his Great Leap Forward notion of 'walking on two legs'. In the full blown imperium of the Son of Heaven, the Chinese, he said, had been arrogant in their conception of the relation between the inside and the out; they had presumed that China was morally at the centre of the known world. This changed during the nineteenth century, and Mao, the historian, claimed: 'By the end of the Ch'ing Dynasty [i.e., at the turn of the twentieth century] when the foreigners attacked and entered China, the Chinese were frightened, became slaves, and felt inferior. Arrogant before, now we are too humble. Let us have the negation of the negation.'[69]

Mao believed that technical development could occur simultaneously at different levels of organizational experience; he deplored any 'dogmatic' tendency of 'copying' which failed to take into account China's distinctive conditions. It was necessary to walk on two legs, one of foreign technology and the other of native technology. These 'legs' were not only to be coordinated, but dialectically integrated in China's specific economic reality. One need not worship foreign technology, but one should, within this scheme, adopt an utilitarian attitude whereby foreign technology is adapted to Chinese economic reality. This view is still hardly understood in the West.

In discussing relations with the outside world, Mao distinguished between 'seeking the truth from the facts' and 'dogmatism'. He wished to study not only the Soviet Union, but western technology and culture. In 1956, he stated that the Chinese people would accept neither 'national nihilism' nor 'left-wing closed doorism'. He rejected the decadent 'bourgeois system' but insisted on filtering out those positive aspects of 'bourgeois' culture and technology which could be usefully deployed in the case of Chinese economic development.[70] In a general policy statement of April 1956, Mao clarified his position:

Our policy is to learn from the strong points of all nations and all countries, learn all that is genuinely good in the political, economic, scientific and technological fields and in literature and art. But we must learn with an analytical and critical eye, not blindly, and we mustn't copy everything indiscriminately and transplant mechanically.[71]

Mao emphasized the learning of the strong points of *all* countries and instructed his cadres not to adopt the same arrogance which allegedly characterized some Soviet comrades whose conceit he traced to 'Tsarist Russia' and the fact that the October Revolution had occurred in Russia.[72]

In this relatively open frame of mind, he commented on the late nineteenth century strategy of prominent imperial officials, namely, *zhongxue wei ti, xixue wei yong* (Chinese learning for essence and foreign learning for practical use). Marxism-Leninism as *ti*, which originated in the West was acceptable to Mao as 'essence', and in this instance he made no distinction between West and East: 'Some people advocate "Chinese learning as the substance, western learning for practical application". ... It is wrong. ... How can we make a distinction between what is Chinese and what is western in this respect?'[73]

Mao had already in 1949 abandoned his emphasis on the 'sinification of Marxism and Leninism' in his quest for ideological legitimacy and Stalin's recognition, but he returned with a vengeance to the idea of *tiyong* in 1964 when he proclaimed himself to be a 'native philosopher'. 'The substance was like our General Line, which cannot be changed. We cannot adopt western learning as the substance, nor can we use the substance of the democratic republic. We cannot use "the natural rights of man", . We can only use western technology.'[74]

CONCLUSION

Until very recently, western scholarship has assumed that Confucianism was truly a dead weight which held China back from participating in modernity.[75] There is even some measure of agreement between this assumption and Mao's own critique of Confucianism. Seemingly, the latter did not value scientific technique and invention, but instead exclusively focused on the question of 'benevolence'. This has been described as a recipe for stasis, especially in the light of Weberian assumptions. The latter contrasted the vital social and economic benefits of the Protestant ethic with the assumed stagnation of a languid Chinese tradition which, despite its intense focus on transcendent moral principle, reportedly suffered from a lack of creative moral tension in its relation to the economy and society. Confucianism, for example, reduced commerce to 'profit', which was in its very nature antithetical to *li*, or social decorum and rites. The latter had alternatively focused on mutual social obligations.

Some of the popular assumptions concerning Mao Zedong and Chinese modernization need careful and more balanced examination. Mao is often thought to have espoused iconoclasm and a closed-door attitude towards the rest of the world. In particular, his correlation of 'red and expert' and politics to economic development has been described in terms of a shortsighted hostility towards science and technology.

Mao, however, argued that it would be inappropriate for contemporary Chinese to 'lop off' their own history. The latter is to be subjected to critical analysis on the basis of Mao's dialectical conception of 'seeking the truth from the facts'. In relation to the outside world, Mao urged an attitude of 'modesty compatible with reality'. As an intrepid dialectician, he was ready for cross-cultural borrowing from the West, but only on his own Chinese terms. Certainly, Mao was very much in favour of the use of western technology provided there were no strings attached.

Mao rejected the social doctrine of Confucianism, but he, himself, may have communed with the Confucian past in terms of his perspective on the significance of internal consciousness as the basis for politics and his organizational focus on the party's 'workstyle'. His emphasis on modesty and honesty is suggestive of Chinese tradition, as his agreement with Confucius in the rejection of 'bookishness'. Mao too wished to discuss 'essence'.

However, Mao, himself, did not deliberately contrast his own interest in consciousness and self-realization to the predilections of the Confucian scholar, and it is, therefore, difficult to establish his relation to the Confucian focus on internal moral virtue with textual precision. His Marxist-Leninist interest in class consciousness evolved within an historically complex emphasis on the unity of Marxist-Leninist theory with Chinese praxis. His strategy of revolution was focused on the attitudinal change which accompanies 'self-reliance' and *fanshen*.

As a Marxist-Leninist, he valued technology, but as a Chinese thinker he would not give it priority over politics and the subjective element of consciousness. He deplored Stalin's fixation with technology and emphasized 'essence' and creative thinking as the fundamental basis for the development of China's new, modern culture.

Mao, himself, however, became the central paradox of China's quest for such modern culture. His personal leadership in the Cultural Revolution disputed the requirements of his thought which called for democracy and collective wisdom in the face of ever-changing configurations of social and economic contradictions. In the midst of leadership crisis Mao, himself, did not always consciously 'seek the truth from the facts'.

In life, Mao was no mere 'teacher', and, in death, his own contradictions caught up with him. There was heated and unseemly leadership dispute over the disposal of his corporeal remains, and, despite the explicit requirements of his own political thought, Mao's body was entombed in a Tiananmen Square mausoleum as befitting the emperor of the Chinese Revolution.

Deng posthumously invoked Mao own ideas on 'seeking the truth from the facts' and 'emancipation of the mind', in order to repudiate Mao's leadership of the Cultural Revolution and the continuing 'leftist' emphasis on 'class struggle as the key link'. Deng attacked rivals in the leadership for their lack of 'scientific attitude' and 'feudal' subscription to 'two whateverists', namely, 'we will resolutely uphold whatever policy decisions Chairman Mao made, and unswervingly follow whatever instructions Chairman Mao gave'.[76] Somewhat prophetically Deng also urged the Party to exorcise the 'feudal' spirit of 'one man rule' by reinforcing and entwining socialist democracy and law so that institutions and laws do not change'...whenever the leaders change their views or shift the focus of their attention.[77]

However, the multiplying contradictions of modern China could not be critically contained within the mere repetition of 'seeking the truth from the facts'. While the selective reference to Mao's political thought in the heady context of accelerated modernization appeared to provide a rational element of ideological continuity it became increasingly difficult to synthesize competing emphases relating to 'socialist spiritual civilization', economic reform, commodity production, 'self-reliance' and the 'open door' to foreign culture and technology. Deng fervently sought the development of 'socialist spiritual civilization' in opposition to 'wholesale Westernization' and 'bourgeois liberalism' but in his reading of Chinese reality the primary aspect of each contemporary contradiction was not always clear.

Seeking the truth from the facts sanctioned 'to become rich is glorious', *zhi fu guangrong*. However, Deng's alleged 'cat theory', *mao lun*, suggesting that the colour of a cat is immaterial to whether it can catch mice, obscured the dialectical tension between the primary and secondary aspects of the contradiction between market efficiency and a strong collectivist sense of Chinese socialist morality. The Tiananmen Square events of 1989 represented a poignant irony in the annals of modern Chinese history. When the top Party leadership, itself, seriously split over how to resolve the contradictions of China's modernization, Deng stepped into Mao's Hunanese sandals to act as the one 'above the emperor', *taishang huang*.

NOTES

1. Mao made this remark to Edgar Snow on 9 January 1965. See Edgar Snow, *The Long Revolution*. New York: Vintage Books, 1973, p. 222.
2. Even in the extreme circumstances of the Cultural Revolution adulation of his 'Little Red Book', Mao told Zhou to eliminate this term. See Ronald C. Keith, *The Diplomacy of Zhou Enlai*. London: Macmillan Press, 1989, p. 162.
3. Mao subsequently dropped this term to avoid a confrontation with Stalin, but it does indicate his real thinking as well as the audacity of his view of Marx. See Stuart R. Schram, ed., *The Political Thought of Mao Tse-tung*. New York: Praeger, 1977, pp. 169–74. Also see Schram's analysis in *Mao Zedong: A Preliminary Reassessment*. Hong Kong: Chinese University Press, 1983, p. 34.
4. Stuart R. Schram, ed., *Mao Tse-tung Unrehearsed*. Talks and Letters: 1956–71. Harmondsworth: Penguin Books, 1974, p. 225.
5. Mao Zedong, 'On the Ten Major Relationships', *Selected Works of Mao Zedong*, Vol. V. Beijing: Foreign Languages Press, 1977, p. 306.
6. Schram, *Mao Tse-tung: A Preliminary Reassessment, op. cit.*, p. 79.
7. Snow, *The Long Revolution, op. cit.*, p. 66.
8. *Ibid.*, pp. 71, 169.
9. Mao claimed that the legendary Monkey was capable of up to 72 metamorphoses. The legend was celebrated in the Song dynasty novel, *The Journey to the West*. The Monkey therein accompanied the Buddhist pilgrim, Xuan Cang, to India.
10. Snow, *The Long Revolution, op. cit.*, p. 175.
11. Wang Gungwu, 'The Chinese', Dick Wilson, ed., *Mao Tse-tung in the Scales of History*. Cambridge: Cambridge University Press, 1977, p. 295.
12. Schram, *Mao Tse-tung Unrehearsed, op. cit.*, p. 214.
13. *Ibid.*, p. 214.
14. Snow, *The Long Revolution*, p. 169. For an extended account of his early education and experience see Stuart R. Schram, *Mao Tse-tung*. Harmondsworth: Penguin Books, 1966, pp. 19–58, esp. p. 57.
15. 'Analysis of the Classes in Chinese Society', *Selected Works of Mao Zedong*, Vol. 1. Beijing: Foreign Languages Press. 1967.

16. Texts in Mao Zedong, *Selected Readings from the Works of Mao Zedong*. Beijing: Foreign Languages Press, 1967, pp. 54–69, and pp. 70–108.

17. Texts in *ibid.*, pp. 162–70, and pp. 171–87. For more of Mao's Yan'an writings in English translation see Boyd Compton, ed., *Mao's China. Party Reform Documents*. Seattle: Washington University Press, 1966.

18. Deng Xiaoping, 'Setting Things Right in Education', *Selected Works of Deng Xiaoping (1975–1982)*. Beijing: Foreign Languages Press, 1984, p. 81.

19. Mao, 'On the Ten Major Relationships', *op. cit.*, p. 291.

20. See 'Talk of January 27', Mao, *Selected Works*, Vol. V, *op. cit.*, pp. 367, 169.

21. Mao Zedong, 'On the Correct Handling of Contradictions Among the People', *Selected Works*, Vol. V, *op. cit.*, p. 388.

22. *Ibid.*, p. 402.

23. *Ibid.*, p. 393.

24. Mao Zedong, 'Talk at an Enlarged Central Work Conference', (30 January 1964), Schram, *Mao Tse-tung Unrehearsed*, *op. cit.*, p. 173.

25. *Ibid.*, p. 86.

26. *Ibid.*, p. 85.

27. *Ibid.*, p. 87.

28. Mao, 'On People's Democratic Dictatorship', *Selected Readings*, *op. cit.*, p. 304.

29. Mao, 'On New Democracy', *Selected Works of Mao Zedong*, Vol. II. Beijing: Foreign Languages Press, 1965, p. 340.

30. *Ibid.*, p. 380.

31. Maurice Meisner, *Marxism, Maoism and Utopianism*. Madison: University of Wisconsin Press, 1982, p. 207.

32. Mao, 'On New Democracy', *op. cit.*, p. 381.

33. Schram, *Mao Tse-tung Unrehearsed*, *op. cit.*, pp. 93–94.

34. Mao Tse-tung, Speech at the Conference of Provincial and Municipal Committee Secretaries, 2 February 1959, *Miscellany of Mao Tse-tung Thought (1949–1968)*, Part 1, henceforth *Miscellany*, I. Arlington: Joint Publications Research Service, 1947, p. 155. The texts for this period are taken from Mao Zedong, *Mao Zedong sixiang wansui* (Long live Mao Zedong thought) henceforth, *MZDWS*. Taipei: Institute of International Affairs, 1969, here p. 276. These 'wansui' materials are discussed at length in Stuart R. Schram, *Mao Tse-tung Unrehearsed*, *op. cit.*

35. Mao, First speech, 2nd Session of the Eighth Party Congress, 8 May 1958, *Miscellany*, I, *op. cit.*, p. 92; *MZDWS*, *op. cit.*, p. 187.

36. Mao Tse-tung, 'The Chinese Revolution and the Chinese Communist Party', *Selected Works*, Vol. II, *op. cit.*, p. 306.

37. *Ibid.*, p. 309.

38. First Speech at the 2nd Session of the Eighth Party Congress, 8 May 1958, *Miscellany*, I, *op. cit.*, p. 98 and *MZDWS*, *op. cit.*, p. 195.

39. 11 January, 1958 Nanning speech, *Miscellany*, *op. cit.*, p. 79; *MZDWS*, p. 147.

40. Schram, *Mao Zedong: A Preliminary Assessment*, *op. cit.*, pp. 5, 27.

41. Confucius, '*Lunyu*', (The analects), p. 18, in *Sishu* (The four books). Macao: Juwendangshu, 1962.

42. Mao's speech at the Hankow Conference, 6 April 1958, *Miscellany*, I, *op. cit.*, p. 90; *MZDWS*, *op. cit.*, p. 186.

43. Deng Xiaoping cited Mao, 'Rectify the Party's Style of Work', in 'Uphold the Four Principles', *Selected-Works of Deng Xiaoping, op. cit.*, p. 185.

44. Mao's second speech, 17 May 1958, *Miscellany*, I, *op. cit.*, p. 104; MZDWS, *op. cit.*, pp. 202–3.
45. Mao, 'A Letter to Chou Shih-chao', 25 November 1958, *Miscellany*, I, *op. cit.*, p. 126; *MZDWS*, *op. cit.*, p. 246.
46. Confucius, 'Lunyu', *op. cit.*, p. 18.
47. Speech to the Conference of Provincial and Municipal Committee Secretaries, 2 February 1959, *Miscellany*, *op. cit.*, 152; *MZDWS*, *op. cit.*, p. 272.
48. Mao,'Talks with Directors of Various Cooperative Areas, 12 December 1958, *Miscellany*, I, *op. cit.*, p. 137; *MZDWS*, *op. cit.*, p. 257.
49. Mao, Second speech, 17 May 1958, 2nd Session, Eighth Party Congress, *Miscellany*, I, *op. cit.*, p. 107; *MZDWS*, *op. cit.*, p. 206.
50. Mao, 'Summary of Chairman Mao's Talks with Responsible Comrades at Various Places during his Provincial Tour', Schram, *Mao Tse-tung Unrehearsed, op. cit .*, pp. 293–94.
51. Mao, Speech at the Nanning Conference, 11 January 1958, *Miscellany*, I, *op. cit.*, p. 77 ; *MZDWS*, *op. cit.*, p. 146.
52. Mao, Speech at the Nanning Conference, 12 January 1958, *Miscellany*, I, *op. cit.*, p. 80; *MZDWS*, *op. cit.*, p. 149.
53. Mao, Speech at the Hankow Conference, 6 April 1958, *Miscellany*, I, *op. cit.*, *MZDWS*, *op. cit.*, p. 183.
54. Mao, Speech at the Conference of Provincial and Municipal Committee Secretaries, 2 February 1959, *Miscellany*, *op. cit.*, 152; *MZDWS*, *op. cit.*, p. 272.
55. Mao, Third Speech, 20 May 1958, 2nd Session, Eighth Party Congress, *Miscellany*, *op. cit.*, p. 111; *MZDWS*, *op. cit.*, p. 216.
56. Confucius, 'Lunyu', *op. cit.*, p. 14.
57. Mao, Instructions at a Discussion Meeting...of the All-China Federation of Industry and Commerce, 8 December 1956, *Miscellany*, I, *op. cit.*, p. 39.
58. Mao, First speech, 2nd Session, Eighth Party Congress, 8 May 1959, *Miscellany*, I, *op. cit.*, p. 93; *MZDWS*, *op. cit.*, pp. 189–90.
59. Mao, 'Remarks at the Spring Festival', 13 February 1964, Schram, *Mao Tse-tung Unrehearsed, op. cit.*, p. 208.
60. Mao, 'Talk on the Question of Philosophy', 18 August 1964, Schram, *Mao Tse-tung Unrehearsed, op. cit.*, p. 214.
61. Mao, First speech, 2nd Session, Eighth Party Congress, 8 May 1958, *Miscellany*, I, *op. cit.*, p. 95; *MZDWS*, *op. cit.*, p. 192.
62. *Ibid.*, p. 192.
63. As quoted and analyzed in a summary of Deng Xiaoping's position on Party reform in *Renmin ribao*, 2 November 1981, p. 1. The discussion here on the meaning of 'seeking the truth from the facts' is taken from my article, Ronald C. Keith, "Egalitarianism" and "Seeking the Truth from the Facts" in the People's Republic of China', *Dalhousie Review*, Vol. 63, No. 2 (Summer, 1983) pp. 327–28.
64. Mao, 'Talk on the Question of Philosophy', Schram, *Mao Tse-tung Unrehearsed, op. cit.*, p. 226.
65. *Ibid.*, p. 240.
66. See Klaus Mehnert, 'Mao and Maoist: Some Soviet Views', *Current Scene*, Vol. VIII, No. 15 (1970), p. 8.
67. Mao, 'Talk at the Hangchow Conference of the Shanghai Bureau', April, 1957, *Miscellany*, I, *op. cit.*, p. 70; *MZDWS*, *op. cit.*, p. 108.

68. Mao, Speech at the 8th Session of the Sixth Central Committee of the Chinese Communist Party, 19 December 1958, *Miscellany*. I, *op. cit.*, p. 144.
69. *MZDWS*, *op. cit.*, p. 264.
70. Mao, Speech at the Conference of the Heads of Delegations to the 2nd Session, Eighth Party Congress, 19 May 1958, *Miscellany*, I, *op. cit.*, p. 123; *MZDWS*, *op. cit.*, p. 225.
71. This explanation of Mao's views on foreign culture and technology is taken from Keith, *The Diplomacy of Zhou Enlai*, *op. cit.*, p. 92.
72. Mao, *Selected Works*, Vol. V. Beijing: Foreign Languages Press, 1977, p. 303.
73. Keith, *The Diplomacy of Zhou Enlai*, *op. cit.*, p. 92.
74. Schram quotes this passage and analyses it in his introduction to *Mao Tse-tung Unrehearsed*, *op. cit.*, p. 35.
75. This interpretation, which largely originates with Weber's comparative analysis was challenged in the debate over Thomas A. Metzger, *Escape From Predicament. Neo-Confucianism and China's Evolving Political Culture*. New York: Columbia University Press, 1977.
76. This two-fold position was originally touted in a leading editorial 'Study the Documents Well and Grasp the Key Link', *Renmin ribao*, 7 February 1977.
77. Deng Xiaoping, *The Selected Works of Deng Xiaoping*, *op. cit*., pp. 158–59.

6 What Good is Democracy? The Alternatives in China and the West

Robert X. Ware

The attempt to read Chinese institutions in terms of Western ideas has resulted in failures of understanding and of action from the very beginnings of our contact.

John Dewey, 'Chinese National Sentiment', 1919.

The development of democracy in China is a widely debated issue both in China as also in the West. This debate gained momentum after the demonstrations for democracy and freedom in Tiananmen Square and the subsequent massacre of 4 June 1989. Not surprisingly, the reactions to those events have been framed in unexamined conceptions about the nature of democracy—conceptions which after all are drastically different. Any questions about democracy are already plagued with vagueness and confusion in any particular social context, but the problems are confounded when we ignore the differences of fundamental political, cultural, economic, and moral ideas that underlie our alternative conceptions of democracy in different societies. I want to look behind the events of 1989[1] and even the demonstrations for democracy in 1986–87 which first prompted me to investigate the contrasts in conceptions of democracy. Too often western theorists have looked at China through western ideas, a practice which is also found amongst some Chinese. While the power struggle continues in the Chinese Communist Party there is also a struggle of ideas, including a struggle over the kind of democracy that should prevail. Until now very little has been said about the nature of democracy most appropriate for China.

This essay first considers the need for a deeper conceptual analysis of the contrasting visions of democracy in China and the West before turning to some evidence that there are indeed some deep and significant differences in the dominant conceptions of democracy. The core of the ensuing discussion is an investigation of five areas which clearly reveal differences in the prevailing theories of democracy. I conclude with a discussion of the implications of these differences for theory and practice.

DEPTHS OF COMPARATIVE POLITICS

Political institutions, practices, and ideas are varied throughout the world and internally complex in each country. They are subjects of contention internationally and domestically. In fact they are so contested in a single society that we have to expect them to be the source of disagreement between two societies. Moreover, they are closely tied to cultural and moral practices where differences are familiar. We should expect differences and contrasts whatever the depth of comparison.

So often, however, the comparison (or contrast) is made superficially on the basis of the behaviour of political agents, existence of political institutions from congresses to constitutions, or a simple count of parties and elections. Such comparisons with respect to democracy are questionable when the very conception of democracy is unknown and when the economic foundation and moral and cultural framework are unanalyzed. Arne Naess and his associates might have been extreme in claiming that there are 311 definitions of the world 'democracy',[2] but I think it is quite clear that there are many that differ in very significant ways, even where there is a dominant notion. Some of the differences revolve around competing moral ideas about kinds of freedom, the importance of equality, instrumental goods, rights, participation, etc. Different emphases are put on different aspects of democracy depending on our values. Moral differences strongly affect our conceptions of democracy. The difference of conceptions in western investigations is a very good reason for expecting there to be differences of significance between western and Chinese conceptions of democracy.

As in many cases we should be suspicious of a comparison where the foundation and framework are assumed and ignored rather than investigated. The very basis of our comparison may well be inappropriate and misleading. John Dewey, for example, drew attention to the following pitfall:

> We merely forget that we think in terms of customs and traditions which habituation has ingrained; we fancy that we think in terms of mind, pure and simple. Taking our mental habits as the norm of mind, we find the ways of thinking that do not conform to it abnormal, mysterious and tricky.[3]

Or in the case of democracy in China, we ask whether China is like us or our 'totalitarian' opposite. Thus Harry Harding says '...one can usefully ask whether China has moved toward a more liberal, pragmatic, and pluralistic political order, or whether it has simply become a routinized authoritarian system similar to the post-Stalinist Soviet Union.'[4] I disagree. Just as John Dewey said seventy years ago: 'The attempt to read Chinese institutions in terms of Western ideas has resulted in failures of understanding and of action.'[5]

Dewey was also right about the reason: 'Neither our political science nor our history supplies any system of classification for understanding the most characteristic phenomena of Chinese institutions.'[6] That is what I try to show here with respect to the theory and practice of democracy. However, the differences have to be ferreted out just because they concern basic conceptual frameworks that are usually assumed rather than studied. For example, many of the most perceptive and sympathetic western accounts of Chinese democracy misplace and overemphasize the role of rights and elections.[7] This is also true of many Chinese discussions of democratic theory which have a tendency to draw on western ideas. This is not surprising from someone like Fang Lizhi, who says 'I think that complete Westernisation is the only way to modernize.... I believe in thorough, comprehensive liberalisation because Chinese culture is primitive'.[8] Nor is it surprising from the Chinese Alliance for Democracy when we see that its president participates in a forum of the Heritage Foundation as pictured in the Chinese language journal, *China Spring*.[9] Such ideas are promoted by the Voice of America and the National Endowment for Democracy in the States.[10] Among these sources, rights and elections receive exclusive attention.

This western emphasis is also found amongst supportive intellectuals and other ordinary people in China, as I found in interviews throughout China during 1986–87. The lack of certain kinds of elections is often taken as a reason for saying that China lacks democracy. This view is reflected in the following remark from the preface to a new book, *On Democracy*: 'Although today's China still lacks a high degree of democracy, democracy is not completely absent in China as some people have claimed.'[11] Indeed there are problems about elections in China, but the emphasis misrepresents an alternative Chinese vision of democracy.

No country creates a politics on borrowed ideas, least of all China. Political ideas are obviously attached to economic, cultural, and moral ideas with different perspectives that have strong influences. This is especially true in China where ideas are not simply copied but instead borrowed, studied, and adapted.[12] As the authors of the preface to *On Democracy* say, '...it is hardly possible for us to mechanically transplant the Western democracy to China...we should only build the Chinese democracy by proceeding from the realities of China and in accordance with China's own theories and measures relating to democracy building.'[13] It is time to turn to some ways in which those realities and theories are characteristically Chinese.

DEMOCRACY WITH CHINESE CHARACTERISTICS

A good indication that there are different conceptions of democracy in China and the West is that from the western perspective the Chinese hold some very perculiar notions about democracy. This is true not just of the authoritative literature on democracy but also of offhand remarks in passing. Even dissenters from the so-called 'democracy movement', which is not the only force for democracy in China, say unusual things when seen from the western perspective. I will begin with some of the peculiar things that are said. It is in the peculiar that we can find the understandable. Then I will try to characterize what I consider to be the dominant conceptions of democracy in China and the West.

One of the more peculiar things in the discussion of democracy in China is the importance that is given to scientific decisions. Wan Li discussed the importance of science in a speech entitled 'Making Policies Democratically and Scientifically—An Important Problem of Political Restructuring'.[14] The suggestion is that democratic decisions are scientific decisions, or as was reported from *China's Youth News* '...without scientific application, democracy cannot really be achieved.'[15] Mao Zedong put a similar point very succinctly: 'Constitution-making is a matter of science.'[16] The authors of the preface of the new book on democracy even speak of 'the science of democracy'.[17] In western thought, democracy and science are virtual opposites. Democracy is a matter of choice and the will of the people, not a matter of science.

No doubt such claims are connected with the view that democratic decisions should be objectively correct. As it was put in one article, government decisions should '...reflect objective reality and not subjective opinions'.[18] In western thought, subjective opinions seem to be exactly what voting, and thus democracy, is about. However, in China only by the development of science, including social science and the scientific study of organization and management,[19] is it thought that correct democratic decisions can be made. The emphasis is on what does in fact benefit the people and the society and not on what people might choose especially if it is out of ignorance. Decisions in China arise more out of knowledge than choice.

The emphasis on objective reality helps explain the emphasis on political reform, greater democratizing, as a means to achieving economic modernization and development. Democracy is not so much an ideal in itself as a means to the ideal of a better society. 'In essence', according to Deng Xiaoping, 'the purpose of political restructuring is to stimulate the initiative of the people and of the grass-roots units' to promote the growth of productive forces and modernization.[20] A commentator in the *Renmin ribao (People's Daily)* put it the following way: 'the development of socialist democracy is basically an internal requirement for the development of the socialist commodity economy.'[21] This kind of linkage with the economy is certainly more prominent in Chinese discussions of democracy than in western discussions.

Another rather peculiar goal is the development of a democratic spirit in people.[22] A democratic attitude of the people is thought to be very important for a democratic society. And such an attitude is said to be achieved through democratic practice. Furthermore, this democratic practice should be found everywhere: in the workplace, in the research institute, in the university, even in the army, and in the family. Zhao Ziyang says that such practice exists 'in all spheres of activity'.[23] The practice is promoted by encouraging citizens to carry out their duties to participate. The greater the participation, the greater the democracy.

A distinctive feature of discussions of democracy in China is the acknowledgement of and attention to degrees of democracy. In China, democracy is something to be developed and expanded. As Zhou Enlai said, 'We must constantly pay attention to expanding democracy because it is of essential significance.'[24] More recently Zhao Ziyang has said that the long-range goal is 'a socialist political system with a high degree of democracy'.[25] In most western thinking on democracy, a government is either democratic or not, and there is no question of developing a fuller or better or more dynamic democracy. These are all examples of remarks on democracy in China that I consider unusual from the western perspective. In some cases they can be understood in connection with the ruling conception of democracy, which is explicitly opposed to the western conception of democracy.

DOMINANT CONCEPTIONS OF DEMOCRACY

The dominant conception of democracy in China is strongly influenced by historical materialism. According to historical materialism politics is thought to be a part of the superstructure which is explained primarily by the economic base. It is not uncommon in China for people to think that the Chinese political system must be undeveloped as long as the economy is. Also according to historical materialism the state is said to be a class structure defending the interests of the ruling class. This leads to the view that there is a difference between bourgeois democracy and proletarian democracy, that the two classes use different systems to defend their interests.

The ruling conception of democracy in China has been relatively permanent under the rule of the Chinese Communist Party, and the main outlines can be put succinctly.[26] The former party General Secretary, Zhao Ziyang, put it in the following general way:

The essence of socialist democracy is that the people are masters of the country, genuinely enjoying all citizens' rights and the power of administering the state, enterprises and institutions [and] [t]he system of the people's congresses, the system of multi-party co-operation and political consultation under the leadership of the Communist Party, and the principle of democratic centralism are the characteristics and advantages of our system.[27]

The Chinese political system is also said to be a people's democratic dictatorship,[28] a paradoxical expression for most in the West. Democracy is a form of government by the people, but as a form of government it is necessarily a class phenomenon involving control over the enemies of the ruling people. The great majority of people in China, about 95 per cent, are thought to constitute the people who rule themselves democratically and over the others dictatorially. When it is understood that the dictatorship is over the few enemies of the people and that the people should decide things democratically, the expression may seem misleading but not paradoxical.

The actual events of the summer of 1989 have not affected the *conception* of democracy that prevails. The party leaders did appeal to the constitutionally recognized conception of the people's democratic dictatorship and took steps against the counter-revolutionary enemies of the state. The tragedy, conceptually, is that they considered some students, intellectuals, and even hooligans to be counter-revolutionaries. Of course, acting dictatorially where it is obviously unnecessary affects the practice of democracy. Still, my point has been one about the conception of democracy that guides behaviour when that behaviour can be democratic. The use of dictatorship on one occasion affects the use of democracy on many other occasions, but it does not annihilate democracy everywhere and forever—a point that the Chinese have made about the War Measures Act being instituted nationally in Canada in 1970.

It is important that the people be led by an advanced organization, the Chinese Communist Party, which can best understand the knowledge culled from the masses and the scientific theory that explains the development of state and society. Zhao Ziyang has elaborated on this saying that the views of the people are important and should be 'easily and frequently transmitted'. Zhao stated: 'The basic principle for establishing a system of consultation and dialogue is to carry on the fine tradition of "from the masses, to the masses".'[29] Regardless of leadership changes it has been a constant theme that leaders should learn from the masses and then take ideas to the masses, once again learning from them and then continuing the process. As Mao said, the democratic method is 'the method of letting the masses speak out.'[30] This 'mass line' is the basis for the policy, re-emphasized in recent years, of 'letting a hundred flowers blossom and a hundred schools contend', calling for the open discussion of different ideas.

This conception of democracy also requires devolution of power, hence Zhao reminded the party: 'In the relations between the Party and the government on the one hand and mass organizations on the other, it is essential to give full play to mass organizations and to self-managed mass organizations at the grass-roots level so that people will handle their own affairs'.[31] The goal is to achieve a harmony of interests that will serve the revolutionary classes, i.e., the great mass of the people. This suggests unity and a single party as well as the patient development of understanding amongst the people and in the party. In fact this is carried out through a multi-party system with consultation and supervision. Besides the Chinese Communist Party with about 45 million members, there are also eight 'democratic' parties with about 300,000 members most of whom are intellectuals or professionals. Members of these democratic parties are by no means irrelevant to the system. About a dozen are vice-governors or vice-mayors. Many are active in the Chinese People's Political Consultative Conference, which meets regularly to advise on legislation. It is also said that many are now being selected for leading posts in ministries and commissions.[32] They have a consulting and supervisory role with the goal of understanding and working for the good of the people and the country.

The conception of democracy discussed previously is found throughout Chinese literature and from Mao to Deng. It is perhaps less clear since the Cultural Revolution what should be said about class, but the concept of class has been unclear from the beginning and the changes in democratic theory are minor. There is also more in the present literature about the importance of laws, and amongst various critics, of rights, but again I think the differences in the conception of democracy are minor. It would certainly be wrong to think that the ideas of Mao about democracy have been over-thrown in the ruling conception of democracy. There is much talk about political reform, but so far there has been little change in the main outlines of the dominant conception of democracy.

One also finds many aspects of the dominant conception in the dissenting literature such as Chen Erjin's *China: Crossroads Socialism*.[33] It also affects the conception of democracy held by young people in Chinese universities. Consider, for example, some of the results of a questionnaire that was answered at Beijing University shortly before the student demonstrations in 1986.[34] The respondents reflected on the widespread attraction of the United States as almost 80 per cent of them said that the United States is the most democratic country in the world. (Such a view is sometimes suggested even by authoritative intellectuals, although with some qualifications and while making other criticisms.) Still over two-thirds of the respondents thought that democracy always has a class character and almost three-quarters of them thought that democracy does not require multi-party governments. These are views that are very different from those expressed by western respondents, even many who are opposed to the dominant conception of democracy in the West.

I can be even briefer about the western conception of democracy even though details are vague and/or contested. Still the general conception is widely familiar at least at an intuitive level. Democracy is a system of governmental representation of pluralistic interests promoted by competing parties and decided by vote. It is through voting that a government is democratically legitimized and subjec-tive wishes expressed. It is enough that the vote is periodic even if infrequent. It is not necessary, or even expected, that everyone be satisfied, but virtually everyone (perhaps excluding criminals and enemies of the state) should have a full range of citizen's rights to act as they wish. This conception does not involve a class character, and it requires more than one party. It emphasizes public protection of individual rights and private pursuit of individual benefits. Moreover, it combines representation and consequently non-participation with an expectation of differences and an emphasis on the political being a matter of public administration and not of financial policy or economic management.

These conceptions are very different. The differences notwithstand-ing, they both involve theories lacking in detail and full justification, and no doubt they both also involve incoherencies or inconsistencies. They also involve claims (for example about social structure) that would most certainly be contested. Moreover, they include values that would not be shared in the other society. Finally, it is important to remember that even within the society in which a conception is dominant, China or the West, there are critics and dissenters.

Still I have maintained about China, and do also about the West, that many of the dissenting views contain elements of the dominant conception, for example, about the class nature of democracy, about the necessity or not of more than one party, and about the importance of citizen's rights. The differences in the general conceptions that I have sketched serve as part of the explanation for some of the unusual things that are said about democracy by virtually all Chinese democrats. No doubt westerners also say unusual things from the Chinese perspective which can also be explained partially by the difference in the general conceptions. But it is my contention that there are conceptions about deeper and even more general matters that can give us a greater and more general understanding of our political differences. That is the burden of the next section.

SOME CONCEPTUAL DIFFERENCES

I want to indicate five areas in which there are significant differences which I think help make the differences discussed in the previous section more understandable. The five areas are: (*a*) goods vs. rights; (*b*) collectivism vs. individualism; (*c*) objective vs. subjective interests; (*d*) the domain and degree of democracy, and (*e*) practice vs. procedure. I do not contend that these are in any way exclusive or exhaustive areas. It is also important to note that each of them cover problems and issues that deserve far more attention than I can give them here. This is merely a sketch designed to alert the readers to differences of perspective. Furthermore, if I am right in contending that the differences in these areas are significant for understanding democratic conceptions, they will almost certainly be significant in understanding other social or political conceptions.

Goods vs. Rights

First, Chinese culture and society is much more oriented to goods and benefits than to rights. In Chinese morality the emphasis is on what would be the resulting goods or benefits rather than what should be done according to duty or obligation. This is fundamental to the virtue-centred morality of Confucianism, which continues to have an influence in the framework of moral thinking.[35] The virtues are those human qualities that best promote the good as it is conceived in the society. In Confucian thought, they include respect and benevolence as exhibited in the rites and practices. The quality of one's relations with others is important in developing the good of the individual, which can only be achieved with the good of others and of society as a whole. It is fundamental to achieve these goods, which are achieved only by the participation of all. Confucianism involves both a social conception and a social realization of the good with both diversity and harmony.

This is different from a rights-based morality that looks to duty and obligation as fundamental because of the categorical imperatives found in reason (as in Kantianism) independent of the benefits or goods promoted. What is right is prior to what is good. Such a theory is also rights-centred in that it emphasizes our rights, which impose duties on others not to interfere. In western thought, these have been individual rights of non-interference imposed on others and society as a whole. People then have a right to pursue whatever is in their personal interest.

The alternative western view to rights-based morality is consequentialism, according to which moral assessment depends on consequences, both intended or aimed at and unintended. Utilitarianism is the most commonly recognized form of consequentialism. It is based on the satisfaction of wants, i.e., the goods, which are to be maximized. What is right is then defined (in terms of the good) as the maximization of goods. It is a common misimpression to think that utilitarianism is concerned exclusively with what is useful or pleasurable. The higher wants are never ignored and sometimes even emphasized. A more prevalent and more misleading mistake is to think that utilitarianism is a selfish doctrine, advocating that we maximize our own happiness. This is decidedly not the case for the classical authors, for example, J.S. Mill. As a utilitarian, one should help another rather than oneself if that would most increase the good in the world.

Chinese moral thinking is not theoretically developed, at least not in the abstract way that it is developed in western philosophy, but it does contain strains of consequentialism parallel to western consequentialist thinking. Marx was a consequentialist[36] and of course has been influential in contemporary Chinese thought. Marx was concerned about the wealth of society and its just distribution, but he was also an historicist who emphasized the importance of the growth of wealth. Both features are found in the thought of Mao and in contemporary Chinese thinking. Mao commonly wrote of being a utilitarian, although I think he used the term rather loosely. He spoke of the communists being the real utilitarians because they bring 'real benefit to the masses of the people.'[37] In other words, they serve the people. He also wrote about the development of the economy since it was that which would show the progress of socialism. These are themes that continue to prevail in both official and unofficial Chinese thinking. It was expressed in a column in the *People's Daily*:

> Some people hold the foreign theory of 'natural rights' and talk freely about democracy; some other people interpret democracy with the democratic ideology of Mencius which stresses that 'the people are the most important element in a nation and the sovereign the least important'.[38]

What is important is whether interests are served, whether there are benefits from the system that is established. But it is more than a maximization of benefits, and in this way I think the Confucian strains show through.

The good cannot just be maximized; it must be rightly distributed in a harmonious whole. Even in times of greatest emphasis on some getting rich first there has been the policy of prosperity for all, a policy of increasing prominence. It is also seen in the voting policy followed in China of electing deputies to fit a predetermined 'proportion of positions among nationalities, sexes and professions',[39] rather than the electors simply choosing the deputies without limitation. For the Chinese, the benefits are more important than unconstrained choice.

Thus, for the Chinese it is essential to be able to say what good democracy is. Democracy is right only if it best serves interests and is to the benefit of the people. On this matter, Andrew Nathan is right in saying that for the Chinese 'democracy is a matter of the interests rule serves rather than of procedures for selecting rulers'.[40] And there are ethical reasons for them not to put so much emphasis on rights as is done in the West. If there are rights, they must be for some good. Thus, it is natural for them to ask what good democracy is. This is not, however, a natural question from the western perspective, which assumes that democracy has its benefits, but the important thing is that it is the right system to establish. It is not judged according to its benefits.

The emphasis on consequences also connects well with a more European, and Marxist, notion of freedom according to which it is the knowledge of necessity. We are free to the extent that we know the objective laws of nature and society. To that extent we can achieve our goals and avoid attempting the impossible. This view which comes from Hegel via Marx was also held by Mao: 'Freedom means the recognition of necessity and it means transforming the objective world.'[41] The emphasis is on what can be done rather than on the right to non-interference, the conception of freedom central to western liberalism since Locke. We may have a right to do something without being able to do it. That it is a right without the full benefits of the right. A consequentialist morality inclines one to what in the end can be done. It is a different notion of freedom which allows the 'interference' of assistance and the requirement of mutual aid. The alternative conceptions of freedom link up to alternative conceptions of the foundations of morality.[42]

An implication of thinking in terms of consequences is that it is reasonable to formulate ideals, consequences that can at best be only approximated or achieved in the future. Here is a recent example of attention to ideals. 'Today, our common ideal is the creation of a modern and powerful socialist country, characterized by a high level of both civilization and democracy.'[43] It is not unintelligible that the constitution and laws contain ideals that are not applied because they cannot be achieved at the time. Historical materialism as a theory about social progress also encourages this embedding of ideals in the juristic system. The present is marked by the faults of the past but encouraged by ideals for the future and the possibility of development. Such embedding of ideals makes goals for the future explicit, but it also makes failures to reach those goals evident. From

a western perspective this is a curious thing to do, but it makes sense
if a conception of the good is fundamental.

Collectivism vs. Individualism

This is another area where there is universal dispute and unclarity in
social theory, but we can be confident in attributing greater collectivism to the Chinese. There is a continuum of views in different
domains ranging from pure collectivism with the collective being
supreme to pure rugged individualism. In both Chinese and western
societies one finds a variety of views along sections of this continuum.
The sections are different, however, with the Chinese thinking and
practice being much more collective, despite recent Chinese pro-
paganda honouring individual extrepreneurs. The family, the village,
and the society have established roles and interests in the social
conceptions in China. A modern discussion of this can be found
in Mao, 'On the Ten Major Relationships', where he said, '...we
should consider not just one side but all three, the state, the collective and the individual'.[44]

Thus, combining this area with the previous one, we find attention
being given to the benefits for the family, group, or society. A good
society is more than a collection of good people, just as a good
orchestra is more than a group of good instrumentalists. The society
or group as a whole must be considered in order to achieve peace
and harmony, and the Chinese are certainly more attentive to non-
individual properties and interests. The attribution of interests
to groups or collectives can be called ethical collectivism. Ethical
collectivism seems to me a way of thinking that is thoroughly Chinese
since the time of Confucius. Chinese philosophy is pervaded by
ideas of the family and the society, but the Chinese also have
different conceptions of the family and perhaps of the society. In
Chinese philosophy, the individual is sustained in the groups to
which he or she belongs, at least the family, the neighbourhood, the
village, and the society.

Some would say that too much importance is given to groups like
the family and society, but at least it should not be said that the
individual is irrelevant or has no interests. Families and other groups
can be important without being the only centres of importance.

Individuals also have their interests which must be served. The point is that the interests of individuals and their groups must be compatible, and in a good society they will be in harmony. It has often been said that the interests of the individual should always be subordinated to the interests of the group,[45] but this is an extreme position compared to the practice. The important point is whether group interests are acknowledged at all. If they are, then the priority or weighing of interests necessarily becomes much more complex. The comparing and weighing of interests will be made between individuals, between groups, and between individuals and groups. But the emphasis has always been on all individuals and groups living in harmony with benefits accruing to all. These are ideas that are much more Chinese than Marxist. Marx had little to say about collective interests and even less about harmonious collectives. His emphasis was on individuals living together rather than on the collective features or harmony of the group as a whole.

There is another way in which Marx *was* a collectivist rather than an individualist, and this is true of most Chinese thinking as well. Marx's social theorizing was in terms of collectives, most importantly classes, as well as individuals. He attributed explanatory importance to classes, parties, movements, bureaucracies, etc. He was opposed to methodological individualism[46] and thus was a methodological collectivist in that he theorized in terms of collectives as well as individuals. The same can be said for most social theorizing in China, where all theorists are much more inclined to refer to groups and their effects.

Whatever notion of collectivism is used, there are clearly implications. In the sense of ethical collectivism there do appear to be collective interests and rights that must be taken into account. Earlier I mentioned interests of the party, but I think there is also greater inclination in China to consider rights of minority nationalities and interests of groups of all kinds. Some attention has also been focused on the representation of groups or sectors of the society, in the case of voting. In the sense of methodological collectivism there are also implications. Here the implications are more in the realm of theory and explanation, but there are implications for practice as well. Mao's methodological collectivism made it natural for him to say that exercising 'dictatorship over the reactionary classes does not mean that we should totally eliminate all reactionary elements, but rather that we should eliminate the classes to which they belong.'[47] The collective can be eliminated while its members are saved. In methodological collectivism it is also natural to give importance to campaigns, movements, and mass organizations. Collective work and the effects of collectives are important.

Objective vs. Subjective Interests

The Chinese tend to speak of benefits, while western theorists tend to speak of wants. For the Chinese, interests of people as well as collectives are objective and can be determined scientifically. This seems to me to have roots in Chinese philosophy as well as encouragement from Marx's writings. In Chinese philosophy, superiors have certain responsibilities for looking after the needs of the people. In Marx's writings, much attention is given to needs, as in the communist slogan 'from each according to ability, to each according to need'. The point is strengthened by the view, widespread in China, that Marxism is scientific and that society can be studied scientifically. In the May Fourth movement in 1919, science and democracy were the two overriding goals, and since that time they have been interrelated much more than in the West. Democracy is thought to be scientific just because the interests are objective and can be investigated scientifically. Mao, and leaders since him, have given great importance to investigations in order to determine the objective interests of the people and of the collective units. This fits nicely with the consequentialist emphasis on goods. Democracy is judged by the interests it serves.

An implication of the view that interests are objective is that people are sometimes helped without their consent, which has both positive and negative features. At least it is not a case of being asked but not being helped or of being permitted to do something that one cannot do. A drawback of course is that people may be helped when or in a way that they do not want to be helped. Here I think of the people of Daqing (the model oil city) each getting reading glasses at 45 whether they want them or not or of everyone in workplace getting mooncakes for Mid-Autumn Festival. But it is not that people are not consulted. In fact in China there seems to be more weight put on consultation and less on voting than in the West. Consultation is considered very important as I mentioned before in my discussion of democratic parties. More and more consultation is being used to decide whether local leaders should stay in office or not. I suspect the truth about interests is somewhere in between, but the point that I want to make here is that there is a difference between China and the West in the conception of interests, a difference which has a clear implication for the role of consultation or voting in democratic decision-making. It also gives more sense to the Chinese thinking that democracy can be objective and scientific.

Domain and Degree of Democracy

It is part of the framework of democratic thinking in China that democracy is something that can be established in any domain and that the more democracy there is the better. Thus the Chinese speak of democracy in the family and, more so, in the workplace. Wherever there are decisions to be made democratic processes should be applied. Where the domains of democracy are in question we can think of the extensiveness of democracy, and where the amount of democracy in any one domain is in question the intensiveness of democracy is at issue. The Chinese speak of increasing both the intensiveness and extensiveness of democracy.

After the student demonstrations in late 1986 it was said that the students should be involved in democratic decision-making in the universities as a way of developing a democratic attitude. It may well be that after the events of 1989 the party will become afraid of encouraging too much democracy for fear of losing privileges and power. Democracy in the workplace, however, is underdeveloped. It is something that clearly should be developed, according to all Chinese conceptions of democracy. Whatever the truth of the matter is at this time, it is significant that an official would say, 'More democracy will make workers become true masters of their factories.'[48] As Zhao Ziyang said, there should be 'a high degree of democracy' (intensive democracy) and 'in all spheres of activity' (extensive democracy).[49]

I do not know of any detailed Chinese discussion of this issue, but Frank Cunningham has suggested some standards for comparing degrees of democracy.[50] As he claims, one society is more democratic than another if more people have control over more aspects of their social environment that are important to them. The standards will have to be quite complex, but it does make it clear that democracy can be expanded and be fuller. This is quite different from the standard western conceptions of democracy according to which a country is either democratic or not. Moreover, in the dominant western view, non-participation is acceptable or even beneficial, while the ruling Chinese view calls for full participation especially at the local level. It is an important implication in the Chinese conception that there might be fuller or more developed democracy.

This makes sense in the context of Chinese cultural history. The central group has been the family, with the village being of next greatest importance and the central government being distant and unimportant. The important decisions have to be made locally, and if good decisions are made there then the country as a whole will live harmoniously with little governing from the centre. This was noted by Dewey seventy years ago: 'Yet her deepest traditions, her most established ways of feeling and thinking, her essential democracy, cluster about the local units, the village and its neighbours.'[51] It is in the local groups that participation is most feasible, although one can also conceive of ways of expanding it outwards. With the focus on the local units, it is not surprising that less attention is given to the central government and to institutions, although they are not ignored. This is part of the tradition that M.J. Bau also observed at the time that Dewey was in China. For him there was '...no doubt that China has been a great democracy for centuries with the monarchical autocracy superimposed.... The village life in China has always been a democracy: the people maintain their own corps of defence and settle their own disputes as far as feasible.'[52] Many have noted the importance of local politics in contemporary China, particularly during the time of Mao.[53] The point here is that the extension of democracy in China may be totally different from that in the West and that in some of those different domains it may be quite intensive. In any case, the ideal in China is for democracy to be both intensive and extensive.

There are a couple of sources of resistance to the idea of full democracy, but they do not seem to have been developed. The Cultural Revolution is criticized for being a time of 'extreme [great] democracy' (da minzhu). For example Zhao Ziyang has said: 'We shall never again allow the kind of "great democracy" that undermines state law and social stability.'[54] The expressed concern is with

anarchism and lawlessness, but I know of no theoretical development of this point. Another point that is not developed is the
Marxist-Leninist one that democracy is a form of state, i.e., a class
phenomenon,[55] and thus should be transcended in a communist
society. This would be an embarrassment to the idea that China
should develop the fullest democracy. In fact I think there are two
different ideas and that it is the latter idea that prevails in contemporary thinking. The difference turns on differences in the
corresponding notion of politics, which sometimes applies only to
matters of government and sometimes to any matter of power or
decision-making. The dominant conception of democracy seems to
be the non-Marxist-Leninist one of people's decision-making.

Practice vs. Procedure

In the dominant western conception of democracy voting is the core
of democracy. In most Chinese discussions of democracy, on the
other hand, the emphasis is on consultation, manner, style, and even
spirit. Democracy is more non-procedural and non-institutional. In
theory the concern is with establishing good policies through
consultation and experimentation. Again Mao is representative and
influential. He put it briefly: '...we can only use democratic methods,
the method of letting the masses speak out.'[56]

Recently it has been said about the development of democracy in
China that China has '...gradually perfected the system of the
people's congress, opened up various channels for conducting
political consultative dialogues, developed a multi-party co-operation
system under the leadership of the Communist Party, mobilized the
initiative of all sectors to participate in and discuss political affairs,
strengthened social supervision by means of various forms, and so
on.'[57] This is a very different list than any found in western discussions of democracy. Participation is important in the Chinese
conception of democracy, but it has a different role and even the
conception of it is different in China compared to the West.[58]

The importance of consultation and mobilization derives from
the important notion of the mass line. The government must learn
from the masses, take ideas to the masses, and continue to listen to
their ideas. This is why it is so important to carry out investigations

amongst the people, a central part of both government theory and practice. Consultation and mobilization are also important to the consultative and cooperative work of the democratic parties under the leadership of Communist Party. They also encourage experimentation, which plays an unusually large role in contemporary China. Political and economic experiments are carried out in selected localities, and draft regulations are applied selectively.[59]

The emphasis on practice and style has its connections with Chinese tradition. The best way to rule, according to Daoism, is through inaction or unforced action (*wuwei*). A good government brings harmony through good examples rather than through good commands. The people would then concentrate on local activities and observe good democratic practice in their local units. As Dewey observed: 'The central factor in the Chinese historic political psychology is its profound indifference to everything that we associate with the state, with government. One inclines to wonder sometimes why the anarchists of the pacifist and philosophic type have not seized upon China as a working exemplification of their theories.'[60] Many things are still happily left to the state today, although there is much more concern about what it does. Nevertheless, I think there is much that is anarchistic about China today from the unregulated flow of traffic to the illegal non-payment of taxes by state companies. Anarchistic ideas are not necessarily incompatible with a high degree of democracy, especially if one emphasizes the natural and harmonious life of the society.

The Chinese think that a good society is promoted by a high degree of democratic consultation rather than by an exclusive concern with voting and procedures. Of course they can be combined as they are in both China and the West, but China is unusual in the emphasis that it puts on consultation. The dominant Chinese conception of democracy emphasizes practices like consultation rather than procedures like voting. If Gramsci was right that 'the counting of "votes" is the final ceremony of a long process,'[61] then we could say that the West tends to emphasize the ceremony while the Chinese tend to emphasize the process before it.

CONCLUDING REMARKS

One cannot simply compare one political system or theory with another. Societies and theories pertaining to them are complex and significantly affected by deeper theories and ideas that form a framework that is more often assumed than studied. When comparing societies as different as the Chinese and the western on an issue so important and contested as democracy, there are many factors to be taken into account. It is not that the societies and people are so different and alien to each other as that the differences apply to so many things that are relevant to democratic theory and practice. Any conception of democracy, or of any form of decision-making, is complex and related to many other conceptions, including those of parties, voting, politics, legislation, and many other political terms. I have tried to show that conceptions of democracy are also related to many other non-political conceptions and ideas that are even more general.

The Chinese emphasize the good to be achieved by democracy rather than the rights to be protected. Their democracy is more oriented to benefits determined through consultation than to responding to choices determined by a vote. The benefits that are relevant are affected by their differing conception of freedom. The Chinese also have a different conception of interests, which have a complex relation to democratic practice. This conception encourages a more scientific approach to social issues and correspondingly a more prominent role for social scientists. Furthermore, the decisions are applied to collectives in ways that have both positive and negative effects on individuals. The focus on degrees of democracy encourages a concern for development and is connected with the historical materialist view of a correspondence between the state and the level of economic development. This allows the view that China can tolerate a less developed democratic state than can be tolerated when their economy is more developed.

These differences help explain a lot of differences that are noted in Chinese democratic theory and practice. It helps explain the importance of the principle of serving the people and the emphasis on economic modernization. It explains the need to show real improvement and security in the lives of the people. It gives reason for less importance and different roles being given to rights, voting, and alternative parties than one finds in the West. It also makes understandable that both officials and dissenters would call for reforms and the expansion of democracy. The Chinese have a very different conception of democracy than is usually found in the West partly because they have different ideas about ethical and social issues.

I have concentrated on general conceptions without criticizing the basic outlines of the theory, but I do not want to give the impression that I think that the dominant Chinese theory of democracy is without inconsistency or confusion. There are indeed problems about many of the areas and especially about the nature of interests and the expectation of social harmony. More attention should also be given to procedural matters. There are many things in the theory of democracy in China that need full discussion. A great failing in Chinese literature, both official and dissenting, is a lack of theory to clarify what democracy in China should involve. Vagueness has prevailed in ideas expressed by student critics of the government. This has been obvious in wall posters in China and the critical and dissenting literature that we have seen in the West. This vagueness is also ignored by most westerners who applaud such Chinese demands for democracy. But vagueness also pervades the official literature on democracy and political reform. Guidance is not being given on how to promote democracy. Official Chinese thinking should give more attention to some of the differences between western and Chinese ideas as well. Moreover, the practice lags far behind the theory, and not just because of an ideal that is out of reach. (Of course, the events of 4 June 1989 had nothing to do with democracy. It is to be hoped that it was an aberration.) Undoubtedly, there are many ways the practice could change to better apply a reasonable theory.

The same thing could be said of western theory and practice which contains many inconsistencies, confusions, and mistakes, particularly about parties, voting, and participation. Similarly, practice falls far short of theory. But my interest has not been to clarify one conception or another of democracy. I have tried to show that there are two genuine and significantly different conceptions of democracy that relate to differences of non-political conceptions. Understanding these differing conceptions helps us understand the differences of theory and practice in the other country. It is not a simple comparison.

It is certainly a mistake to look to China and think that they have a dictatorship and thus not a democracy because they do not have one of the systems established in the West. It is not enough simply to say that they have a different system. It is much more revealing to compare the rights granted and the benefits of democracy expected in the two countries, as Nathan does for China and the United States.[62] Nathan even considers some of the connections of political ideas in China with ideas of morality and culture in the past. Unfortunately, he does not see some of those non-political ideas as genuine alternatives to those in the West. He is too inclined to see the American conceptions of freedom, rights, law, and the press as the model for a similar democratic pluralism elsewhere and a basis for a change in the 'undemocratic' ways of China. He seems to disallow the fact that there can be alternative conceptions of democracy embedded in different economic systems and different moral cultures.

The discussion above is a call for considering genuine alternatives including the alternative frameworks in which they are developed. A comparison of political systems has to go beyond the political structures themselves, hence the foregoing analysis highlighted China's consequentialism, collectivism, objectivism of interests, developmentalism, and emphasis on practice in order to understand its democratic theory. These are social and moral issues that are outside political issues, but they have a significant effect on the vision of politics and democracy in China. The issues that are relevant are by and large part of the framework that is assumed rather than the ideas that are discussed and developed. Each political theory assumes a background, but comparative political theory must compare the alternative backgrounds, which this essay has attempted in comparing China and the West on what good democracy is.[63]

NOTES

1. I discuss the events themselves in 'What Does the Statue of Liberty Mean in China?', *Canadian Dimension*, Vol. 23, No. 6 (September 1989). The massacre of 4 June reveals the hypocrisy of some of the statements from leaders quoted below, but it does not change the fact that there is a deep-seated conception of democracy influencing their views. There will be a change of leaders faster than a change of the Chinese conception of democracy.
2. As mentioned in Frank Cunningham, *Democratic Theory and Socialism*. Cambridge: Cambridge University Press, 1987, p. 25.
3. John Dewey, 'Transforming the Mind of China', *John Dewey: The Middle Works, 1899–1924*, Vol. 11: *1918–1919*. Carbondale and Edwardsville: Southern Illinois University Press, 1982, p. 210.

4. Harry Harding, 'Political Development in Post-Mao China', in A. Doak Barnett and Ralph N. Clough, eds., *Modernizing China: Post-Mao Reform and Development*. Boulder: Westview Press, 1986, p. 13.
5. John Dewey, 'Chinese National Sentiment', *op. cit.*, p. 215.
6. John Dewey, 'Transforming the Mind of China', *op. cit.*, p. 210.
7. For example, see Andrew J. Nathan, *Chinese Democracy*. Berkeley: University of California Press, 1986.
8. In his 18 November 1986 speech in Shanghai, 'Democracy, Reform and Modernization' as quoted in *China Spring Digest* (published by the Chinese Alliance for Democracy), Vol. 1, No. 2.(March-April 1987), p. 12. Fang Lizhi is the physicist who was removed from the party and dismissed from his university position for comments like this.
9. *China Spring*, No. 47, May 1987, p. 22.
10. On the National Endowment for Democracy, see Laurien Alexandre, 'In the Service of the State: Public Diplomacy, Government Media and Ronald Reagan', *Media, Culture and Society*, Vol. 9, No. 1, January 1987, who reports (p. 38) that one of its projects in 1985 was $200,000 for a US-based Chinese language quarterly published by a group of writers and scholars from the People's Republic of China.
11. Quoted from *Renmin ribao*, 30 December 1988, p. 5 in Foreign Broadcast Information Service, *Daily Report: China*, No. 4, 6 January 1989, p. 26. (Henceforth: FBIS-CHI, followed by year, issue, and page.)
12. For a clear argument to this effect, see Ronald C. Keith, 'Mao Zedong and the Chinese View of Modernity,' this volume.
13. FBIS-CHI-89-004, p. 28.
14. Reports in *Beijing Review*, Vol. 29, No. 39, 29 September 1986, pp. 28ff.
15. In *China Daily*, 16 September 1986.
16. In *Selected Works of Mao Tse-tung*, Vol. 5, Beijing: Foreign Languages Press, 1977, p. 146.
17. FBIS-CHI-89-004, p. 25.
18. Reported in *China Daily*, 16 September 1986.
19. This view is clearly expressed by the physicist Qian Xuesen in *Beijing Review*, vol. 30, No. 11, 16 March 1987, pp. 14–17. Zhao Ziyang, in his report to the 13th Party Congress, calls for 'a scientific system of management', *Beijing Review*, Vol. 30, No. 45, 9–15 November 1987, p. 40.
20. Deng Xiaoping, *Fundamental Issues in Present-Day China*. Beijing: Foreign Languages Press, 1987, p. 150.
21. FBIS-CHI-89-090, p. 22.
22. For example, see the *China Daily* opinion piece, 30 August 1986, p. 4.
23. Report to the 13th Party Congress, *Beijing Review*, Vol. 30, No. 45, 9–15, November 1987, p. 43.
24. In 'Dictatorship Should Be Continued, Democracy Expanded' (1956) as quoted in *Beijing Review*, Vol. 31, No. 51, 19–25 December 1988, p. 18
25. Report to the 13th Party Congress, *Beijing' Review*, Vol. 30, No. 45, 9–15 November 1987, p. 37.
26. Two important sources are the following two essays by Mao Zedong: 'On New Democracy' (1940), *Selected Works of Mao Tse-tung*, Vol. 2. Beijing: Foreign Languages Press, 1967, pp. 339–84 and 'Talk at the Enlarged Central Work Conference' (1962), *Chairman Mao Talks to the People*, Stuart Schram, ed. New York: Pantheon Books, 1974, pp. 158–87.

27. Report to the 13th congress, *Beijing Review*, Vol. 30, No. 45, 9–15 November 1987, p. 37.

28. See, for example, 'On the People's Democratic Dictatorship', *Selected Works of Mao Tse-tung*, Vol. 4. Beijing: Foreign Languages Press, 1967, pp. 411–24 and Deng Xiaoping, *Fundamental Issues in Present-Day China*. Beijing: Foreign Languages Press, 1987, p. 162.

29. Report to the 13th party congress, *Beijing Review*, Vol. 30, No. 45, 9–15 November 1987, p. 41. (The party obviously failed to follow this basic principle in 1989).

30. *Chairman Mao Talks to the People*, Stuart Schram, ed. New York: Pantheon, 1974, p. 160.

31. Zhao Ziyang, Report to the 13th Party Congress, *Beijing Review*, Vol. 30, No. 45, 9–15 November 1987, p. 39.

32. FBIS-CHI-89–012, p. 22. For more on the democratic parties, see James D. Seymour, *China's Satellite Parties*. Armonk, NY: M.E. Sharpe, 1987.

33. Chen Erjin, *China: Crossroads Socialism* (An Unofficial Manifesto for Proletarian Democracy). London: New Left Books, 1984.

34. I am drawing upon a questionnaire prepared by students at Beijing University answered by 257 students there. The questionnaire was completed before the demonstrations in Anhui province in November and about a month and a half before the demonstrations in Beijing involving many students from Beijing University. As far as I know, the questionnaire and results have not been made public or reported elsewhere. The following discussion also depends on numerous discussions I had in several cities with demonstrators and others.

35. For a good discussion of Chinese virtue-centred moral thinking see David B. Wong, *Moral Relativity*. Berkeley: University of California Press, 1984, esp. chapters 9–13. This is an important source for my comments here.

36. Whether Marx even had a moral theory is much contested, but I think Richard Miller argues convincingly that Marx was a consequentialist (although not a utilitarian) in 'Marx and Aristotle: A Kind of Consequentialism', K. Nielsen and S. Pattern, eds., *Marx and Morality, Canadian Journal of Philosophy*, Supp. Vol. 7 (1981). The whole volume is worth consulting on Marx's moral thinking.

37. Mao Zedong, 'Talks at the Yenan Forum on Literature and Art', *Selected Works of Mao Tse-tung*, Vol. 3. Peking: Foreign Languages Press, 1967, p. 85.

38. FBIS-CHI-89–090, p. 21.

39. See *China Daily*, 23 March 1987, p. 3, which also reported that the practice would be abandoned in the Beijing municipal elections of that year.

40. Andrew Nathan, *Chinese Democracy*. Berkeley: University of California Press, 1985, p. 124. It is for this reason that I think it is misleading for Nathan to have compared China and the U.S. on the basis of the rights provided for (see pp. 112ff).

41. *Chairman Mao Talks to the People*, Stuart Schram, ed., New York: Pantheon, 1974, p. 180. This dialectical relationship between freedom and necessity is discussed at length by Yu Guangyuan, *On the Objective Character of Laws of Development*. Beijing: CASS, 1982.

42. For more on this, see Wong, *Moral Relativity, op. cit.*, pp. 162–68.

43. Shao Hanming and Wang Yankun. 'Picking out the Pieces', *Beijing Review*, Vol. 32, No. 4, 23–29 January 1989, p. 22. They add that it is 'an ideal for a person, a nation, and the entire humanity', thus indicating collective agents, the second area for my discussion.

44. *Selected Works of Mao Tse-tung*, Vol. 5. Beijing: Foreign Languages Press, 1977, p. 289.
45. For example, see Liu Shaoqi, *Selected Works of Liu Shaoqi*, Vol. 1. Beijing: Foreign Languages Press, 1984, pp. 135–42, where he talks about personal interests being completely subordinated to the interests of the party.
46. In recent years Jon Elster and other analytical Marxists have been arguing that Marx was a methodological individualist at least in his most careful writings. See Elster's *Making Sense of Marx*. Cambridge: Cambridge University Press, 1985. I have argued against an aspect of methodological individualism in 'Group Action and Social Ontology', *Analyse & Kritik*, Vol. 10, No. 1 (1988), pp. 48–70. See also section 2 of Kai Nielsen and Robert Ware, eds., *Analyzing Marxism*. Calgary, Canada: University of Calgary Press, 1989.
47. *Chairman Mao Talks to the People*, Stuart Schram, ed., New York: Pantheon, 1974, p. 169.
48. Reported in *China Daily*, 17 September 1986, p. 3.
49. Report to the 13th party congress, *Beijing Review*, Vol. 30, No. 45, 9–15 November 1987, pp. 37 and 43.
50. Frank Cunningham, *Democratic Theory and Socialism*. Cambridge: Cambridge University Press, 1987, pp. 25–34.
51. John Dewey, 'Transforming the Mind of China', *op. cit.*, p. 212.
52. Mingchien Joshua Bau, *Modern Democracy in China*. Shanghai: Commercial Press, 1923, p. 115.
53. See especially Vivienne Shue, *The Reach of the State: Sketches of the Chinese Body Politic*. Stanford, CA: Stanford University Press, 1988. She emphasizes the importance of localism in such an enormous underdeveloped country, but is especially good at indicating some of the subtle changes in structure. See her fourth chapter on the change of structure in the 1980s from a honeycomb to a web.
54. Report to the 13th party congress, *Beijing Review*, Vol. 30, No. 45, 9–15 November 1987, p. 37.
55. Lenin talked about people's decision-making, but he didn't call it democracy.
56. *Chairman Mao Talks to the People*, Stuart Schram, ed. New York: Pantheon, 1974, p. 160.
57. FBIS-CHI-89–090, p. 22.
58. There is now a new and important literature on the nature of participation in socialist societies as compared with capitalist societies. See especially the articles by Donald Schulz and Victor Falkenheim (on China) in Donald Schulz and Jan Adams, eds., *Political Participation in Communist Systems*. New York: Pergammon Press, 1981. Also of recent interest is John P. Burns, *Political Participation in Rural China*. Berkeley, CA: University of California Press, 1988.
59. The relevance of the mass line to democracy has a close parallel in the relevance of the mass line to socialist legality. The subtlety of that connection is discussed by Ronald C. Keith in 'Law and Society in the Confucian and Natural Law Traditions', this volume.
60. John Dewey, 'Chinese National Sentiment', *op. cit.*, p. 216.
61. Antonio Gramsci, *Selections from the Prison Notebooks*, New York: International Publishers, 1973, p. 193.
62. See Nathan, *Chinese Democracy*, *op. cit.*, pp. 111ff and 224ff.
63. Many people have helped me correct confusions and lapses in my ideas on this subject and in a previous draft of this article. Besides many Chinese informants and discussants of the earlier paper, I particularly want to thank Ron Keith, who has commented extensively on my work on this subject.

7 Of Artha and the Arthasastra

K.J. Shah

This science (*arthasastra*) brings into being and preserves spiritual good, material well-being, and enjoyment of pleasures; and destroys spiritual evil, material loss and hatred (ill-will).
Arthasastra.

INTRODUCTION

In this paper I want to present a structure of thought, pertaining to the management of the affairs of the state, with reference but not confined to the *Arthasastra*.[1] I do so, however, in my own fashion. Various issues are raised: some internally (e.g., does the *Arthasastra* work out a scheme of *artha* according to *dharma*?) and others externally (e.g., does it escape being authoritarian and an obstacle to the freedom of the individual? If it does, why is there no mention of rights?) It is my hope that this many-sided (though brief) exploration of the structure of thought in the *Arthasastra* will throw some new light on the text and that a study of the text will help us in our enquiry to understand traditional thought.

Acknowledgement: I am grateful to my friend Dr. K. Raghavendra Rao whose comments on the successive drafts of this paper proved extremely valuable.

I would like to add that I have taken the thought of the past seriously: i.e., I have allowed it to speak for itself before judging it to be more or less adequate compared to any contemporary understanding of the same issues. This approach reveals that the thought under examination is not merely a collection of maxims, but has a structure and focus capable of presenting to us at least one way of realizing the values or goals, individual and social, of human life—the *purusartha*.

In brief, our purpose is to present a broad outline of the nature and scope of the thought, and to make a beginning in the dialogue between the past, the present and the future. Pursuantly, I discuss, in the next section, the account of the sciences and their interrelationship as presented in the *Arthasastra*. Next, I consider the institution of law and its relationship to *dharma* and, in the following two sections, the institution of kingship and the various ways in which it was sought to be kept on the path of *dharma*. In the two sections that follow, I discuss, first, some implications of my argument for the relationship between *dharmasastra* and *arthasastra* and, then, the problem of method in the *Arthasastra*.

THE SCIENCES AND THEIR INTERRELATIONSHIP

For properly understanding *artha* as a *purusartha*, as a goal of life, one must begin, perhaps, where Kautilya himself begins: the consideration of the nature of the sciences and their relationship. The sciences are: *anviksiki* (*darsana* or philosophy); *trayi* (the three Vedas); *vartta* (the science of the means of livelihood); and *dandaniti* (*arthasastra* or the science of politics) (AS.I.ii.1).

The sciences are so called because through them we can know what is material and moral well-being. *Dandaniti* and *vartta* give us knowledge of material well-being, and *trayi* and *anviksiki* of moral well-being (AS.I.ii.9). This raises three questions: viz., (*a*) What is the nature of these sciences? (*b*) What is the relationship between them? (*c*) What are the implications of these relationships?

Beginning with the nature of the sciences, it may be recalled that Kautilya clarifies the notion of *anviksiki* by means of examples. Thus the three philosophical or metaphysical systems, *Samkhya*, *Yoga* and *Lokayata*, are said to illustrate it; but the goal is not stated in metaphysical terms which are not the same for the different systems. It is rather stated in concrete terms; a rational enquiry into *dharma* and *adharma* (good and evil); *artha* and *anartha* (economic and uneconomic); *naya* and *apanaya* (politic and impolitic); and the relative strength of these three. It confers benefit on the people, keeps the mind steady in adversity and prosperity, and illuminates thought, speech and action (AS.I.ii.10).

This account of *anviksiki* gives rise to many questions but my purpose here is to make only some general points. These are as follows:

1. One could say that the goal is to bring into focus, to bring a unity to, the thought, speech and action of the individuals and society. One might, in the usual terminology, say that the goal is self-realization, whatever the theoretical terms in which it may be presented.
2. Insofar as the description of the goal and the theoretical structure to support this are different in different systems, the relationship between the system and its goal cannot be logical in the sense in which this term is usually understood.
3. It is important to note that though the terminology of *purusartha* may have sectarian associations, the issues which are being discussed are not sectarian; in fact, they are universal. This is borne out by the fact that among the systems which can secure unity of thought, speech and action, *Lokayata*—which does not accept either transcendence as *Samkhya* does, or transcendence and God as *Yoga* does—is mentioned. Thus Indian pluralism is more plural than it is often supposed to be and includes a materialistic system (*Lokayata*) also.

The next science, *trayi*, is the three *Vedas*, *Rg*, *Sama* and *Yajur*, which give us the knowledge of *dharma* and *adharma*, of the duties of the four *varnas* and the four *asramas*, and of the duties common to all the *varnas* and the *asramas* (AS.I.iii.1 and 4). Ordinarily the science of *dharma* will be a *dharmasastra*, like the *Manusmrti*, *Yajnayavalkyasmrti*, etc., but here it is said to be the Vedas. This need not be held out as an objection, because among the sources of *dharma*, *sruti* is the one mentioned first in the *Manusmrti* (II. 6); and the *Vedas* are *sruti*. Therefore, it is not necessary to overemphasize such variations in emphasis.

Vartta is concerned with agriculture, rearing of cattle, and trade. It is a science concerned with the techniques of the various means of livelihood (AS.I.iv.1). Not much is said about this; so much so that it is not clear whether it has a separate status, or is only a distinguishable adjunct to *dandaniti*.

The last of the sciences, *dandaniti*, is concerned with the use of power for the sake of the internal and external security of the state (AS.I.i.iv.3). The more frequently used term for *dandaniti* is *arthasastra*, and it is the means of securing the safety and strength of the three sciences. It enables us to gain what we do not have, to protect what we have, to increase what is protected, and to bestow it on a worthy recipient. Thus, the use of power is not narrow and selfish, as it is very often supposed to be, but manifold.

Coming to the relationship between the sciences, this is iinked by Kautilya to the question of the number of sciences, as can be seen from what follows.

The followers of Manu say that the sciences are only *trayi*, *vartta*, and *dandaniti*; and *anviksiki* is only a special aspect of the *trayi*. The followers of Brhaspati say that *vartta* and *dandaniti* are the only sciences; and *trayi* is only a synopsis to one who knows the affairs of the world, that is, *trayi* and *dandaniti*. The followers of Usanasa say that the only science is *dandaniti*; it is the beginning and the end of all the sciences (AS.I.ii 2–8). Does the acceptance of the relationship between the sciences also mean the acceptance of the doctrine about the number of sciences? This is a very important issue as will be seen from the following discussion.

To say that the *trayi* is nothing but a summing up of the principles, which are known already to one who knows the affairs of the world, seems to imply that the exercise of *danda* is brought into focus by the principles of *dharma* and *adharma*—a consideration different from that of mere power, or lack of it, which might determine the exercise of *danda*. This situation can be described in one of two ways: (*a*) It may be said that there are considerations of power (and lack of power) and of wealth (and lack of wealth) and there are considerations of *dharma* and *adharma*. There are, therefore, two sciences, viz., *dandaniti* concerned with power (and economy) and the *trayi* concerned with *dharma*. (*b*) Only *dandaniti* based on the considerations of *dharma* and *adharma* is truly *dandaniti*. Therefore, there is only one science of *dandaniti*, of which *dharma* and *adharma*, on the one hand, and power or the lack of it, on the other, are aspects.

In a similar way we can argue about *anviksiki* and *trayi*: (*a*) It may be said that there are considerations of *dharma* and *adharma*, and there are considerations of unity and lack of unity. There are, therefore, two sciences, viz., *trayi* and *anviksiki*. (*b*) The *trayi* without the considerations of unity and lack of unity is not truly *trayi*. Therefore, there is only one science, *trayi*, with two aspects, of *dharma* and *adharma* and of unity and lack of unity.

If we take the foregoing account into consideration as a whole, we could say either that there are four sciences, which are interrelated, or that there is one science with four aspects: those of *anviksiki*, *trayi*, *vartta* and *dandaniti*.

We may now look at some implications of the relationship between the sciences.

1. It is important to note that the question of relationship is independent of the question of the number of sciences. In one case it can be a relationship between different sciences, and in the other, a relationship between different aspects of a science.

2. It is also an interesting point to note that when a science is eliminated, the consideration relevant to that science is not eliminated. For example, when *anviksiki* is eliminated as a separate science, the consideration of *anviksiki*, i.e., that of bringing unity to thought, speech and action, is not eliminated. It is made part of the *trayi* and so on. Similarly, when it is said that *dandaniti* is the only science, the considerations relevant to *vartta*, *trayi* and *anviksiki* are not eliminated; they are made part of *dandaniti*. As a result, *artha* is not *artha* unless it is sought in the context of these other sciences also.

3. If *artha* and *vartta*, in order to be *artha* and *vartta*, need focusing by *dharma* and *anviksiki*, it is important to remember that the relationship holds the other way also. That is, if *anviksiki* or *dharma* is not to be an empty form, it must have the content of *artha* and *vartta*. Without this content, or a reference to it, they cease to be what they are.

The foregoing would imply that none of the sciences could be truly itself without reference to considerations of all the other three sciences. Insofar as this is so, any one of the four sciences could not be the only science; or any one of the four sciences could be the only science, but each with a different focus from the other, *artha*, or *vartta*, or *dharma*, or unity of thought, speech and action. In other words, there is only one science—the science of man, or the science of human goals (*purusartha*) interacting with one another.

4. It is important to note here that the goals of the four sciences are not the same as the traditional four goals of human life. The goals of the sciences are *artha* (political), *vartta* (economic), *dharma* (moral), *anviksiki* (spiritual). The traditional goals are *artha* (political), *kama* (psychological), *dharma* (moral), *moksa* (spiritual). The first two goals of science are combined into *artha*, the first traditional human goal. (This is partly at the root of the confusion regarding the meaning of *arthasastra*—a science of economics, or a science of politics, or a science of political economy?) I do not know what to make of this discrepancy. However, the more important consideration is the following.

As we have seen, our discussion of the sciences has taken their goals to be interactional, not hierarchial.[2] Is there a mistake here, or does the hierarchy of the traditional four goals need to be understood differently from what is usual? I think that the latter is the case. We must realize that *artha* will not be a *purusartha* unless it is in accord with *kama*, *dharma* and *moksa*; *kama* in turn will not be *kama* unless it is in accord with *dharma* and *moksa*; and *dharma* will not be *dharma*, unless it too is in accord with *moksa*. Equally *moksa* will not be *moksa* without the content of *dharma*; *dharma* will not be *dharma* without the content of *kama* and *artha*. The four goals, therefore, constitute one single goal, though in the lives of individuals the elements may get varying emphasis for various reasons.

If this is so, what becomes of the hierarchy of human goals? When it is said that, if one has to choose between *artha* and *dharma*, one must opt for the latter, the choice does not imply that *artha* be completely sacrificed for *dharma*. It generally means the choice of less *artha* than may be available if one were to ignore *dharma*. In the extreme case, where complete sacrifice of *artha* is entailed, it means that if instead of *artha*, *dharma* were to be sacrificed, the former would cease to be human goal; therefore, one's humanity demands such a sacrifice. The foregoing could perhaps be summed up in the following slogans: *artha* alone as a goal is greed, *kama* alone is lust, *dharma* alone is mechanical ritual, and *moksa* alone is escapism.

5. The account of the relationship between the sciences raises a

number of questions. What is the relationship between the goals of *anviksiki* and *trayi*? In other words, what is the relationship between religion and morality? How does the study of *anviksiki* help in the attainment of the goal of *anviksiki*? Put differently, the question will be, what does a philosophical system do?

Let us return to the implications of the alternative ways of describing the situation. If we say that there are four sciences, it is suggested that each one of them could be studied on its own, and its principles established without reference to the considerations relevant to the others. This brings out the possibilities of a particular science to the fullest extent, and also suggests which of these can be actualized. Alternatively, if we say that there is only one science with four different aspects, all the considerations are brought to bear on a particular problem; therefore, reference to other aspects will prevent the investigation of the full possibilities of any particular aspect. If one or the other of the foregoing two possibilities is adopted, each would fail to take account of the other and would, therefore, have a certain inadequacy. However, it is possible that each one of the possibilities could be pursued keeping in mind the other.

Insofar as Kautilya accepts that there are four sciences, and yet does not deny a relationship between them, we could say that he would want the other possibility of the relationship between the sciences to be always kept in mind. In this respect it would appear that the approach of the *Arthasastra* is different from the modern approach. The latter emphasizes the autonomy of the sciences even when it adopts an interdisciplinary approach; per contra Kautilya emphasizes the unity of the sciences: 'Therefore, the three sciences have their root in the proper administration of the rule (rod)' (AS.I.v.1). But this could mean that only in an ordered society is it possible to pursue the sciences; it need not mean that *artha* alone is the goal independently of other goals. But Kautilya also says: 'Artha (material well-being) is the first-chief of the three—dharma, artha and kama, because dharma and kama are rooted in artha' (AS.I.vii.6,7).

It is true that what we think of as first, we sometimes also think of as the most important; but it need not be so. Without *artha*, there can be no *kama* and *dharma*; but if there is *artha* without *kama* and *dharma*, what is the point of *artha* by itself? Further, *artha* will not be *artha* if it is not in accordance with *dharma*. That Kautilya thinks so, is shown by the following: '...that he (the king) should not be without pleasures, but he should enjoy pleasures which are not against dharma and artha (consistently with the pursuit of dharma and artha). Or he should pursue the three equally which are bound up with one another. If any one is pursued in excess, it harms itself and the other two' (AS.I.vii.3–5). Also, at the end of the Arthasastra (XV. i.72) occurs the statement that I have adopted as the motto for this essay. All this shows that it could not have been the intention of Kautilya to say that artha is the most important goal. If what we have said is right, then arthasastra lays down a structure to establish political institutions which are in accordance with dharma. This does not, however, accord with the reputation of Kautilya and the Arthasastra. He is supposed to be an unashamed advocate of power[3], in both the internal administration and the external relations of the state. Internally he advocates a system of spying where there is no question of morality. Externally he advocates an expansionist policy which is limited only by one's power and circumstances. The justification is to maintain a society in the performance of dharma. The question is to maintain a society in the performance of the dharma. The question is whether this can be achieved by the means suggested in the Arthasastra. If so, the recommendations of Kautilya do not negate, at least in theory, the understanding that artha has to be pursued in accordance with dharma. What are the institutions and structures suggested so that the individual and society may achieve such fulfilment? I will consider only law and kingship to try to show how these institutions are structured to attain both artha and dharma, or artha according to dharma, or dharma consistently with artha.

LAW AND DHARMA

An examination of the Arthasastra reveals that dharma plays a central role in the settling of disputes, in the constitution of the court, and in the rules of evidence.

In the settlement of disputes, according to Kautilya, four factors were regarded as relevant: Dharma (code of conduct), vyavahara (the actual transaction in a particular case), caritra (the history of similar cases, tradition, precedents), rajasasana (the order of the king). Truth is the basis of *dharma*, witnesses of *vyavahar*, history of *caritra*, and the decision of the king of the order of king (AS.III.i.39, 40).

In this context, how is *dharma* understood? This word has been translated as 'law' by Kangle (1972, see note 1) and as 'sacred law' by Shama Sastri (*Kautilya's Arthasastra*. Mysore: Mysore Printing and Publishing House, 1967). I would like to suggest, however, that this concept is best understood in terms of the relationship of *samanya dharma* (*dharma* common to all castes and stages) and *visesa dharma* (dharma specific to various *varnas* and *asramas*). Taken holistically, *dharma* may be said to be the code of conduct. The sources of this *dharma* are *sruti* (the *vedas*), *smrti* (the *dharmasastras*), *sadachar* (the conduct of good men), and *atmatusti* (self-satisfaction) (MS.II.6). These sources have been understood to be hierarchically arranged in decreasing importance. However, the relationship is much more complex, and the sources are better described as a matrix of interacting factors (see K.J. Shah 'The Concept of Dharma', *Journal of the Indian Academy of Philosophy*, Vol. 12, No. 1: 35–45). It follows that it is not correct to translate *dharma* as law, because the code of conduct is not enacted by any one; or as sacred law, because the sources include the conduct of good men and self-satisfaction. This *dharma* is rooted in truth. One might think of it as moral and social consensus.

The terms *vyavahara*, *caritra* and *rajasasana* do not need explanation, but one may point out how the four factors operated in the implementation of *dharma*. It is a matter of commonsense. In the settlement of a dispute, the appropriate rule or law is provided by *dharma*. No law can exhaustively describe all the possible situations. In order to implement the law, therefore, the facts of the transaction (*vyavahara*) must be known. However, such facts or details may not have occurred for the first time. Therefore, it is necessary to have the precedents (the *caritra*), if the implementation is not to vary from case to case even when the facts are the same. But when the facts of the case do not fit into the existing law or precedents, it is the decision of the king or the state that must decide the issue.

What is the relation between these factors? Kautilya says that '*paschimo purvabadhakah*' (ASS.III.i.39–47). This has been translated as: 'the latter factor supersedes, or is superior to the former'. But this is not at all clear: how can *vyavahara* supersede *dharma*? One could possibly mean that if the transaction is not according to *dharma*, then the terms of the transaction should prevail. This does not seem intelligible in view of the following two considerations: (*a*) on the same basis, one would have to say that precedent (*caritra*) should supersede *vyavahara*—the terms of the transaction. But if the terms of the transaction are to be regarded as superior to *dharma*, it is not clear why they should be regarded as inferior to precedent. (*b*) Later on it is said that if *vyavahara* or *caritra* contradicts *dharma*, then it is to be rejected. Surely this is not to say that *vyavahara* is superior to *dharma*.

To avoid the problem arising from this last statement, it is said that it must be an interpolation. This view is sought to be supported by pointing out that the word used here for precedent is different (*samstha*) from the one used earlier (*caritra*). But this is not sufficient ground for thinking that we have here an interpolation. In any case, the question is: is there a need for such an explanation?

There is no such need if we once again go back to the beginning and attempt to understand the kind of relationship that can exist between *dharma* and *vyavahara* and *caritra*. Surely, *dharma* may be implemented only in the context of a particular transaction and the precedents; the latter, in some *ways*, condition, but do not prevent, such implementation. This is the meaning that the phrase '*pascimo purvabadhakah*' can quite easily bear. If this is so, the later statement that, if the *vyavahara* or *caritra* contradicts *dharma*, then *dharma* must prevail, need not at all conflict with the first account; in fact, it is consistent with the understanding of the *Arthasastra* as a whole. But to this pre-eminence of *dharma* there is one apparent exception. When there is conflict between rational or just decision (*dharma-nyaya*) and *dharma*, the former must prevail and not *dharma*. This is only an apparent exception because, in such a context, *dharma* undergoes a change. This possibility is quite in accordance with the four-fold sources or characteristics of *dharma*: *sruti*, *smrti*, *sadachar* and *atmatusti*. We had pointed out that this four-fold characterization shows that *dharma* is not static and that its change can be brought about by persons who are themselves good.

This brings us to the court which was constituted of three members conversant with *dharma* and three officers of the king, providing sufficient knowledge both of *dharma* and administration. The law of evidence gives sufficient scope to the defender as also to the accused, but it is not the same for both. For example, the defender is given time for answering the charges made against him, but not the complainant (ASI. III.i).

From the foregoing account, we can see that *dharma* has a pre-eminent place in the administration of law. But there is one serious difficulty here: is not the king given a dominant position in which he can override *dharma*? It is he who acts in the name of rational law; also it is he who is to establish *dharma* when all sense of duty has disappeared from society (AS.III.i.38). Does this not endanger the role of *dharma*? There can be no doubt that this is a serious possibility and it would have been actualized quite often, and a time may have come when this was generally the case. However, there can be no structure which is foolproof and free from difficulty; what is required is that it should be possible to deal with this difficulty more often than not. And we find that Kautilya has taken precautions to see that this difficulty is prevented as far as possible from getting the upper hand. The manner in which he does this will now be discussed.

THE KING AND HIS TRAINING

At many places in the *Arthasastra* the king is reminded of his duties and of the consequences of his failing to perform them. Thus: 'In the happiness of the subjects, lies the happiness of the king and in what is beneficial to the subjects, his own benefit. What is dear to himself is not beneficial to the king but what is dear to the subjects is beneficial to him' (AS.I.xix.34)

It is not left to chance, or to his good sense, that the king will do his duty. To inculcate in him a sense of duty, an elaborate two-fold course of training is laid down for the king: first, the training in the sciences we have already mentioned: *anviksiki, trayi, vartta* and *dandaniti*; second, the training in the control of the senses. The former is to be received from the respective experts: 'he should learn economics from the heads of departments, and the sciences of politics from its theoretical and practical exponents' (AS.I.v.8). The training in the sciences, especially the *anviksiki* and the *trayi* makes one realize the need for the control over the senses, the need to overcome lust, anger, greed, pride, arrogance and foolhardiness (AS.I.vi.I). Kautilya emphasizes this point further by mentioning the consequences of indulging in each one of the six vices mentioned, giving two illustrations each (AS. I.vi,4–12).

But to suggest or to provide a course of training is not necessarily to secure the intended results. It is not at all clear that competence in the sciences will give one control over the senses. Insofar as they are independent of each other, it is possible that the king has both, neither, or only one of the two. There is no problem when the king has both, or when he has neither; but there is a problem when a king has one but not the other. There will also be a question of preference between one who is good but has no competence and one who has competence but is not good. In any case, one would fail to get a ruler who will uphold *dharma*, in such a situation the problem of choice between different kinds of failings and/or virtues will be there. Kautilya has discussed a large number of possible situations and tried to come to a conclusion. However, it is an attempt to make the best of a bad bargain.

Another way in which Kautilya attempts to avoid such a situation is through advice to the king regarding discipline and competence.

He who when taught understands spiritual good and practices, the same is one possessed of sagacity. He who understands but does not practise them is one with intellect requiring to be goaded. He who is ever full of harm and hates spiritual and material good is one of evil intellect. If such be the only son, he (the king) should endeavour to get a son born of him. Or he should get sons begotten on an appointed daughter. An old or a diseased king, however, should get a child begotten on his wife.... But he should not install on the throne an only son, if undisciplined (AS.I.xvii,44–51).

Thus, there is no doubt that every attempt was made to see that the king who will occupy the throne would be just. But when a king turns out to be bad, the people will have to suffer and they would have no alternative but to wait until he perishes in one way or another. But they may not wait; in fact, there are other tests, besides the *Arthasastra* which advocate that the people should kill the king in such extreme cases. Kautilya does not directly advocate the killing of the king but he does say that an undisciplined, evil and impious king will, by his own negligence and indolence, produce decline, greed and disaffection among his subjects who may then kill him. 'Subjects, when impoverished, become greedy; when greedy they become disaffected; when disaffected, they either go over to the enemy or themselves kill the master. Therefore, he should not allow these cases of decline, greed and disaffection among the subjects to arisè, or, if arisen, should immediately counteract them' (AS.VII.v.19–28).

This indeed is a way out, but it is an extreme way out, involving considerable hardship to the people before they take recourse to such an action. But the alternative could be an invitation to unvirtuous kings to do what they wish and to the people to be long-suffering. This situation arises because the policy of Kautilya suffers from a fundamental defect in that there is no conception of rights—the rights of the citizens, especially against the state—in it.

RIGHTS: PROBLEM OF THE MISSING CONCEPT

One very striking difference between traditional and modern societies is that in the latter alone the rights of the individual citizens, even against the state, are recognized. This is one reason for the assertion that traditional society is authoritarian and modern society, free. What is the real significance of this distinction?

First, let us see what happens to freedom in a traditional society. As already noticed, the king did not make the law in traditional society, except in special circumstances. Law, therefore, was customary, it was the law of the *dharmasastra*. This itself was a great check on arbitrariness. Further, it made it difficult for the king to cover this arbitrariness under the guise of law. Though there were no legal processes against such behaviour, surely the moral and social processes were present; and even if these processes could be controlled by the authorities, the control must have been much more limited than what it can be today. This was the kind of risk that society took: the risk was not, as is sometimes imagined, the total and continuous absence of freedom; it was the possibility of arbitrariness, now and then, getting the upper hand.

What was the scope of arbitrariness? It could have been an unduly high collection of revenues, or personal harassment of one kind or another, which must have been limited to a few. If it went beyond the limit, it was not impossible to deal with it more or less effectively. If the kingdom was small, it was possible to leave the kingdom; if large, the pressure of arbitrariness would have been limited. Thus, on the whole, the freedom of the people would have been maintained on the one hand by the social and moral sanctions, and on the other hand, by the limited nature and power of government.

However, it might be argued that the recognition of the rights of citizens is definitely an improvement on this, and it gives to the citizen greater scope to realize human goals, individual and social. There can be no doubt that there must have been a time when the institution of rights must have facilitated the attainment of human goals—especially when the ruler had become much stronger in many ways, and the citizen much weaker, such that it had become very difficult to challenge the arbitrariness of the ruler. However, this does not mean that this would be so at all times and places; or that this arrangement would not be open to subversions of one kind or another, as the traditional arrangement was open to subversion. For example, even when there are legal rights, many people will lack the time, the energy and the resources to assert these rights and, therefore, the rights will become a tool in the hands of the powerful against the weak.

At a different level, a similar argument can be used against the notion of universal human rights also; for example, freedom of information could become, in fact it is, a tool in the hands of the powerful states against the weak states. Insofar as this is so, the rights of the weak can be ignored with impunity. As greater and still greater efforts are made to avoid such a possibility, law becomes increasingly complicated (including legal assistance at public expense) and even if the situation does not become worse, it continues to be as bad as ever. This sort of development, on the one hand, leads to the acceptance of law as a standard of behaviour, and, on the other hand, social norms take a back seat. Thus there comes about a kind of situation which makes things difficult for the straightforward while easy for the crooked. Further, in such a situation, where the ruler does not merely administer law, but also makes it, he can disguise his arbitrariness in the shape of law. These are the degenerations and risks involved in a society where rights are accepted. Not that there are no safeguards against these, but there are situations in which the safeguards are too weak to counter the trends mentioned above.

The foregoing analysis shows that there is no such thing as a foolproof structure which cannot be subverted, or which cannot degenerate; further, it would be difficult, if not impossible, to reject the traditional or the modern approach as fundamentally, inherently inadequate. Nor can we say that each kind of society has not tried to meet the difficulties that are likely to arise. However, situations might arise that might strain the systems to such an extent that they may break down. It is wrong, therefore, to think that traditional society neglected the freedom of the individual whereas modern society gives him his rightful place. Perhaps the best way of choosing between the two structures will be to opt for one where, in the prevailing circumstances, degeneration is not likely to become uncontrollable.

The crux of the matter seems to be that in traditional society duties are at the centre, whereas in modern society rights are so located. Thus there is the recognition of value in modern society which is not there in traditional society; and in modern society the possibilities and opportunities for the individual have increased immeasurably. It would be impossible and also unnecessary in this context to carry this controversy forward to a conclusion, because my purpose is not to choose between traditional and modern society but to institute a meaningful dialogue between the two.[4]

It has often been held that there are universal human rights, inalienable human rights, or natural rights. These terms may have had different uses, but I take them to mean the same thing: human beings, just because they are human beings, have certain rights, such as the right to life, liberty, equality, etc., irrespective of difference in time or place. There may be differences in the account of what specifically are such rights. However, my purpose is not to determine what these rights are, but to understand the notion of universal human rights.

One could approach the problem by considering the implications of the assertion of an individual's decision or resolve to do something. This raises the issue of personal liberty. Now, personal liberty is an element in one's being oneself in the attainment of happiness, at the achievement of the goals of life, viz., *moksa, kama,* or *dharma* (sometimes said to be individually the only goals of life), or *dharma, artha, kama,* and *moksa* taken together as the goal of life. If this conception of personal liberty is granted, then the assertion of an individual right is also part of one's goals of life.

These goals, it is often held, are both the given and the normative ends of human endeavour. But how do we establish that they are the goals of life? *Artha* and *kama* do not, perhaps, pose a serious problem but that is not·true of *dharma* and *moksa*. However, we have earlier seen how these goals are said to be related, and only in their interrelationship do they manifest their true nature. We might even say that these goals are the *a priori* conditions of being a human being. Insofar as *dharma* and *moksa* are also sought along with *artha* and *kama*, these are the goals and these also ought to be the goals.[5]

To return to our question about the assertion of an individual resolve to do something, does it belong to any one of the elements in its true nature? Our problem is not to answer this question but to see that a right, if there is one, will follow from the fact that certain goals are goals that one ought to pursue. Insofar as this is so, the doctrine of rights is essentially a mode of making duty operative.

The distinction between the traditional and modern societies is thus seen to be not fundamental. In other words, it is not such that one recognizes a fundamental value which the other does not. In fact, the difference is that in modern society, the performance of one's duty requires a right as an instrument. A legal safeguard is needed because a social or moral safeguard does not operate.

DHARMASASTRA AND ARTHASASTRA

So far we have examined Kautilya's account of the administration of law and kingship. But *dharmasastra* also lays down rules in both these respects. If *artha* is to be pursued in accordance with *dharma*, what is the point of having both *dharmasastra* and *arthasastra*? This question has not been raised explicitly but it is possible to consider it in more than one way.

One way of considering it would be to compare the sources of the rules in the *Manusmrti* and the *Arthasastra*. According to the former (as already stated above), the sources of *dharma* are *sruti, smrti, sadachar* (conduct of good men), and *atmatusti* (self-satisfaction). Further, and again as we have seen, the sources of law in the *Arthasastra* are *dharma, vyavahara, caritra* and *rajasasana*. (It is true these are said to be the four factors that are relevant to the settlement of disputes but by being so' relevant they become the source of the *dharma* which is to be implemented.) Moreover, there are rules of conduct and punishment which are there in the one text but not in the other; in some cases the two overlap. The important question to ask would be, what is the significance of the foregoing differences and similarities between the two texts?

I think the reason for the differences/similarities are not always the same, as may be illustrated by considering the rules regarding marriage and verbal and physical injury in the two texts (MS.III.I.44 and VIII, 267–87; AS.III.ii. 1–13; III.xviii. 1–12; and III.xix. 1–36). It will be seen that in some matters, social control is considered adequate—e.g., in the case of advice regarding the kind of girl one should marry. In other cases, it must have been thought that the matter is such as cannot be controlled by law or that law can do precious little in the matter—e.g., the abuse of one's parents. It is some or more of these reasons that would explain why the common code of conduct, which is known as *samanya dharma* and includes such virtues as forgiveness, speaking the truth, etc., are not included in the *Arthasastra*.

Now let us note some of the things which are there in the *Arthasastra* but not in the *Manusmrti*. The most important feature of the rules in the former is that the description and classification of situations, events, offences, etc., are detailed, precise and clear. Thus, in it, different types of marriage are said to be lawful if only the father has approved, or both father and mother have approved, irrespective of the caste of the parties concerned. In the *Manusmrti* a type of marriage is lawful for certain castes but not for others.

As more and more cases arise, there is always a tendency that case-law is built up and so are precedents. This would certainly lead to a more specific and clear definition of situations, events, etc., so that the law is clearly established, there is no ambiguity, and similar situations are dealt with in the same manner. As long as this crystal-lization does not occur, and there is no machinery to enforce the rules and the punishment, it is possible to lay down unrealistic punishments as in the *Manusmrti* but once there is a machinery of enforcement, it seems punishments also become realistic as they are in the *Arthasastra*.

However, there are areas of conduct in which both our texts give details, which are practical, and relate the consequences to the nature of the action; for example, this is so in the case rules stating the duties of husbands and wives, or regarding rules of inheritance. The difference between the two texts here is a matter of detail and not one of nature.

At any time, in any society, there are some kinds of conduct that are not left only to informal social control, but are also formally controlled. This is the beginning of the difference between the rules in the *Manusmrti* and the *Arthasastra*. In any society, it is found necessary to leave certain areas of conduct to only social sanctions or moral sanctions. Equally, it is found necessary not to leave certain other areas of conduct to such sanctions only but to formalize the rules as also the institutional structures for their enforcement. However, there can be no definiteness or universality regarding where the line will be drawn between the formal and the informal. It is not, therefore, surprising that the *Manusmrti* contains some rules which are formal and like the rules of the *Arthasastra* in nature. This is how there are not only differences between the two texts but also similarities. With the passage of time, imperceptibly but inevitably, the generality and informality of the rules must have been replaced by specificity and formality regarding more and more areas. This must have led to the crystallization of the distinction between *dharmasastra* and *arthasastra*. But however much this process goes on it would not be possible to have only an *arthasastra* without a *dharmasastra* because, as we have already seen, in any society, it is not possible to bring all activities under formal control. However, a change from the informal to the formal code of conduct, does not alter the basis of the code of conduct which remains *dharma*; there is change only in the mode of its operation in certain areas of conduct. To describe this process, as is sometimes done, as a change from the religious approach to the secular approach is a grievous mistake.

THE METHOD OF THE ARTHASASTRA

I would now like to consider a methodological objection that may be raised against our approach to the *Arthasastra*. It may be said that this text is merely a manual of rules and maxims and not a systematic treatise: we are imposing a system and method on it, because we want to see in it something which is not there but which we think is necessary if the *Arthasastra* is to claim any value, other than its historical importance.

We began with the discussion of the place of *arthasastra* in the scheme of sciences. This brought out also the place of *artha* as a goal in the traditional scheme of the four *purusarthas*. However, the

Arthasastra does not consider only the principles according to which *artha* is to be attained; it also elaborates the institutional structure required for the realization of *artha*. These details are not only the details of government but also of administration. Thus the *Arthasastra* considers the principles of politics, government and administration as a whole. Not only that; the validity of the principles is not established so much in contrast to possible principles as by means of their relationship to government and administration; it follows that the relationship between the principles of the state, government and administration is reciprocal and not hierarchical, from the principles of the state downwards.

Our account of *Arthasastra* does not involve any distortion of the text; however, we have used only part of what it has to say about the main principles and used only some details for illustrative purposes. But this in no way affects the account of the nature of the goal of *artha*, the related institutions, and their relationship. But can we not say that this kind of account will give a wrong picture of the text and emphasize the presence of a method where it is only present superficially? This objection arises not so much from the fact that we have presented a kind of sketch or outline, but because we have a view of the method where the principles of the state, government, and administration, are not mixed with details but treated separately. However, this is to presuppose and impose a particular view of method. The sort of approach adopted by the *Arthasastra* also could be called a method: it consists of elucidating the principle by its application, and of elucidating a fact by means of a principle. In fact, in the social sciences, more than in the other sciences, this method has its own virtues. Different parts of the exposition illuminate one another; and this prevents the theory from being empty and the facts from being simple facts without a focus.

But it might be said that our account of method goes far beyond the conception of method that Kautilya has described in his last chapter. He mentions thirty-two devices that have been used in the composition of the *Arthasastra*. They are a mixed lot from our point of view (or perhaps even from any point of view including that of Kautilya). But it is possible to classify them into three groups: (*a*) the devices which are used for the establishment of the point of view such as advice (*upadesa*), reason (*hetvartha*), doubt (*samsaya*), the opponent's view (*purvapaksa*), etc; (*b*) the devices which are used to explain the meaning of words such as giving the meaning of a word (*padartha*), the meaning of a word through the meaning of the components of a word (*nirvacanam*), etc; (*c*) the devices which are methods of expounding the subject; these are devices of literary composition or stylistic devices, reference (*apadesa*), reference to a future statement (*anagata aveksanam*), reference to a past statement (*atikranta aveksanam*), etc. (AS.XV.i).

These devices have a two-fold purpose: to counter the statement of those who argue falsely, and to establish one's own position. That they are not classified or considered in their interrelationship within or outside a certain grouping may be taken to show that the thinking in this direction had not progressed far. However, this judgement is itself based on the presupposition that method has to be what we generally take it to be. But when the whole approach is different, as in the case of *Arthasastra*, the devices mentioned cover the text and may have a point which they may not have found it necessary to formulate into a method any further. However, it is useful for us to do so, for more than one reason. Thus it will enable us to see, first, that the text is not unsystematic, and, then, that the method of this text, in relation to what is acceptable as method today, is not incomprehensible although it is not the same.

One main difference between the method of the *Arthasastra* and contemporary discussion of political thought will be that in the former there is no clear-cut distinction between political philosophy, political science and political policy—they are together seen as one process. It is very succinctly brought out in the last verse. 'This science has been composed by him who in resentment, quickly regenerated the science and the weapons and the earth that was under the control of the Nanda king' (AS.XV.i.73).

As against this, modern thought distinguishes between political science, political philosophy and political policy and makes efforts to keep them separate, lest the consideration of one should vitiate the consideration of the other. One could put the matter differently: the *Arthasastra* mentions the goals and their relationship, but it also gives us the structure of government and administration which is required to attain the goals in accordance with the principles. There is no separate discussion of each—the principles, the government and the administration—but presumably they all hang together, each supporting the other two and supported by the other two.

CONCLUDING REMARKS

At this point we shall sum up our discussion, with a few concluding remarks. As indicated at the beginning, we have presented a structure of thought with reference to the *Arthasastra*, but we do not claim that it represents what Kautilya thought, though it will contribute to its understanding. At the same time it is a structure of thought and values which can stand on its own.

What is this structure of thought? What are the principles and presuppositions of *artha* and the *arthasastra*? We find that *arthasastra* is not autonomous in the sense in which we think of a discipline as autonomous. Though it must begin with the considerations peculiar to itself, namely, acquisition and maintenance of land through power (principles of politics), by itself it will not give us the principles of *artha*, because other considerations—those of *vartta*, *trayi* and *anviksiki* must come in to make it truly an *arthasastra*. Similarly, *artha* is not an independent goal; for truly to be *artha* it must be pursued in the context of *dharma*, or more fully, in the context of the economy (*vartta*), *dharma* (*trayi*), and unity of thought, speech and action (*anviksiki*). If we put it in the traditional terminology of *purusartha*, *artha* must be pursued in the framework of *kama*, *dharma* and *moksa*. Though it may be possible to work out some detailed differences between these two formulations, the principle remains that *artha* to be truly *artha* must be part of a larger totality, individual and social. When we probe deeper, the meaning of the two formulations may not be very different.

In theory it may be all right to state the principle that *artha* must be pursued in accordance with *dharma*, but to have institutions which will achieve this is not easy. There is no such thing as a fool-proof institution, and one must provide for remedies when things go wrong. This has been done with considerable care and foresight by Kautilya, in respect of both the institutions of law and of kingship. But these institutions are related to certain concrete conditions, and, therefore, independently of these conditions, these institutions may and did develop problems. But within a framework, they provided a way of living which was conducive to the attainment of individual and social goals. We also found that the society which enables this approach is authoritarian and without the institution of rights. This happens because we think that certain values must be attained only through a particular set of institutions. However, when we consider the society as a whole, we find that social institutions provide for freedom of the individual, and the possibility of degeneration is common both to traditional and modern society.

A similar situation exists in the case of method also. In appearances, the *Arthasastra* seems to have no method, but this again is due to certain presuppositions about what the method should be. If we divest ourselves of such preconceptions, we find that the *Arthasastra* too has method; and perhaps it has advantages of its own which what we today regard as structure that we are presenting can stand on its own, we do not want to say that it can be adopted by us today with or without the institutions. Nor do we want to say that the principles can be adopted and the present institutions can be adapted to those principles. What we want to point out is that there is a structure which has a form and a purpose and which, perhaps, has a bearing on our present situation and problems.

It may be said that all that we are saying was not spelt out, or at least not in the way we have done it. Perhaps there was no need to do so in the past. But in our context, it is necessary to spell out explicitly what is there implicitly; only then may we be fair and hope to establish a meaningful relationship between the past, the present and the future.

NOTES

1. The English translation of the text used here is by R.P. Kangle, *The Kautiliya Arthasastra*. Bombay: University of Bombay, 1972. References to the text are by book, chapter and verses.

2. Prof. Shah's use of the term 'hierarchial' is a conventional one (with reference to the simple ranking and needs to be distinguished from Dumont's notion of Hierarchy). *Editor*

3. For an earlier and unequally worked out challenge to the image of Kautilya, see K. Raghavendra Rao, 'Kautilya and the Secular State'. *Journal of the Karnatak University*, vol. 2, pp. 1–7.

4. Both these themes—viz., the value placed on individualism in modern society and the methodology of cross-civilizational comparison—are, of course, of central importance in Dumont's work. See Dumont, *From Mandeville to Marx: The Genesis and Triumph of Economic Ideology*. Chicago: University of Chicago Press, 1977.

5. There is a big jump here in my argument but Sundararajan ('The Purusartha in the Light of Critical Theory', *Indian Philosophical Quarterly*, Vol. 2, No. 3, pp. 339–50) has argued this point in detail.

8 Mahatma Gandhi's Critique of Modernity

Anthony J. Parel

Mahatma Gandhi (1869–1948) is unquestionably the great innovator of modern India. He is called the father of the Indian nation, and his political philosophy has been subjected to close scrutiny by many scholars. His name is almost synonymous with non-violence. All critics, except the Marxists, have tended to see in him a revolutionary who has demonstrated that non-violence could be effectively practised in modern conditions. Marxists, however, have tended to see him as an important leader, but one who unconsciously reinforced the bourgeois elements of modern India. Rather than rehearse these debates here, I would rather argue that his contribution to political philosophy lies principally in his critique of modernity as such, a critique which has application not just to Indian politics, but politics universally.

Modernity is understood here as a view of life which considers politics solely to be a science of coercive power; economics to be an amoral science of maximizing utilities of individuals and nations; atheism to be the 'metaphysics' of modern humanism, according to which man is seen not only as the measure of things but also as his own maker; historicism to be the new philosophy of truth, and technology to be the right approach to nature and to the question of satisfying human appetites. Historically, modernity has had its origin in the West; but it now threatens the politics of every culture and every nation.

The historical context of Gandhi's political philosophy is constituted by two principal elements: British colonialism and Indian renaissance. He came into contact with the British colonial mentality in Britain itself, where he spent three years as a law student (1888–91), and in South Africa, where he spent twenty-one years as a lawyer and a social reformer (1893–1914), and in India, where he led the struggle for Indian independence until 1947, and where he was assassinated in 1948. He saw modern colonialism as an outgrowth of what he called modern western civilization. This is not to say that he understood and evaluated the West only in terms of its modernity. He had greatly admired the ethics of Christianity, and the western concept of civil freedom and equality. The writings of Leo Tolstoy and *Unto This Last* of John Ruskin had a lasting impact on his thought. His most original contribution to politics, *satyagraha*, had its origin in his struggle against the racial politics of South Africa, and it was applied effectively against the colonial regime in India. Historically speaking, however, it is fair to say that the moderate politics characteristic of British colonial rule in India contributed to the evolution of the politics of *satyagraha*.

Gandhi as an innovator of modern India is historically not imaginable except in the context of the Indian renaissance. Being a cultural movement it affected the religious, literary, social and political consciousness of India. It can be said to have originated in Calcutta by about the middle of the nineteenth century though parallel developments were also occurring in Madras and Bombay. The catalyst for this movement was the acceptance of an English system of education, which, among other things, introduced into India a new vision of civic life cutting across caste and religious lines. The reform movement within Hinduism, spearheaded by such pioneers as Ram Mohun Roy and Swami Vivekananda, was part of this renaissance with the Indian National Congress (1885) giving political expression to it. The founding of the Theosophical Society (1875), the Arya Samaj (1875), and the emergence of the anarchist movement centred mostly in Bengal, Maharashtrà and the Punjab by the turn of the century, can be seen as different expressions of a reawakened India. The 'discovery' of the riches of Sanskrit literature contributed powerfully to a more practical appreciation by Hindus of Hindu ethics, especially that found in the *Bhagavad Gita*.

Gandhi picked up these diverse strands of Indian renaissance, purified them of excess, and gave Indian politics a typically Gandhian character. In this connection it is remarkable that even after the discovery of the text of Kautilya's *Arthasastra* in 1909, the latter exercised no impact on the development of political consciousness in modern India. The man mainly responsible for this, in my view, is Mahatma Gandhi and his interpretation of Indian politics. The *Gita* almost totally eclipsed any impact that the *Arthasastra* might have had on the development of modern Indian philosophy, at least up to now.

Gandhi was not a political philosopher in the formal sense. But he was a political philosopher in the Socratic sense. However, unlike Socrates he wrote incessantly; he has left behind a formidable body of literature, now collected in 90 volumes. But even this mountain of writings does not contain a formal treatise on government and politics. The *Hind Swaraj* (1909)[1] is the closest we have of a formal political tract from him. As Sir Penderel Moon wrote, it is 'the first comprehensive, coherent expression of certain basic ideas that Gandhi never lost sight of throughout all his subsequent political career.'[2] On the surface it is both an analysis of why India lost her political freedom and a prescription for the means of attaining *swaraj* (self-rule). But at a deeper level it is nothing short of an analysis of modernity itself, and a prescription for its cure.

The starting point is an examination of the 'civilization' out of which modernity has emerged. It is a civilization whose humanism misrepresents the human reality of the unity of body and soul. It takes 'man' to be just the body, and considers the soul to be its function. 'Bodily welfare' has emerged as the 'object of life' and the resources of the entire civilization are put in the service of the good of 'bodily happiness'. Its pillars are insatiable possessiveness, 'machinery', mechanization of every aspect of human life, rejection of the virtue of religion, and coercive power.

Perhaps we should pay attention to Gandhi's use of metaphors and myths to describe the nature of this civilization. From Hinduism he borrows the myth of the 'black age', and from Islam, that of 'satanic civilization.'[3] Even more interesting is the metaphor of the Upas tree. 'One writer', observes Gandhi, 'has linked the whole modern system to the Upas tree. Its branches are represented by parasitical professions including those of law and medicine, and over the trunk has been raised the axe of true religion. Immorality is the root of the tree.'[4] The possessive appetite enslaves the self; mechanization of life will gradually destroy human life. 'Under it [modern civilization] the nations of Europe are becoming degraded and ruined every day.'[5] 'It is eating into the vitals of the English nation. The English deserve sympathy. This civilization is such that one has only to be patient and it will be self-destroyed.'[6]

The two most prestigious institutions of liberal democracy—the British parliament and the modern free press—are found wanting. Using sarcasm, Gandhi compares the parliament to a sterile woman and a prostitute, a remark that offended a lady admirer of his, and for that reason, he was later prepared to modify it.[7] The point is that the parliament as an institution does good only 'under public pressure'. Its members act only as their parties want them to act. The 'greatest questions' are debated ideologically. The prime minister is more concerned with maintaining his power than with the good of the nation. 'His care is not always that Parliament shall do right. The Prime Ministers are known to have made Parliament do things merely for party advantage.' Gandhi wonders how 'a true Christian' could be part of such an institution. And he hazards the opinion that 'If the money and time wasted by Parliament were entrusted to a few good men, the English nation would be occupying today a much higher platform.'[8]

The modern free press is not as free or as good as it is taken to be. Political events are interpreted by the press according to the financial and power interests of those who own and edit papers. And the interests of those who own the press '...swing like the pendulum of a clock and are never steadfast.' The media keeps the public in a state of perpetual misinformation and misrepresentation.

Perhaps the most controversial elements in his critique concern those dealing with modern professions, especially those of the lawyers and the doctors. What Gandhi is saying is that the professionalization of various human activities has tended to pervert their true human ends. The true ends of law and medicine are promotion of justice and care of the sick, respectively. Instead, under modernity, these professions have become means of gaining social power and private wealth, and as such, they create a powerful social and political elite that serves its interest first and last. He is aware that there are honourable exceptions to this rule. But his point is that the good they may have done is 'accidental'.[9] Thus the good that lawyers do '...is due to them as men rather than as lawyers.'[10] As lawyers it is in their interest that human beings quarrel. Men become lawyers, he asserts, not in order to help others out of their miseries, but to enrich themselves. Petty pleasers actually manufacture disputes; like so many leeches, they 'suck the blood of the poor people'. They decide what fee they will charge. They frame laws as they frame their praises. The court system only perpetuates the grip of the power elite. 'We, in our simplicity and ignorance, imagine that a stranger by taking our money, gives us justice.'[11] The judges fare no better under Gandhi's gaze; they give 'strength' to the lawyers. Briefly, the professionalization of the judicial system has created a powerful political elite that dominates society.

The doctors, as doctors, do no better in Gandhi's view. The business of the doctor, he avers, is to take care of the body, '...or, properly speaking, not even that. Their business is really to rid the body of diseases that may afflict it.'[12] But diseases, Gandhi points out, often arise out of 'negligence and indulgence', through lack of personal discipline of the individual. Thanks to the professionalization of medicine, individuals become more and more self-indulgent as well as dependent on medicine and the doctors. In this sense, says Gandhi, 'Hospitals are institutions for propagating sin. Men take less care of their bodies and immorality increases.'[13] And the doctors enter this picture, not for the purpose of 'serving' humanity, but to obtain 'honours and riches'. They make a show of their knowledge and 'charge exorbitant fees. Their preparations which are intrinsically worth a few pence, cost shillings. The populace, in its credulity and in the hope of ridding itself of some disease, allows itself to be cheated.'[14]

What Gandhi has said of lawyers and doctors is applicable, in principle, to every other modern profession. Practical knowledge is in danger of becoming an instrument of power and domination; as interpreted by modernity, it has ceased to be a means of service and human fellowship.

'Machinery' and railways—in Gandhi's eyes, its chief symbol—come next for consideration. And what he says of railways, I believe, is applicable, in principle, to all subsequent mechanical inventions. However, we should be clear on one point. Gandhi's attack is not directed against machinery as such, but against what he calls 'the machinery craze' which he compares to 'sexual vices.'[15] Now craze is insanity or the perversion of reason. The craze for machinery then is the perversion of man's natural technical capacity. A natural human capacity becomes a craze when it is not directed towards its proper end, which is, ultimately, the good of the species. But when the natural capacity becomes a craze, technology becomes an instrument of benefit to some and harm to others. Technology as craze becomes an instrument of power and domination and inequality among humans. All technologically advanced nations conquered or sought to conquer less advanced nations, and modernity made the process more efficient. If territorial conquest has ceased to be the goal of technology, it is so because we have run out of territories to conquer. But we have modern substitutes for territorial conquests.

Technology in alliance with industry creates slaves out of workers, dependents out of nations; technology in alliance with war, creates political dependents. Thus, to take a historical example, the modern textile mills of Manchester destroyed the traditional cotton industry of India, leading Gandhi to endorse the conclusion that it was modern machinery that impoverished and enslaved India.[16] Gandhi's solution to the problem was not a simple and straightforward transfer of technology to India, but transfer of technology only after it has been cleansed, after the craze for it has been removed. By reproducing Manchester in India, he wrote, India may secure a better balance of trade, but this can be achieved, he pointed out, only 'at the price of our blood'. This will be so, he argued, '...,because our moral being will be sapped, and I call in support of my statement the very mill-hands (of Bombay) as witnesses. And those who have amassed wealth out of factories are not likely to be better than other rich men. It would be folly to assume that an Indian Rockefeller would be better than the American Rockefeller.'[17]

Here again Gandhi's metaphors are interesting. He compares machinery to a snake-hole, which may contain from one to a hundred snakes.[18] The 'snakes' he mentions are large urban centres, modern systems of transportation, pollution and the risk to health they cause, and the like. But the 'snake' that he takes for vivisection is the railway. For a man who used the railway so much for his work, such a critical attitude is indeed surprising. He first draws a balance-sheet of benefits and harms done to India by the railways. On the benefit side there is increased communication and the emergence of 'the new spirit of nationalism.' On the other hand the railways tightened the grip of the English on India and opened the markets to the outside world. The opening of the market meant that '...people sell out their grain and it is sent to the dearest markets. People become careless and so the pressure of famine increases.'[19]

But what catches Gandhi's attention is the phenomenon of speed in modern communication, and the value modernity attaches to is:

Formerly, men travelled in wagons. Now they fly through the air in trains at the rate of four hundred and more miles per day. This is considered the height of civilization. It has been stated that, as men progress, they shall be able to travel in airship and reach any part of the world in a few hours. Men will not need the use of their hands and feet. They will press a button, and they will have their clothing by their side. They will press another button, and they will have their newspaper. A third, and a motor-car will be waiting for them. They will have a variety of delicately dished up food. Everything will be done by machinery.[20]

What about speed as a modern value? Here Gandhi goes back to the basics: what does our natural constitution intend and what does our technological craze compel? What does the providential order suggest and what does the technological order attempt to create? Gandhi would want nature, providence and technology to work in mutual recognition of each other. He writes:

Man is so made by nature as to require him to restrict his movements as far as his hands and feet will take him. If we did not rush about from place to place by means of railways and such other maddening conveniences, much of the confusion that arises would be obviated. Our difficulties are our own creation. God set a limit to a man's locomotive ambition in the construction of his body. Man immediately proceeded to discover means of overriding the limit. God gifted man with intellect that he might know his Maker. I am so constructed that I can only serve my immediate neighbours, but in my conceit I pretend to have discovered that I must with my body serve every individual in the Universe. In thus attempting the impossible, man comes in contact with different natures, different religions, and is utterly confounded. According to this reasoning, it must be apparent to you that railways are a most dangerous institution. Owing to them, man has gone further away from his Maker.[21]

The value of speed also has to be evaluated ultimately in the light of the notion of the good of man. If it facilitates the human good, it is a blessing. But here Gandhi faces a difficulty. The good in question, the good of character, is acquired by habituation which takes time, and cannot be speeded up. Speed in achieving moral development is not possible. Development of good habits can be achieved only over a long period of time. 'Good travels at a snail's pace—it can, therefore, have little to do with the railways. Those who want to do good are not selfish, they are not in a hurry, they know that to impregnate people with good requires a long time. But evil has wings.'[22]

In the final analysis, technology is a blessing only if it promotes the happiness of all, not just of those who have access to it. Gandhi's approach to technology, art, aesthetics, wealth and power was all guided by his overriding moral concern. As Nehru has observed, 'so entirely was he (Gandhi) a moralist', that he 'would regard even the Taj Mahal as only a vast monument of forced labour.'[23] Whether Nehru is quoted accurately or not, the observation captures the spirit of Gandhi's judgement on modernity, and the civilization that nurtures it. 'Machinery has begun to desolate Europe', he wrote in 1909. 'Ruination is now knocking at the English gates.'[24]

But Gandhi is not a pessimist. 'Civilization is not an incurable disease....'[25] If human beings develop moral character, they may succeed in taking the craze out of technology, and making it into a means of freedom, equality and universal happiness. But how is moral character to be developed? It has to begin with self-reform, or self-rule. It is to Gandhi's concept of *swaraj* that we must now turn.

The basic notions underlying Gandhi's concept of *swaraj* are truth (*satya*), and non-violence (*ahimsa*). Freedom is not Gandhi's starting point; the starting point is truth. On the basis of these, he developed a technique for specific kinds of political action, known to everyone as *satyagraha*. But political action extends beyond *satyagraha* and reaches *sarvodaya*, the improvement of mankind as such. *Satyagraha* and *sarvodaya* require four virtues or stable psychological dispositions—chastity, the spirit of poverty or detachment from possessiveness, courage or fearlessness in the face of opposition or adversity, and the virtue of religion. These dispositions liberate and reorder the self, and a self so liberated, and only such selves, are equipped to reform society and its institutions.

Satya in Gandhi's usage is a many-sided concept. At its most abstract level, it means being; in its ordinary meaning, it refers to honesty in human affairs; at a formal level, it means practical wisdom, i.e., truth as practical, as knowing what to do in a given situation, in a given decision or choice. Truth as practical, or truth of the practical has to be in conformity with *dharma*, the moral law. In a still restricted sense truth means Reality, the Absolute, the foundation of all empirical realities. This is the sense in which truth is discussed in the philosophy of the Vedanta. Finally, when the Absolute is understood as a person, truth means what in ordinary language we mean by God.

One or the other of these meanings of truth can be found in Gandhi's innumerable writings. The meaning that interests us here is the truth of the practical. Gandhi called his autobiograhy *The Story of My Experiments with Truth*. Thus, for Gandhi, life itself is a series of experiments with truth. Political action, accordingly, is grounded in Being, in *dharma*, as well as in the ever changing experiences of life. The experimental character of political action gives it its flexibility while the grounding of political action in *dharma*, and in being, gives it its direction as well as its stability. Moreover, *satya* makes it necessary that both the end and the means be right.

If *satya* is the metaphysical and objective basis of right action, *ahimsa* is its correct psychological basis. *Ahimsa* is variously called by Gandhi as truth-force, love-force, and soul-force. It is important to bear in mind that its source is the soul, and that it is distinguished by him from brute-force or physical force, whose source is the body. The great task of every worthwhile life is to make soul-force prevail over brute-force, guide it and control it. Perhaps the single great contribution of Gandhi to politics is that he showed new ways of making soul-force an alternative to brute-force, in an increasing number of areas of political action. In modernity brute-force, does not recognize its subordination to soul-force. In fact it has asserted its autonomy, and expresses itself in various forms: as economic exploitation, as reason of state, as revolutionary violence, as wars of aggression, as guerrilla wars, as acts of terrorism. 'Those who are intoxicated by the wretched modern civilization,' writes Gandhi, 'think these things.'[26] In modernity these forms of brute-force have acquired the status of a legitimate theory.

The effectiveness of brute-force, Gandhi believes, lies in fear. Fear of punishment restrains the thief. Fear of reprisals restrains an aggressor. In each instance, fear and brute-force do nothing to cure the thief and the aggressor of their habit of stealing and attacking. Brute-force has no solutions to offer in this regard.

Soul-force, on the other hand, being also love-force and truth-force, has the resources of attempting to 'convert' the thief and the attacker, and of curing them of their habit of stealing and attacking. For soul-force is the force of mutuality: it sees another human being, not as a potential competitor, but as a potential cooperator. Where cooperation becomes practically impossible, or where oppression is the reality, soul-force has resources that can be mobilized. This brings out an important aspect of *ahimsa*: *ahimsa* is more than not injuring others; it is also a capacity to accept sufferings voluntarily in the name of justice. As such, as one commentator has pointed out, *ahimsa* implies self-sacrificial love, whose archetype is God's love for man. Thus *ahimsa* shares in certain features of *agape* rather than in those of either *eros* or *philia*.[27] T.K.N. Unnithan has convincingly argued that *ahimsa* as love-force is also the basis for discovering an alternative to coercive force. Soul-force, he argues, though only persuasive and not coercive, is nevertheless, a force. The thief is 'moved' to change his habits by techniques of love-force; an unjust ruler or a rapacious industrialist is moved to change their ways, on their own and on the basis of the enlightenment that soul-force generates. We are so accustomed to identifying the social effectiveness of coercive force in terms of fear of punishment that we find it difficult to see that soul-force can be even more effective than brute-force.[28]

But the pursuit of *satya* and *ahimsa*, as noted earlier, is not possible unless the soul is habituated in certain stable dispositions. The cultivation of these dispositions is difficult. Gandhi's challenge to modernity is that unless men and women are prepared to acquire these dispositions in some degree or other, the prospects for human happiness are dim.

Chastity or *brahmacharya* is one of the four dispositions singled out by Gandhi as being indispensible for both inner *swaraj* and political *swaraj* rooted in *ahimsa*. Gandhi's war against the flesh forms an important (some, like Erik Erikson would say, the crucial) part of his experiments with truth, and the story is fully recorded in the literature. Gandhi came to recognize the importance of chastity for public life only in mid-life, in 1906, when he was 37, happily married and the father of four. He held the view that the sexual act should be limited to procreation in marriage. But his teachings on chastity extend to embrace a re-evaluation of sexuality as a positive source of non-violent social and political behaviour. Gandhi does not employ the vocabulary of repression or sublimation. But he does require openness and honesty in understanding our motivation, control of diet, use of fasting and prayer, regulation of imagination and fantasies by 'reality-tests' or truth-tests. A true *satyagrahi* has to be sexually mature.

Erikson saw in Gandhi's achievement in regard to sexuality a counterpoint to Freud's and modernity's position regarding sexual instinct, violence and the prospects for civilization. 'The truth of *satyagraha* and the "reality" of psychoanalysis come somewhat nearer to each other', writes Erikson, 'if it is assumed that man's "reality testing" includes an attempt not only to think clearly but also to enter into an optimum of mutual activation with others.'[29]

Modernity taps sexuality for purposes of financial gains, as an extension of brute-force. Gandhi taps sexuality as a subordinate ally of soul-force for purposes of respecting and serving the other as the other, with no hidden agenda for control or sexual exploitation.

The virtue of voluntary poverty is the second stable disposition that *swaraj* required. This disposition had nothing to do with involuntary poverty, the lot of India's millions. In fact, in Gandhi's thought, involuntary poverty was an obstacle to the practice of voluntary poverty; and only when human beings had a sufficiency of material possessions could they practise voluntary poverty. Further still, the spirit of voluntary poverty was a means of bringing about economic justice, and of ultimately removing involuntary poverty. Gandhi wanted to bring the right to private property under the guidance of the soul-force. This meant that private wealth was only conditionally legitimate, the condition being the welfare of all, *sarvodaya*. The spirit of voluntary poverty would tolerate a limited amount of disparity in material possession between individuals. Any excess wealth was potentially for the use of others: this was basically the substance of his notion of trusteeship.

Gandhi believes that the spirit of voluntary poverty has to be nourished by daily manual labour. No matter what one's station in life, one had to engage in some limited kind of manual labour, if one took *swaraj* seriously. Just as physical exercise was good for the body, so manual labour was good for the soul. It had a socially levelling effect and, as Basham points out, in India it was tantamount to being a revolutionary concept. Traditional sources did not value the dignity of manual work.[30]

Gandhi saw the modern corporations as obstacles to the practice of voluntary poverty and to social justice. In alliance with modern technology, they tended to centralize not only wealth, but also social and political power, in fewer hands. He believed that where the majority of the people suffer from involuntary poverty, it was better for industries to be decentralized. And the majority of people everywhere in the world do suffer from involuntary poverty. While Gandhi saw that structural changes were necessary if the welfare of all was to be secured, he saw two things even more clearly: first that these changes have to be brought about voluntarily, and secondly that if they were to be brought about voluntarily, the soul had to be reformed first. Each individual has to come to terms with his or her possessive instinct, much the same way he or she will have to come to terms with his or her sexual instinct. Hence the importance of the virtue of voluntary poverty.

Fearlessness or courage is the third disposition that *swaraj* required. Fearlessness is a function of the soul-force. It is exercised at several levels. At the most fundamental level it is exercised against the fear of death. Gandhi was remarkably free of the fear of death. 'That nation is great which rests its head upon death as its pillow. Those who defy death are free from all fear. For those who are labouring under the delusive charms of brute-force, this picture is not over-drawn.'[31] At less fundamental levels, it is exercised against tyrants, unjust laws, unfair economic and social conditions. 'Passive resistance cannot proceed a step without fearlessness. Those alone can follow the path of passive resistance who are free from fear, whether as to their possessions, false honour, their relatives, the government, bodily injuries or death.'[32]

In an illuminating comment on Gandhi, Jacques Maritain points out that the Mahatma has brought out something new here, namely, courage, as the capacity for endurance rather than as the capacity for attack. Traditionally, courage is associated with soldiers and war leaders, with a Churchill or a de Gaulle. But this, according to Maritain, is only one aspect of courage. The other aspect, and here he finds similarity between Aquinas and Gandhi, is something which modern 'Western civilization is hardly aware', namely, that power of the soul or the power of love or power of truth can be made an instrument of political and social action. According to Aquinas, the principal act of the virtue of courage is not the act of attacking but of enduring, bearing, suffering with constancy. For there are two kinds of warfare, the coercive and the spiritual. Similarly there are two kinds of courage, the courage that attacks and the courage that endures, 'the force that inflicts suffering on others and the force that endures suffering inflicted on oneself.' Gandhi's 'work of genius has been the systematic organization of patience and voluntary suffering as a special method or technique of political activity.'[33] Here again, as in the case of voluntary poverty, acceptance of suffering has to be voluntary. For, as Gandhi points out, 'To suffer under pressure is no suffering.'[34]

Finally, *swaraj* required the practice of the virtue of religion. Modernity has the greatest difficulty in accommodating Gandhi on this point. Gandhi was and remains an implacable enemy of Indian Maoists. Gandhi's religious politics nauseated Winston Churchill. 'It is alarming and also nauseating', he wrote in 1929, 'to see Mr. Gandhi, a seditious Middle Temple [*sic.*] Lawyer, now posing as a fakir of a type well-known in the East, striding half-naked up the steps of the Viceregal palace, while he is still organizing and conducting a defiant campaign of civil disobedience, to parley on equal terms with the representative of the King-Emperor.'[35] To the left-wing British establishment, slightly more receptive to Gandhi than was any other group in Britain, his religiosity was no more edifying. George Catlin reports the account of a London meeting of British left-wing intellectuals, including Harold Laski, with Gandhi. They 'dismissed him as "too much of a Jesuit for them." His religiosity offended their Fabian commonsense, their Marxist prejudices, and indeed their Bloomsbury good taste.'[36] Even George Orwell, who appreciated the good *effects* of Gandhi's politics, could not stomach the *religious principles* from which they flowed. For him Gandhi's religious-politics was fundamentally anti-human. It was so because it demanded of men, Orwell believed, as condition for practising it, a theocentric conception of man and the universe, and a saintliness of human conduct. For Orwell such a demand would only diminish man: for him man had to choose between God or Man; man cannot have both. The error of Orwell's judgement was, of course, that he thought that for Gandhi too, man could be served only on condition that one rejected God. 'Gandhi's thought cannot be squared with the belief that Man is the measure of all things and that our job is to make life worth living on this earth, which is the only earth we have.'[37] The doctrine of indifference to possessions,'Orwell believed, went against the secular doctrine of 'the full acceptance of earthly life.' He could not see why the average man should be measured against a saint; and why, accordingly, the average man should be considered a 'failed saint'. Orwell ultimately concluded: 'One must choose between God and Man, and all "radicals" and "progressives", from the mildest Liberals to the most extreme Anarchist, have in effect chosen Man.'[38] But even Orwell grants that despite Gandhi's alleged anti-humanism, he did better, even in politics, than did the whole lot of humanists and progressives: '...regarded simply as a politician, and compared with the other leading political figures of our time, how clean a smell he has managed to leave behind!'[39] But is it possible to consider him, as does Orwell, 'simply as a politician' and still account for the 'clean smell' that he has left behind? Orwell does not, perhaps cannot, answer this question. Gandhi's 'clean smell' and atheistic humanism are not compatible entities.

To understand why Gandhi left a clean smell, we must understand precisely what he meant by religion. Religion, like truth, for him had several meanings. At the most ordinary level, it meant the organized religions, such as Hinduism, Islam, etc. Religion in this sense divided human beings culturally and sometimes even socially. At a more restricted level, religion meant religious beliefs and doctrines, such as, *karma, incarnation, resurrection, prophecy.* Religion in this sense also divided men, though rather intellectually than socially. At a third level religion meant the virtue, or the virtues of religion, religion as a moral, not theological, virtue. Religion in this sense is articulated in the West, among many others, by such writers as Cicero, Macrobius, Aquinas. It articulates a theistic view of man and nature which requires of men to treat one another with kindness, respect, humility and charity. Religion in this sense is indistinguishable from ethics, and it can unite people in such areas of activity as economics and politics, social service and works of charity.

I would suggest that it is religion in this third sense that underlies Gandhi's politics. When, for example, Gandhi says 'Religions are diferent roads converging to the same point,'[40] he means religion in the first and second levels we mentioned, and not the third. But when he says that by religion he means 'that religion which underlies all religions', [41] he means religion in our third sense. It was his conviction and also his practice that religion as ethics could bring about the political unity of a multi-religious entity such as India. It was also on the basis of religion in this sense that he could work with the British or any other nation. He believed that 'at heart' the British belonged to a 'religious nation'. 'If you will abandon your so-called civilization and search into your own scriptures', he wrote in 1909, 'you will find that our (Indians') demands are just.'[42] Religion in this sense did not pose the false alternatives between God and Man; indeed humans were better treated by humans if an *ethic* of religion was universally practised.

The fact is that Gandhi showed that religion as ethics can remove at least some of the stench from politics. How Gandhi achieved this is best explained by an American Catholic monk, Thomas Merton:

> The religious basis of Gandhi's political action was not simply a program, in which politics were marshalled into the service of faith, and brought to bear on the charitable objectives of a religious institution. For Gandhi, strange as it may seem to us, political action had to be by its very nature 'religious' in the sense that it had to be informed by principles of religious and philosophical wisdom. To separate religion and politics was in Gandhi's eyes 'madness' because his politics rested on a thoroughly religious interpretation of reality, of life, and of man's place in the world. Gandhi's whole concept of man's relation to his own inner being and to the world of objects around him was informed by the contemplative heritage of Hinduism, together with the principles of Karma Yoga which blended, in his thought, with the ethic of the Synoptic Gospels and the Sermon on the Mount. In such a view, politics had to be understood in the context of service and worship in the ancient sense of *leiturgia* (liturgy, public work). Man's intervention in the active life of society was at the same time by its very nature *svadharma*, his own personal service (of God and man) and workship, *yagna*. Political action therefore was not a means to acquire security and strength for one's self and one's party, but a means of witnessing to the truth and the reality of the cosmic structure by making one's own proper contribution to the order willed by God. One could thus preserve one's integrity and peace, being detached from results (which are in the hands of God) and being free from the inner violence that comes from division and untruth, the usurpation of someone else's *dharma* in place of one's own *svadharma*. These perspectives lent Gandhi's politics their extraordinary spiritual force and religious realism.[43]

So far we have considered the principles of *satya* and *ahimsa*, and the four virtues of chastity, voluntary poverty, courage and religion. It remains to be considered how they become practical, both in the life of the individual and in relation to public institutions. It is the great insight of Gandhi that no improvement of society can occur unless there is improvement of the self. The self has to gain control over itself, and this control has to be *experienced:* mere *knowledge* of ethics would not do:

> It is Swaraj when we learn to rule ourselves. It is, therefore, in the palm of our hands. Do not consider this Swaraj to be like a dream. There is no idea of sitting still. The Swaraj that I wish to picture is such that, after we have once realized it, we shall endeavour to the end of our life-time to persuade others to do likewise. *But such Swaraj has to be experienced, by each one for himself.*[44]

The process of inner reform, to be successful, needed the assistance of an appropriate type of education and an appropriate community environment. Gandhi held that the aim of education should include character-building and acquisition of knowledge of letters and sciences, in that order. For him, ethics had priority over technical knowledge. Ethics was the foundation on which such knowledge must build. He considered the modern concept of education that stressed the priority of technical knowledge and left ethics to each individual's choice, to be rotten in its very foundation. Knowledge of the sciences and letters has 'its place' only 'when we have brought our senses under subjection and put our ethics on a firm foundation.'[45]

The need for an appropriate community environment for the acquisition and development of the spirit of inner improvement was recognized by Gandhi early in his career. This is why he established several ashrams both in South Africa and India. They were to be the nurseries for the training of Gandhian 'guardians' who in their turn would go out and carry out Gandhi's social mission.

The same insight was applied to the process of political reform as well. That is why he paid very close attention to the question of the relationship between politics and civilization. His critique of modern civilization was the *via negativa* of his great project. Only when one realized how corrupt modern civilization was, could one begin the process of self-reform and social reform. True civilization, as he envisaged it, was that mode of life which produced self-reform and which defined for each one his or her duty. 'Civilization is that mode of conduct which points out to man the path of duty. Performance of duty and observance of morality are convertible terms. To observe morality is to attain mastery over the mind and our passions. So doing, we know ourselves.'[46]

Without being a reactionary, Gandhi believed that each major civilization of the world had something original and good in it, and that it was foolish to destory it in the name of modernity. We have seen how he appealed to the British to integrate what was good in modern science in terms of their own Christian culture. In his own case he wanted to take ideas from outside only if they could be creatively integrated within the framework of what was good and original in Indian civilization. George Woodcock makes the acute observation that of all the Third World revolutionaries Gandhi was the only one who did not make a mental surrender to the modern western civilization. Mao and Ho Chi-minh, Che Guevera and Franz Fanon, while rejecting the political and economic domination of the West, adopted its modernity. And in doing so they rejected the traditional ways of life of their own people, and especially the religious elements that provided the foundations of their traditional culture.[47] Gandhi, by contrast, was very clear on one point: he did not want the modernity of the British replaced by modernity of the Indians, 'English rule without the Englishman. You want the tiger's nature, but not the tiger; that is to say, you would make India English. And when it becomes English, it will be called not Hindustan but Englistan. This is not the Swaraj that I want.'[48]

We have seen from the foregoing that the critique of modernity requires a re-evaluation of the concept of coercive political power both in its *reason of state* form and in its *absolute sovereignty* form. Given this, would Gandhi still recognize the modern state as a legitimate institution? This is a question to which no easy answer can be found. My own tentative answer is that he would accept the modern state, so long as the state can be seen as subject to the principles of *satya* and *ahimsa* and so long as its seeks *sarvodaya* as its true end. The crucial question, however, is whether the state may legitimately employ coercive force in such specified areas as self-defence and in the interest of domestic justice. Gandhi does not give a systematic treatment of these issues. But one could gather a more or less coherent answer from his behaviour and from his various utterances. For example, he organized medical corps in support of soldiers in the Boer War, in the Zulu Rebellion and in the First World War. He raised no objection to India's use of military force in Kashmir in 1947. It would seem that his theory of *ahimsa* is compatible with a strict form of just war theory.

As for the legitimacy of use of force domestically, it is obvious that Gandhi recognized the moral value of the preservation of India as a territorial entity. He did not object to the existence of a police force. *Satyagraha* itself presupposes the existence of the state as a legitimate entity. In other words, the state in Gandhi's thought is not a purely voluntary organization, it may, under certain conditions, use coercive force. The value of his theory of *ahimsa*, when applied to the modern state, lies in this: as much as possible the state should leave to voluntary agencies the task of settling disputes; it should encourage a system of education that will promote development of character, and the spirit of *ahimsa*, but where voluntary achievement of social peace fails, the state has to intervene.

There is no indication in Gandhi's thought that human nature will be radically transformed. His system of non-violence does not require such a theory of radical human transformation. Reform by means of virtues is not the same as radical transformation of the self. Insofar as this is true, the state will have to retain, even on a permanent basis, a limited range of coercive powers. Just as Gandhi does not require a total radical transformation of the individual, so he does not require the withering away of the state. As Woodcock has noted, Gandhi may have underestimated the 'extent and the reality of evil' in this world.[49] And as Orwell has remarked, Gandhi 'did not understand the nature of totalitarianism and saw everything in terms of his own struggle against the British government.'[50] Hence he may have exaggerated on the one hand the power of love-force, and, on the other, undervalued the positive good that coercive power of the state can do in certain areas of human experience.

In this connection the discussion of brute-force in *Hind Swaraj* is worthy of close scrutiny. First of all, the focus of the discussion is on what *private* individuals may do in the face of the exercise of brute-force by a colonial regime. He may resist such force only with soul-force, even if this may involve the sacrifice of his life. The focus is not on the question of what a legitimate government may do against an unjust aggressor. There is no suggestion in Gandhi that a country should surrender to the unjust aggressor.

Secondly, though soul-force is superior to brute-force, there may be circumstances where soul-force may be ineffective and brute-force may be legitimate. Gandhi introduces the qualification of 'the majority of cases, if not indeed in all' into the discussion. His point is that 'only fair means alone can produce fair results, and that, at least in the majority of cases, if not indeed in all, the force of love and pity is infinitely greater than the force of arms.'[51]

Finally, there is the question of the play of self-interest in the use of brute-force. Force exercised 'entirely' in one's own interest and without consideration of the requirements of love and pity is properly speaking the exercise of brute-force. This leaves open the suggestion that force used for motives other than self-interest, and used according to the requirements of love and pity, may not be allied to the exercise of brute-force. Thus forcibly preventing a child from rushing towards the fire certainly involves the use of physical force—but it would be physical force 'of a low order' and its exercise may not be considered reprehensible,[52] the reason being that the action in question is prompted by love and pity.

CONCLUSION

We have now seen Gandhi's critique of modernity and the outlines of his alternative to it. But we have also seen an excellent example set by Gandhi of how comparative political philosophy may be studied. Throughout, Gandhi had modern western political philosophy in mind. But the basic analysis is conducted with the aid of ideas taken from Indian moral philosophy. The outcome is an original theory of politics, many elements of which have applicability outside his own particular tradition.

NOTES

1. *Hind Swaraj*, revised new edition, Ahmedabad: Navajivan Press, 1939, p. 29. Hereafter, HS.
2. Penderel Moon, *Gandhi and Modern India*, London, 1968, p. 52.
3. HS, *op. cit.*, p. 37.
4. HS, *op. cit.*, p. 58. Upas tree, 'a fabulous Javanese tree so poisonous as to destroy all life for many miles round'. The Shorter Oxford English Dictionary. Gandhi took the metaphor from one of Madame Blavatsky's writings: see Raghavan Iyer, *The Moral and Political Thought of Mahatma Gandhi*. New York: Oxford University Press, 1973, p. 23.
5. HS, *op. cit.*, p. 34.
6. HS, *op. cit.*, p. 37.

7. See Gandhi. *Collected Works*, New Delhi: Government of India Publications Division, 1963, Vol. X, p. 17.
8. HS, *op. cit.*, p. 32.
9. HS, *op. cit.*, p. 58.
10. HS, *op. cit.*, p. 55.
11. HS, *op. cit.*, p. 57.
12. HS, *op. cit.*, p. 58.
13. HS, *op. cit.*, p. 59.
14. HS, *op. cit.*, p. 60.
15. HS, *op. cit.*, pp. 94, 96.
16. HS, *op. cit.*, p. 93.
17. HS, *op. cit.*, p. 94.
18. HS, *op. cit.*, p. 96.
19. HS, *op. cit.*, p. 45.
20. HS, *op. cit.*, pp. 35–36.
21. HS, *op. cit.*, p. 48.
22. HS, *op. cit.*, p. 45.
23. Cited in George Catlin, *In the Path of Mahatma Gandhi*. Chicago: Henry Regnery, 1950, p. 29.
24. HS, *op. cit.*, p. 94.
25. HS, *op. cit.*, p. 38.
26. HS, *op. cit.*, p. 69.
27. Margaret Chatterjee, *Gandhi's Religious Thought*. Notre Dame: University of Notre Dame Press, 1983, p. 89.
28. See T.K.N. Unnithan, *Change Without Violence: Gandhian Theory of Social Change*. Ahmedabad: Gujarat Vidyapith, 1987, pp. 38–45.
29. Erik H. Erikson, *Gandhi's Truth*. New York: Norton, 1969, p. 439.
30. A.L. Basham, 'Traditional Influences on the Thought of Mahatma Gandhi', in R. Kumar, ed., *Essays on Gandhian Politics*. Oxford: The Clarendon Press, 1971, p. 40.
31. HS, *op. cit.*, p. 83.
32. HS, *op. cit.*, p. 85.
33. Jacques Maritain, *Man and State*. Chicago: The University of Chicago Press, 1951, pp. 69–70.
34. HS, *op. cit.*, p. 104.
35. Cited in Catlin, *op. cit.*, p. 208. Gandhi belonged to the Inner Temple, not Middle Temple, as Churchill stated.
36. Catlin, *op. cit.*, p. 201.
37. Orwell, 'Reflections on Gandhi', *Partisan Review*, Vol. 16 (1949), p. 88.
38. *Ibid.*, p. 89.
39. *Ibid.*, p. 92.
40. HS, *op. cit.*, p. 50.
41. HS, *op. cit.*, p. 41.
42. HS, *op. cit.*, p. 100.
43. Thomas Merton. 'A Tribute to Gandhi', Gordon C. Zahn, ed., in *The Non-violent Alternative*. New York: Farrar, Strauss, Giroux, 1980, pp. 180–81.
44. HS, *op. cit.*, p. 65. Emphasis added.
45. HS, *op. cit.*, p. 89.

46. HS, *op. cit.*, p. 61.
47. George Woodcock, *Gandhi.* London: Fontana, 1972, p. 15.
48. HS, *op. cit.*, p. 30.
49. Woodcock, *op. cit.*, p. 106.
50. Orwell, *op. cit.*, p. 90.
51. HS, *op. cit.*, p. 75.
52. HS, *op. cit.*, p. 76

9   Farabi and Greek Political Philosophy

Yusuf K. Umar

Abu Nasr Muhammad ibn Muhammad ibn Tarkhan Al-Farabi (870–950 AD) was born in Farab in the province of Transoxiana. Farabi's early life is shrouded in mystery. Very little is known about him in general, and what is known is not certain.[1] At about the age of forty he left Farab and migrated to Baghdad, where he studied under Abu Bishr Matta ibn Yunus, the well-known translator of some of Aristotle's writings into Arabic. From Baghdad, Farabi migrated once again to Harran (ancient Carrhae) in northern Mesopotamia. Harran was the major philosophical centre after the demise of the philosophical school of Alexandria. One of Farabi's teachers in Harran was Yohanna ibn Hailan. He subsequently returned to Baghdad, and studied Arabic under the famous Arab grammarian Abu Bakr As-Sarraj.[2]

Farabi preferred the life of solitary study and ascetic contemplation. In AD 940 he left Baghdad for Damascus where he lived as a recluse and worked as a night watchman in an orchard. At night, Farabi used to meet with his students and teach them philosophy. Towards the end of his life, the Shi'ite prince of Aleppo, Saif ud-Dawla, became Farabi's patron. However, Farabi was content to live modestly on a salary of 4 dirhams per day, and perferred the traditional Sufi attire.

Farabi was a prolific writer and a commentator of Aristotle's work. In the Islamic philosophical tradition, Farabi is considered the 'second teacher' after Aristotle. Many of his writings are presumed lost. This essay focuses on Farabi's political writings, such as *Tahsil as-Sa'ada* (*The Attainment of Happiness*), *Fusul al-Madani* (*Aphorisms of the Statesman*), and the two well-known books *Al-Madina al-Fadila* (*The Virtuous City*) and *Al-Siyasa al-Madaniyya* (*The Political Regime*).

Farabi lived at a time when the Abbasid empire was experiencing a decline. With the reign of the Caliph al-Wathiq (842–847), the golden age of the Abbasids had come to an end. With the Caliph al-Mu'tadid (892–902), the Abbasid caliphate came to a virtual end. It lingered on until the final blow at the hands of the Mongols in 1258.[3]

Farabi lived at a time of crisis in the history of the Islamic state. The empire was racked with upheavals, uprisings, religious and sectarian wars, and the instabilities of political succession marred by palace intrigue and arbitrary deposition. The caliphs became virtual prisoners of their wazirs and military commanders. They increasingly ran the risk of assassination. Al-Mu'tazz (d.908), for instance, ruled for one day. The Abbasid empire disintegrated into mini-states which exercised virtual independence. Local rulers continued to offer nominal allegiance to the caliph, but had no real power or authority.[4]

This crisis of the Islamic empire greatly influenced Farabi's political theory. It was, in all its manifestations, a reflection of a central theologico-political problem. Islam offered its adherents an integrated system of religious beliefs, as well as the basic outline of an ideal community based on Islamic law (*Shari'a*). The doctrine of the legitimate and rightful Imam has ever since been a contentious issue in Islamic political thought and culture. It was also the main reason why Islam split into two major sects, the Sunnis and the Shi'is. In Farabi's time, the conflict between the two sects was at its height, both theoretically and practically. The last 'hidden' Imam of Twelver shi'ism, the dominant sect in contemporary Iran, disappeared during Farabi's time.

An elaborate and integrated religious, political and social system such as Islam leaves little room for the role of natural reason in human things. Theological reason in Islam limits itself to the task of interpreting the present in light of an ideal community in the past. The present is always confronted as a deviation from the ideal. At the same time, the ideal is always perceived as a frozen moment that lasted no more than thirty years in Islamic history.

Political philosophy for Abu Nasr Al-Farabi was essentially the pursuit of human happiness. It encompassed the search for the truth about human things. However, philosophizing more generally is the search for the truth about the whole. The human mind begins with cultural and religious categories peculiar to the society in which one lives. These are relative and yet necessary categories if man is to be made fit for living in a human community. Philosophy is the activity that helps certain men transcend societal limitations in their search for the universal truth. Philosophy, in other words, begins with a confrontation with what is given, received, or transmitted through a particular tradition or religion.

This distinction helps explain the result of the tension between Farabi the Muslim and Farabi the philosopher, between Mecca and Athens. As a result of his study of Greek philosophy Farabi, the Muslim, had to think through several central issues dealing with philosophy and revelation, political philosophy and Islamic *Shari'a*, God, the philosopher and the prophet, and the solution to the Sufi doctrine of unity with God.

CONFLICTING CLAIMS

Political philosophy, according to Farabi, delineates the main elements of the ideal regime and should offer the means of realizing the ideal in actual human cities. Political philosophy, accordingly, begins with a critique of existing political arrangements in order to approximate the real with the ideal. Political philosophy must, therefore, begin with the assumption that what exists is not the best regime. For political philosophy to be possible at all, it must begin with a sense of a problematic situation or crisis situation. The crisis need not be universally perceived; it is the political philosopher who determines whether a crisis exists or not.

Farabi, like other Islamic political philosophers, begins with an existential dilemma that is centred around the generally accepted premise that the ideal has been revealed for all time. He begins with the nature of the ideal community as revealed in the *Quran*. He must confront not the principle of being only, but also the manner in which the ideal city is organized on the basis of the Islamic *Shari'a*. The philosopher, from the outset, finds himself in confrontation with the prophet. The claims of the prophet are grounded in divine revelation while those of the philosopher stem from theoretical reason.

The issue in Farabi, as in Islam, boils down to one simple question. Who has the right to perceive the ideal community and on what grounds should that community be brought into being? It is a simple platitude that the ideal *qua* ideal does not permit the existence of two conceptions of the ideal. The central question then is: Who is the rightful law-giver? Is it the prophet or the philosopher? The possible alternatives are narrowed down to a choice between political philosophy and theology.

A reasonable choice cannot begin with a dogmatic belief in the truthfulness of one's wilful decision. One's choice is predetermined or at least conditioned by the corresponding grounding principles of philosophy and theology. One must choose between reason or revelation. Stating the problem in this manner tacitly assumes that there must be an inherent conflict between the claims of reason and the claims of revelation. Siding with revelation implicitly or explicitly assumes that the truth has already been revealed. Whatever reason submits and accords with revelation is accepted, and whatever contradicts revelation is rejected. The theologian does not really have a problem.

Siding with reason, in turn, implies that the philosopher has solved the riddle of being and has attained knowledge of the truth about the whole. To argue that revelation is an untruth entails by definition that it contradicts reason. But we know as much as Farabi is willing to admit that the claims of reason have not been consistent. Choosing between these contradictory claims necessitates a principle that transcends the particular reason of individual philosophers. One must begin with a concept of absolute reason (*al-áql al-Kulli*) that transcends particular revelation and particular reason of this or that philosopher.

The *falasifa* (philosophers) in general and Farabi in particular do not perceive the claims of reason and revelation to be mutually exclusive, because a contrary premise inevitability leads its holder to a dogmatic position. Farabi resolves the apparent contradiction between philosophy and revelation by adopting the position that each presents the truth in a language that suits the natural division between the elect and the multitude which one finds in the cities. Farabi's position, in other words, leads to a state of conscious openness to the claims of reason and the claims of revelation. All philosophers begin with a certain culture and tradition, from which they gradually move to the culture of reason. If the philosopher is to remain open and continue being a philosopher he can neither rest assured that the findings of reason are final nor can he continually dismiss the claims of revelation without continually re-examining his premises and conclusions. Needless to say that this is an intolerable mode of existence because, it seems that the philosopher as a human being always longs for certainty and belief in what he argues. The philosophic way of life, to use Platonic imagery, is a continual journey to and out of the cave.

This state of openness is predicated on the following. Man's search for true knowledge about the whole remains relative to the abilities of the philosopher in question. Those abilities reflect traits peculiar to the philosopher himself, such as the breadth and depth of his knowledge, his comprehension and the extent of his learning. More important is the philosopher's ability or inability to receive emanations from the 'Active Intellect' (Aql fa'al) and whether he receives those emanations through the rational or the imaginative faculties of his soul.

The philosophical search for certain knowledge of the truth about the whole is also dependent upon the development of the sciences in general in a certain historical epoch. Philosophy, in other words, must continually revise and criticize its claimed knowledge of the truth about the whole in light of new developments in the human and natural sciences.

Political philosophy, on the other hand, occupies a less exalted position than philosophy. The end of political philosophy is the attainment of the ideal city and the attainment of happiness. Happiness must be understood in two senses: the happiness of the philosopher and the happiness of the non-philosophical multitudes. The philosopher's happiness must in turn be understood in relation to the distinction between happiness that is derived from the philosophical activity, which is the supreme form of happiness and happiness that is derived from the existence of an ideal city suitable for human living and suitable for the philosophical way of life.

Therein, one has to find a dialectical relationship between philosophy and political philosophy, for without the proper political philosophy to organize and attain the ideal city, the philosophical way of life itself becomes almost impossible. Without the philosophical way of life and without a true philosophy, political philosophy itself becomes impossible. On its own, the latter could only bring forth the corrupt city that would neither heed the philosopher's advice nor respect his right to philosophize. Consequently, political philosophy, although less exalted than philosophy, remains of crucial importance for the philosopher because his philosophical happiness remains dependent upon his ability to philosophize, which is, in turn, dependent upon the existence of a truly human city.

The philosopher's attempt to implement his understanding of the true order in the cosmos depends not only on his own personal abilities, but also on the readiness of the city to accept his version of the ideal order. The readiness and willingness of the city to implement his ideas reflect in turn the quality of the human component of the city. Human beings are the essential element of the city. To begin the task of realizing the ideal city, i.e., to make political philosophy possible and feasible, one must begin with human beings. The moral uplifting of the human element is the quintessential requisite for political philosophy and ultimately for philosophy itself. Moral principle, for Farabi, is an essential starting point, without which life itself becomes impossible. What distinguishes the human from the beast is the element of sociability. Sociability implies much more than congregating into herds. It entails the need for certain moral principles that would make life in the city qualitatively different from life within, say, a pack of wolves. It is in this sense that the moral, the political and the philosophical become inseparably linked. Without the moral life, the political life is impossible, and without political life the philosophical way of life becomes impossible.

The moral fibre of any city resolves itself in opinions about good and evil which will vary from one city to another. The reason for this is simple. What is good or evil by nature does not necessarily coincide with the city's opinions about them. Opinions about good or evil reflect the culture of the city in question, while the idea of good and evil reflect the philosophical understanding of that which is good or evil according to nature. The foundation of culture itself is the revealed doctrine. Religion in particular and revelation in general give people opinions about good and evil. This is necessarily so because revelation or prophecy reflect an emanative process from the Active Intellect through the imaginative rather than the rational faculty, hence the differences in revealed doctrines. Philosophical conceptions of good and evil are emanations from the Active Intellect through the rational faculty. Different philosophical conceptions of the divine order seem to reflect either differences in philosophical abilities or the fact that the philosopher in question is not a genuine philosopher. The perfect man is he who combines perfect imaginative and rational faculties. The imaginative faculty expresses itself in allegories and symbolic language, while the rational faculty expresses itself in precise philosophical discourse that may not be readily comprehended by those who are not philosophically trained to receive it and comprehend it. Philosophy, after all, is the domain of the elect.

Life in the city will always reflect a tension between two dominant ways of life, the philosophical way of life and the way of life of the multitude. This in turn reflects the two different conceptions of good and evil. The city represents the eternal tension between the two conceptions, or the tension between philosophy and revelation. The tension is eternal because a resolution presupposes the disappearance of one or the other. The disappearance of philosophy may come about either violently or through the abandonment of reason itself. The human city in its historical-cultural manifestations will only reflect a potentially violent clash of opinions and mutually exclusive conceptions of the divine. The disappearance of opinion on the other hand, presupposes an equal ability of all to understand the philosophical understanding of the truth about the whole, and to live by it. This presupposition appears ludicrous in light of the fact that philosophy is an arduous pursuit of knowledge, whereby men are either by nature or inclination prepared or unprepared for it.

The solution to the tension must not be sought in the destruction of one or the other of the two cornerstones of life in the city. The solution must be sought in an accommodation between the two. This accommodation is not an automatic result of an artificial and superficial mutual recognition, which accords a pluralistic equal value to philosophy and revelation or a nihilistic dismissal of both as valueless opinions. For Farabi, political philosophy, therefore, must accommodate culture and history, and yet it must also attempt to transcend both. A political philosophy that suits a certain city at a certain stage of history may be destructive of another city. What makes political philosophy reasonable or unreasonable is its ability to reflect and deal with the type of human beings that predominates in a city. Political philosophy, in other words, must deal with different people differently if the desired goal is to be attained. This simply means that rulers and ruled alike begin with 'the commonly shared opinion among all'.[5] The multitude must remain satisfied with that first shared opinion. The elect, understood as philosophers and political leaders, must not be satisfied with that opinion and must graduate to a higher understanding of the truth which the multitude understand through symbolisms and imagery. This process of transcending the commonly shared view must not be a public one, because that will involve the multitude in debates and arguments that can only lead to schisms. Needless to say Farabi has in mind the schisms that divided the Muslim community fighting over images. The solution lies in the recognition of political rulers that their public debates, squabbles, and violent affirmations of their images will ultimately lead to self-destruction as well as the elimination of the very foundation of a shared life.

Farabi, as far as I know, was the first philosopher to articulate a dynamic and realistic solution to the dilemma of the conflict between reason and revelation. He recognized the essential need for revelation in order to transcend it philosophically. His solution required an initial belief in and acceptance of the revealed moral code of the city, without which man may not succeed in transforming himself from an ordinary mortal into a divine man. Revelation became the foundation for philosophy. Philosophy, in this sense, may be defined as the activity that seeks to transform the small 't' truth into the capital 'T' Truth.

This dynamic recognition flowed from the following important considerations. Life in the city would be impossible without the opinions of revelation. Equally important is the fact that it is extremely difficult for one man to combine two perfect imaginative and theoretical faculties. Since combining these two perfect faculties in one man is a rare occurrence, and since not all philosophers are genuine philosophers and, since philosophy must remain open to the truth, reason must leave room for revelation in the life of the city. Philosophy must remain firmly rooted in the city, while permanently pointing to something higher than the city itself.

The process of transforming one's self from a mere moral man is accompanied by a gradual transformation of the city. Self-transformation is a wilful act that requires arduous study, while transforming the city is something that is outside the will of the philosopher and cannot be attained by study only. Gradual enlightenment of individual men is not the same as the gradual enlightenment of cities. The latter implies politics by definition.

Farabi discusses the ideal city in two separate books: *Al-Madina al-Fadila* and *Al-Siyasa al-Madaniyya*. Both books share a common format. They are divided into two major sections, each section dealing with one dominant theme. It is noteworthy that Farabi begins with metaphysics, and concludes with political philosophy. This supports the hypothesis that political philosophy should only be attempted after a mature philosophy is attained.

One of Farabi's cardinal principles that was adopted by subsequent Muslim philosophers is the parallelism between philosophy and divine revelation. The ultimate aim of philosophy is knowing the sublime creator; knowing that He is One, unmoved, and the efficient cause of all things, and that He in His generosity, wisdom, and justice gave order to this world.[6] The actions of the philosopher aim at '...*imitating the Creator as much as it is humanly possible.*'[7] Philosophy '...gives an account based on intellectual perception or conception, whereas religion gives an account based on imagination. In everything demonstrated by philosophy, religion employs persuasion.'[8] Consequently, religion in Farabi's system is *the* philosophy of the multitude. Its function is to provide for their moral uplifting and education.

In order to imitate God, the philosopher must know that God is and must also know God's intentions. Farabi's philosophy may be described as 'theistic rationalist objectivism.'[9] This explains his rational Sufism, which aims ultimately at knowing God in order to achieve unity with Him.[10] It explains also the reason why Farabi maintained the unity between philosophy as the science of the beings that will bring happiness to the philosopher, and political philosophy as 'the royal art' that will bring happiness to men and to cities in accordance with their abilities to know and experience happiness.

Farabi's metaphysics and political philosophy reflect the highly structured and unified cosmic whole, whose order was given by the First Cause. That is the reason why his metaphysics and his politics are presented as a unity; his political theory is meaningless without considering his metaphysics. The philosopher's ultimate goal is to achieve separation from matter and become pure and infinite intellect.

Beings are ranked in terms of their excellence; excellence is understood as self-sufficient thought conscious of itself; it is separate from matter and can never be in matter. This order of excellence descends from the most perfect to the least perfect beings beyond which being ceases to be.[11] The first rank is occupied by the First Cause; the second rank is reserved for the 'second causes'; the Active Intellect is in the third rank; the soul is in the fourth rank; the *sura* (form) is in the fifth rank; matter is in the sixth and final rank. The first three are not in bodies and cannot subsist in bodies, and the last three exist in bodies but they are not bodies—these are the soul, form, and matter which is nothing in and by itself. This totality constitutes the cosmos.[12] Divine bodies (the ten celestial spheres) end at the lunar sphere; terrestial bodies exist in the sub-lunar world.[13] The entities of the sub-lunar world are ranked from the lowest to the highest, man being the most excellent entity of the sub-lunar world.[14]

Being is classified into necessary being that which cannot but exist or be, and contingent being that which may or may not be. 'The most excellent, noble, and most perfect of existents is that existent whose non being is impossible', and the least perfect is that which can or cannot exist. Imperfect beings are those that need another being in order to exist, are members in a genus, or have contraries. Finally, all composite beings have imperfect existence since their being is dependent on the composing elements and on the efficient cause, and because they are potentially reducible to their original constituent elements. It follows that existence in the sub-lunar world will always be imperfect.[15] Final and complete perfection, therefore, can never be attained on this earth.

All existents point towards the First Existent. Accordingly all human sciences that investigate the beings are prerequisites of the science that aims at knowing the Necessary Existent and the intelligibles that are separate from matter. Farabi divides the sciences into two main categories: *juzv' iyya* (particular) and *kulliyya* (universal) sciences. Particular sciences investigate the essential or the accidental qualities of 'some existents or some imagined existents'. None of the particular sciences examine being as a whole.[16] Universal science, or total science examines the thing that is common to all existents, as well as the common principle of all beings, which is the thing that must be called 'the One', 'Allah the exalted' who is 'the principle of absolute being not of one being but not another.'[17]

The excellence of the sciences and the arts can be determined on the basis of the nobility of the subject, demonstrative investigation, or on the basis of immediate or long term utility. What is of great utility and higher in rank than any particular science are the 'legal sciences' and the arts that are needed over time and by all people. Metaphysics surpasses all.[18] Metaphysics is the only science whose rank and excellence is tied to the excellence of its subject, its utility, and as the source of demonstrative truths.

The ultimate aim of Farabi's philosophy is to arrive at *al-Sa'ada al-Quswa* (Supreme happiness). This is what constitutes human *kamal* (perfection). Perfection is understood in two senses: perfection in this world which is predicated on theoretical and practical virtues; and perfection in *al-Hayat ul-Akherah* (the after life), which is predicated on the first perfection. Man's final perfection can be attained only in the after life. This is what Farabi calls 'the absolute good that is choice-worthy for its own sake', and the happiness that is truly happiness. This must be the '...goal and aim of the true king who manages the cities to attain true happiness for himself and for all the inhabitants of the city, because this is the aim and the goal of the royal art.' The royal art, i.e., political philosophy, is inseparable from philosophy. The separation is only for analytical purposes. '*Hikmah*' (wisdom, philosophy) is that which leads to true happiness, while political philosophy ('practical wisdom') is that which leads to what must be done to realize happiness. These two are therefore the constituting elements of man's perfection if *hikmah* is to be attained.[21] Philosophy is impossible unless the philosopher is willing to offer his programme for the improvement of human societies.

Political science entails knowledge of the '...things by which the citizens of cities attain happiness through political association in the measure that innate disposition equips each of them for it.'[22] The social world must mirror the order of the cosmos if human happiness is to be possible at all.[23] Hence, the most perfect and most 'powerful virtue' that a human could attain is the 'combination of all the virtues'. It is the kind of virtue that 'when a man decides to fulfil its functions, he cannot do so without making use of the functions of all the other virtues.'[24] The genuinely virtuous man, in other words, is he who has combined in himself the theoretical and practical virtues.

True human happiness entails a harmonious unity; one cannot be a true philosopher, strictly speaking, because one cannot be perfectly happy without the existence of a virtuous city.[25] Theoretical and speculative excellence is the *telos* of the practical virtues. But theoretical excellence is not possible without the moral virtues.[26] In all of Farabi's works, philosophy as a theoretical activity and political philosophy as the art of managing human cities are causes of human happiness. But given the fact that Farabi also believes in the strict hierarchical structure of being, the abilities of men to understand difficult logical arguments and complex metaphysical proof of

God's existence will vary accordingly. Hence their abilities to attain true happiness and true perfection in this world and in the other world will vary also. Farabi's view on varying degrees of human happiness in the after life do not seem to contradict the apparent meaning of a number of Quranic verses.[27]

FARABI'S GOD

Just as the God of revelation appears in the world through the prophets, the God of philosophy appears in the world through the philosopher. The ruler of the virtuous city is equivalent to or 'similar to the First Cause whose being is the cause of all beings.' The ideal ruler is the one in whom the Active Intellect 'resides'.[28] Farabi's stringent requirement of moral, practical, and theoretical perfections make the man who attains them the natural ruler of mankind.

Farabi's epistemology conceives knowledge as unity between the intellecting subject and the object of intellection. The intelligible exists in the objects of sense perception *in potentia*, and once it is abstracted from the senses through intellection it becomes an existence *in actu* in the mind. The crucial distinction between rational conception and sense-perception is that the first is a kind of inspiration and illumination. The process of intellection flickers what amounts to a light that exists in the intellect *in potentia* and transforms it into a light *in actu*. To imitate God, who is always intellect *in actu*, is to know what God knows. What God knows is the whole, and, by knowing God, the philosopher knows the whole. To imitate God on the level of action means to give order to the city that is an image of the order that God gave to the whole.

Knowledge of God and His order is attained through emanations from the Active Intellect. Emanations may be received through the imaginative faculty or the theoretical faculty, or both combined. The 'perfect man' is the one who has attained perfection in both faculties. This is the man 'who is said to receive inspiration'. He is truly the divine man and the true king. Farabi is silent on whether he considers himself to be such a man; however, the fact that he wrote two books on this theme speaks louder than any explicit claim.[29] Political philosopher is nothing short of the reflection of the philosopher's divine obligation and moral responsibility, similar to or even higher than that of the mere prophet. If Muslims in particular, and all human societies in general were ever to attain the human happiness that is natural to them, political philosophy as the true image of philosophy must replace theology. This is one way to transcend the sectarian conflicts of Islam, which are grounded in an imaginative rather than a true conception of the divine order.

Farabi's conception of God is at the heart of what he considers to be an esoteric teaching that can be discussed with the elect, but it must be represented symbolically and rhetorically to the multitude.[30] Farabi refers to God as the One, the First Cause, the cause of all causes, the First Principle, and the First Originator. His God is changeless, simple and indivisible. God's original action is timeless and without motion, because He is outside time and because motion implies change.[31] Farabi's God has no form because form only exists in conjunction with matter. His existence has no end outside Himself. He is the end of all things. His existence is different from and more excellent than that of any other existent.[32] His essence is intellect or mind *in actu* and never *in potentia*. The First Existent '...is intelligible by virtue of its being intellect; for the One whose identity is intellect is intelligible to the One whose identity is intellect.'[33] It is wise because wisdom consists in knowing the most excellent thing with the most excellent knowledge.[34]

Farabi's God had no choice, it seems, in originating all the categories of being, hence we may speak of divine determinism. His mere existence entails the existence of all beings. Farabi rejects the Aristotelian thesis that the world is *qadim* (pre-existent, eternal). He relies on the apocryphal Aristotle's *Theology* to harmonize the opinions of Aristotle and Plato. God *abda'a* (originated) the world in one act; and with the movement of the spheres time originated.[35]

The theory of *ibda'* or origination seems to have been Farabi's first attempt to explain the existence of the beings. *Ibda'* means, '...the origination of something from nothing, and whatever is made of something is by necessity reduced to that thing. Since the world is originated from nothing, it degenerates into nothing.'[36] *Ibda'* is not merely the origination from nothing; it is also '...the continued existence of contingent beings whose essence and existence are not one.'[37] The 'marvelous order' that exists in the world reflects the presence of a First Cause that is both efficient and just.[38]

The second Farabian attempt at explaining being is the theory of emanation that was developed in his last works. The First Cause, upon its thinking of itself, causes to emanate the first intellect which, in turn, causes to emanate the second intellect. The chain of emanating intellects and spheres ends in the tenth or the Active Intellect, and the sub-lunar world.[39] Every existent, whether perfect or imperfect, emanates from the First Excellent.[40]

In his early work, *Harmonizing the Opinions of the Two Sages Plato and Aristotle*, God appears to resemble the Islamic omniscient and providential God. God's knowledge encompasses everything. He is the one who governs the whole universe. Nothing escapes his attention not even 'the measure of a mustard seed.' God's omniscience encompasses all beings, in the sense that He knows the particular in a universal way. Evil, in the sense of material corruption and in the sense of moral corruption, is as necessary as the good. Evil is the necessary property of all contingent being. It is necessary, and 'praiseworthy' because without evil the good that exists permanently would not be known and would not be possible. Evil does not exist in the world of divine intellects. It is peculiar to the sub-lunar world, the world of man, the world of becoming and degeneration.[41]

These are not Farabi's final ideas on the subject of God's omniscience and providence. This change may be explained in a Straussian way as deliberate esoteric contradictions, or it may be attributed to philosophical maturity.[42] It is clear that Farabi disagrees with the traditional Islamic conception of God's omniscience, because it leads its holders to maintain 'ugly' or repugnant absurdities that lead to 'great evils'. Farabi is referring to the *kalam* schools in his time, and to the intra-Islamic schisms that resulted from such debates. What is not clear, however, is whether Farabi considers the second position to be unacceptable as it leads to great evil. Does God or the First Cause know anything outside himself? This is the question that seemed to lead to great mischief and difficulties for Islamic medieval philosophy. Ibn Rushd and Ibn Sina argued that God knows the universal intelligibles and that He knows the particulars in a universal way. There is evidence to suggest that Farabi also subscribed to this position. This solution, however, as Ghazzali pointed out, does not save God from not knowing that a particular person did a particular thing in a particular place and time. Farabi poses intermediaries between his God and man. The tenth intellect is the one that has a semblance of a relationship with the sub-lunar world, in the sense that man is capable of receiving its emanations and uniting himself with it.[43]

Farabi's attempt to make God transcend all beings and all imperfections led to a stringent de-anthropomorphism that permits only an indirect but not immediate relationship between God and man.[44] This appears to be the ultimate Farabian contribution to the theological debates on the nature of the One that plagued the dialogue between the Mu'tazilites and the orthodox Sunnis. Such a conception is at the heart of Farabi's esotericism, which does not convince or benefit the multitude.

THE PHILOSOPHER AND THE PROPHET

The 'marvelous order' and God's knowledge in Farabi's discourse are not those of a providential God, but a wise God. But Farabi could not do without some kind of providence or mediation between the world of the divine and the human world. The human soul is made up of five faculties: the nutritive, the sensory, the imaginative, the appetitive, and the rational. What interests us here are the imaginative and the rational. The imaginative faculty is that which retains the images of sensible things; it combines those images and representations when man is awake or asleep in ways that are sometimes truthful and sometimes false.

This definition is important to Farabi's theory of prophecy. The rational faculty, on the other hand, is that through which man intellects things and deliberate on them.[45] The rational faculty is divided into two parts: practical and theoretical. The first is what Farabi calls reason, which is nothing but experience. The theoretical part enables man to know '...the beings that we cannot make or change from one state to the other.' The virtues, accordingly, are rational and moral. Rational virtues are the virtues of the rational faculty such as wisdom, intelligence, cleverness, and excellence of understanding. The moral virtues are the virtues of the appetitive part of the soul such as temperance, continence, courage, generosity, and justice. The vices are similarly divided.[46]

Virtue is distinct from self-control, as it is a second nature and effortless, whereas the latter requires effort. Moral perfection in speech and in deed is the prerequisite to learning to philosophize.

The philosophical initiate must have the moral virtues as a second nature before he commences to pursue the higer virtues of the theoretical faculty.[47]

Man is moral and rational *in potentia*. Religion transforms man from a potentially moral being into an actual moral being. To become rational in deed, man goes through different stages, which reflect the different categories of intellect, which Farabi elaborated in practically all his writings. The first is the potential intellect with which every man is endowed in his capacity as man.[48] The potential intellect has the inherent ability to intellect the essence of all existents. Once the intellect and the objects and the images of the objects of intellection become one, man develops into the second stage of intellect *in actu*. The intellect *in actu* does not need any longer the beings as objects of intellection; it works with the beings as ideas. It becomes intellect, intellection, and intelligible all in one. When the intellect intellects the intelligible as an idea, the human mind develops into the stage of the acquired intellect.[49] The last stage is the stage of the Active Intellect, which is 'separate from matter and was never in matter'. The effect of the Active Intellect on the acquired intellect is analogous to the sun and its effect on the eye which is sight potentially without the presence of light.[50]

The Active Intellect is Farabi's solution to the problem of how man gets to acquire knowledge of the divine, of prophecy and revelation, and to the Sufi problem of seeking oneness with God. Man, according to this solution, does not seem to have an immediate relationship with God; the prophet does not receive his message directly from God but rather indirectly through the Active Intellect, which is referred to, in the language of Islamic theology, as the Archangel Gabriel.[51] The doctrine of emanation from the Active Intellect offers also a rational justification for the Shi'i claim regarding the twelve recognized Imams. Even though they were not prophets, they received indirect inspiration as opposed to the prophet's direct message from God. This makes the Imam as infallible as the prophet. The doctrine of the Active Intellect sheds a different light on the Islamic firm belief that Muhammad is the last prophet, and on the claim that the Islamic law is suitable for all time. The doctrine theorizes that mankind will always be in need of a new lawgiver, because of the corrupting influence of time on all legal systems. Finally and most importantly, the doctrine of emanation offers a solution for the dogmatism that grounds itself in an absolute teaching revealed for all time, and the requirements of human reason. The philosopher has the right to be a law-giver as much as the prophet does. This is the essence of Farabi's philosophic teaching, which seems to lead naturally to the conclusion that Farabi may have thought of himself as being divinely inspired in a manner analogous to that of the Imam if not the prophet.[52]

This becomes clearer in Farabi's conception of the 'perfect man'. Not every philosopher is a prophet, and not every prophet is a philosopher. A true philosopher is a lawgiver, and every true prophet is a law-giver. Every true philosopher and every true prophet is a 'perfect man' in his own way. Farabi's metaphysics demands the presence of ten intellects and the First Cause who is pure intellect. This brings the number of intellects that govern the cosmos to eleven. This number combines the Pythagorean belief that ten is the perfect number that symbolizes harmony, order and unity, with the Aristotelian doctrine of the First Cause. Eleven (11) symbolizes a parallelism between the cosmic One and the one in the human world. Farabi's depiction of the perfect man is an exact image of a perfect deity. God's rule in the world, in the theological sense, is absolute. Similarly, the philosopher in Farabi's virtuous city rules absolutely. Theologically, God's absolute rule is grounded in His wisdom and compassion; the philosopher's rule in the virtuous city is also grounded in wisdom and compassion for the city. The prophet's claim to legislate for the city is grounded in his claim to know God and his intentions through a revealed message. The philosopher's claim to legislate is grounded in his knowledge of the First Cause and the marvelous order in the cosmos. The philosopher's claim is grounded in a rational emanation from the Active Intellect, whereas the prophet's claim is grounded in revelation from God.

Additional direct evidence to support the hypothesis that the role of the philosopher in the human world is analogous to that of the One in the cosmos is found in a terse statement of Farabi that is written very clearly but modified slightly in two places in two different books, *The Virtuous City* and *The Political Regime*. The first depicts a relation while the other indicates the similarity between the First Cause and the virtuous ruler. The first reads:

> For the relation of the First Cause to the other existents is like the relation of the king of the virtuous city to all its other parts.[53]

The second, modified version states:

> The ruler of the virtuous city is similar to the First Cause through which all beings come into existence.[54]

The hypothesis concerning the philosopher's claim to prophecy, Farabi's claim in this case, is proven also by Farabi's conception of the perfect man. The perfect man, the true king of the virtuous city, is the supreme ruler whose will cannot be subjected to any other human. He is the *telos* of all the actions in the virtuous city. His imaginative faculty has reached its perfection also, to the extent that it is capable of receiving, whether awake or asleep the particulars in themselves or their similitudes. The perfect man is one with the Active Intellect. He is the man 'on whom the Active Intellect has descended', thus he receives divine revelation.[55] Whatever emanates to his acquired reason makes him *'a wise man and philosopher'* with a *'divine intellect'*. What emanates from the Active Intellect to his imaginative faculty makes him a *'prophet* who foretells what will be and tells of particular things that exist now.'[56]

The philosopher-prophet, who is also referred to as the 'Imam' and 'the first ruler' of the virtuous city is the most excellent and the happiest of all men. He is the one who knows every act that leads to happiness. This is the first attribute of the philosopher-prophet-Imam. He must also have a developed rhetorical ability to convince others through imaginative representations and guide them to actions that bring happiness.[57]

Such stringent attributes are difficult to find combined in one man. The difficulty does not mean that it is impossible to find men with such a nature 'one at a time only', albeit rarely, but what is rare is not impossible.[58] Such a man is superior to all other human beings, and he attained a rank higher than the human. This is the man the 'ancients used to refer to as the divine.'[59]

The prophet receives emanations from the Active Intellect through his imaginative rather than rational faculty. The imaginative faculty occupies the middle position between sense-perception and the rational faculty; it is influenced by the senses and retains the images of the objects of sense-perception.[60] The prophet's imaginative faculty receives also the particulars as they are or images of them. What the mere prophet receives then are images of what the philosopher receives.[61]

The philosopher-prophet emerges as a more virtuous man than the mere prophet.[62] He equals the prophet in terms of a perfect imaginative faculty, but he surpasses the prophet in his theoretical faculty. Prophecy is the image of philosophy; the prophet is the image of the philosopher; revelation is the image of rational emanation. Religion is an imitation of philosophy. Philosophy knows the divine world as it really is, whereas revelation represents the divine world in images, symbolisms, and similitudes. Prophecy or revelation *per se* are not denied by Farabi; they are merely given a philosopical meaning that satisfies Farabi's Shi'ism and rationalist Sufi tendencies. Farabi wants to know God and to be one with God through knowledge of being; the traditional Sufi sees these beings as mere epiphenomena because there is nothing in the world but God. The traditional Sufi looks for inspiration in his own soul and discovers that it is either God or of God's nature, whereas Farabi looks for inspiration in theoretical reason and finds it to be the essence of God.

The true philosopher-prophet is not just one who has mastered all of 'Aristotle's books', the natural sciences, logic, theology, and political philosophy. He is the one whose morality and virtue are in accordance with what is truly moral or virtuous according to the divine world. The false philosopher is the one who knows all the theoretical knowledge there is to know, but whose morality falls short even of the commonly held view of morality. Farabi does not seem here to be denigrating morality; he wants to raise the standard of morality to a higher level than what is generally accepted by the multitude. This is again a Sufi notion that seeks to know the *baten* (inner or real meaning) of the *zaher* (apparent) meaning of the moral virtues and the requirements of divine worship. The virtues are essential if one is to know God and imitate God, in contrast to the ordinary believer who is virtuous only to please God. The happiness of the philosopher, on the other hand, is grounded in his knowledge of oneness with God.[63]

If revelation is an image of rational emanations, and if the prophet is an image of the philosopher, all religions will have an equal status, depending on the perfection of the imaginative faculty of the prophet in question. They are more or less accurate images of the divine world and the order that exists in the cosmos.[64] It is not surprising therefore that Farabi describes the philosophical knowledge of the beings and the religious knowledge of the beings as 'two kinds of knowledge except that the knowledge of the wise men is necessarily better.' Virtue is not limited therefore to the followers of any particular religion.[65] The divine world is more than a salutary myth. The God of the philosopher and the God of the prophet are equally needed in both cases as the source and the ground for the *nomos* or the revealed law.

The truly virtuous and happy city is the city in which the philosopher, the prophet and the king are combined in one. Genuine human happiness will not be complete unless the perfect man rules. This means that philosophy or philosophers cannot wait 'until the cities recognize their rightful claim to rule and duplicate the just and harmonious order that exists in the world. Philosophy must be involved in the world. The coincidence of philosophy and politics is the prerequisite for true happiness`and true perfection. Contemplation is not possible without action inasmuch as action is not possible without contemplation. Philosophy must be cognizant of the fact that politics aims at reproducing the good in the city. Philosophy seeks to align itself with a prince in order to realize itself as a possible rather than an impossible *eros*. Philosophy cannot afford to ignore the city, as Socrates did, nor become haughtily indignant, as Plato did, nor withdraw from the world as the traditional Sufi taught.[66] Happiness is not possible without the city and without human cooperation. The truly virtuous city in which the cooperation philosopher rules is the condition for the philosopher's 'first perfection' without which 'the final perfection in the hereafter' becomes untenable.[67]

If the philosopher's genuine happiness is dependent upon his rule in the city, and if everything that stands between him and that perfection is an absolute evil, and if his happiness will remain imperfect as long as he does not bring about the coincidence of philosophy and politics, and if the city does not either understand or appreciate his divine right to order the human cosmos on the basis of his understanding of the cosmic order and the good that prevails in that order, then he is left with no other choice but to resort to different means—means which practically all prophets employed. Prophets resorted to rhetoric, promises, and force. Farabi does not hesitate to advocate that the philosopher must in this case have 'a moral virtue' that will enable him to '...exploit the acts of the virtue possessed by all others. This, then, is the leading practical virtue that is not surpassed by any other in authority.'[68] Philosophers must either become actual rulers or align themselves with actual rulers in order to realize their own happiness that is natural to them and to realize the happiness of the multitude that is peculiar to them. Farabi devised a programme for action that will bring about this leading virtue.[69]

Farabi's programme includes training the perfect prince who must master the virtues that are truly virtues, not the virtues that are considered true in the opinion of one religion; the prince must be a prince by nature and not by will; subordinates are also subordinates by nature. The method that the prince may use is the duality of instruction in the theoretical virtues, and formation of character which aims at introducing the moral virtues and practical arts in nations and cities through a process of habituation that will arouse the citizens to do the right things with 'resolution' 'by speech or deed'. The princes and the leaders who will be instructed in all the theoretical arts constitute the '...elect who should not be confined to what is in conformity with unexamined common opinion...', as it is manifest in any religion or any city. The habituating method employs persuasive arguments, and 'compulsion'. The multitude must be instructed in theoretical matters through images. The elect are those 'with prominent ancestors and...possess great wealth'. They are the holders of political office and masters of the various arts.

This early programme seems to have gone through some modification in its final version. Farabi's despair of ever finding the right prince, and his despair of genuine happiness and perfection except in cities ruled by philosophers seem to be the reasons behind the modification. The ideal ruler is reinstated as the philosopher-king-prophet. In the absence of such a man, the legitimate 'second ruler' is 'a wise man' who knows the laws and the ways of life of the original founders of the city following their example in all his actions.[70] This is a call for a return to the original sources and the original morality. In the absence of a man with such qualities, Farabi is willing to accept a regime controlled by a maximum number of six wise men. If the city is corrupt enough not to have at least six virtuous men among its inhabitants, it ultimately perishes.[71]

Justice is the harmonious unity of a city that functions and cooperates together like the organs of the body; the city reflects the harmony that prevails in the world headed by the wise man. Natural justice and natural right demand that the men of knowledge rule. Shying away from direct rule is dictated by the frustration the philosopher experiences with the city that is not willing to grant him the same free hand as enjoyed by the prophet, Muhammad.

RATIONAL SUFISM

The soul may attain perfection and may become separate from the body as its tool even when man is still alive. It is the theoretical part of the soul that is capable of attaining separation from the body of a living rational being. When theoretical reason is not in need of sense perception or imagination, '...it has already reached the after-life and then its representation of the First Principle is more perfect....' This is the case because the intellect is 'seizing' its own essence without the need to represent it by example or analogy. 'This is the after-life, in which man perceives in it his God and will not be wronged in perceiving Him.'[72] Death reduces the soul to its simplest essence or substance, the speculative or theoretical faculty that is unique to man. Hence intellection of the First Principle becomes more perfect upon the soul's separation from matter. Man can perceive his God in life or in death.[73] Farabi's Sufism aspires to perceive God not through the imaginative faculty but rather through the rational faculty, which is predicated on knowledge of being.[74] Philosophy, in its Farabian Sufi sense becomes a preparation for death, after which the soul is freed from the body, and its desires and passions in order to enter the realm of eternal and silent contemplation.[75]

It is clearly misleading to suggest that Farabi believes in the Islamic conception of the immortality of all souls, which entails bodily resurrection, personal immortality, and sensual divine rewards and punishments in heaven and in hell. Farabi's teaching on the soul is consistent with the general structure of Farabi's philosophy and world-view.[76] What is imperishable in man is the theoretical part of the soul, which enables him to know and be one with the highest object of his intellection.[77] Since the main function of theoretical reason is to know the intelligibles that are separate from matter, and since knowledge is a unity between the subject and the object of intellection, and since those intelligibles are eternal, it follows, therefore, that what is eternal in man is his theoretical reason, which survives after man's death. This is the logical conclusion that follows from Farabi's premises.[78]

Farabi's ideas on the survival of the soul are characterized by vagueness and what appears to be a contradiction. Farabi seems to argue for both the survival for some souls and the *fana* or *adam*, that is, annihilation of others.[79] The souls that suffer total annihilation are the souls of the wicked who lack all the moral virtues. The souls of such people remain close to the *hyle* state; they cannot become separate from matter, and when matter is annulled such souls go through an automatic and total disintegration.[80] If theoretical perfection requires moral perfection, the theoretical knowledge attained by the wicked soul would not be true knowledge of the intelligibles. On the other hand, the morally virtuous soul, which has not attained perfect theoretical knowledge, does not seem to go through total disintegration. Collective rather than individual immortality can be attained even when the multitude of the inhabitants of the virtuous city have true images or opinions that are founded on a demonstrative and hence true knowledge of the divine.

Farabi's final teachings of the soul are found in *Al-Madina al-Fadila* and *Al-Siyasa Madaniyya*. The soul, according to Farabi, is not indestructible or eternal by nature. Eternal life is attained through right moral action and philosophical cognition of the whole. Man, upon the separation of the soul from the body, reverts to primordial matter, matter without a form. This means that matter accepts different souls and, through its eternal combinations, disintegration, and reconstitution, may enter equally into the bodies of humans, animals, or plants. This makes bodily resurrection impossible since different bodies share the same matter.[81] There is no cataclysmic end of all forms of life where everything returns to God.[82] But if form can only exist in matter, his doctrine of eternal bliss for certain souls becomes untenable, if not a myth. The philosophical way of life would be no different from any other way of life. The happiness that one derives from philosophy as well as the happiness one derives from religion are both equal temporal goods. Either Farabi overlooked a colossal contradiction, or his philosophy leads to a nihilistic will to power.

The question is then which souls achieve eternal life upon death and which souls disintegrate into their material components? Farabi's cosmology and political philosophy seem to be predicated upon a genuine rather than an esoteric belief in a collective rather than individual eternal life.[83] We are told by Farabi that happiness varies according to kind, quantity and quality. The happiest soul in all respects is that of the wise man who knows the First Cause and the separate intellects and whose acts are the virtuous acts. The same hierarchy that prevails in temporal life prevails also after death. The souls of wise men are united with the souls of other wise men. The second degree of happiness is that of the souls of the multitude who live in virtuous cities and are ruled by the wise or virtuous man. Their happiness after death is an image of the happiness of the wise men, because their knowledge of the First Principles is not true knowledge strictly speaking. It is knowledge through imagination, representations, and imagery. The souls of those who had knowledge of the First Cause and the intelligibles but their acts are wicked suffer eternal misery, because their wicked acts and bodily desires will continue to impinge on their souls after death. They can never be fully separate from matter.[84]

The philosopher's happiness after death is dependent upon being virtuous morally and theoretically, while the eternal happiness of the multitude is dependent upon right action that reflects the true knowledge of a virtuous philosopher whose knowledge and way of life are organically linked. That is why the fourth category of souls is comprised of those souls that are neither guided by right action nor by true knowledge. They can neither be happy nor miserable. Thus the inhabitants of ignorant cities '...are annihilated into nothingness exactly like cattle, the beasts of prey, and vipers.'[85] The souls of the inhabitants of corrupt or wicked cities suffer great distress upon death. The distress results from the fact that virtuous opinions would free the souls from their material grounding. Their souls survive their bodily death, but they remain in eternal misery because their acts were incongruent with the virtuous opinions they knew. It is a distress that results from knowing and not doing.[86] As to the souls of the inhabitants of cities that have gone astray, their souls revert to nothingness. It is the soul of the one who led them astray that suffers eternal distress. Similarly, the souls of the inhabitants of cities that have deliberately changed and deviated will face annihilation and nothingness.[87]

It is the absence of bodily resurrection and bodily rewards and punishments that Farabi wants to keep hidden from the multitude. The multitude can understand happiness only in bodily pleasures and pains. A state of nothingness after death does not seem to Farabi to be a sufficient deterrent for the multitude. The multitude is motivated only by hope and the fear of death. The absence of fear and hope will make most men beastly.

There would be no order at all in human affairs, neither in legal nor in political things. For without fear, no one would gain something for his tomorrow, no ruled will obey the ruler..., no one will be kind to another, and no one will obey God.[88]

CONCLUSION

Politics is at the centre of Farabi's philosophical system. This is not surprising in light of the fact that Farabi lived in an epoch of crises. The theologico-political problem is the cause of these crises. Human societies cannot be organized on the basis of revealed law only. Human reason will not have any role to play when it is reduced to the mere task of interpreting divine revelation. Philosophy must take its rightful place in social life. The human cosmos must be harmoniously organized to reflect the harmony that prevails in the whole. Farabi's political theory strives to show the possibilities rather than the limits of political action. Farabi's encounter with Greek philosophy reflects his manner of transcending the commonly held opinions of Islam and his solution to the sectarian feuds that have plagued Islam since its inception. The encounter illustrates also his solution to the problems of a community whose existence, existence and truthfulness are intertwined with the revealed law that simply refuses to admit the reality of time and history.

Farabi lived during a period of political instability and religious schisms that ultimately destroyed the Islamic empire. It is not surprising then to find the theme of social unity a dominant one. Moreover, Farabi seeks to overcome all the sectarian squabbles about the nature of God and the true religious beliefs by reducing revelation to the realm of the imagination, which is a mere reflection of theoretical reason.

Farabi's political cosmos is an image of the cosmic order. Farabi's political philosophy is a true image of his metaphysics. The city does not exist merely to make the philosophical way of life possible. The city, any city, is impossible without philosophy and the philosophic way of life. It is equally impossible without a theology that mirrors the philosophical conception of the whole. Political life cannot be based on religion only or on philosophy only. Both are needed for human happiness and perfection.

The philosopher in Farabi's virtuous city organizes the city for the good of the city and rules openly. God's essence and existence and the 'marvelous order' He gave to the world are not contingent. Similarly, the philosopher is a necessary existent for the city irrespective of whether he rules openly or secretively, irrespective of whether he is recognized as such or not, and irrespective of whether his laws and orders are carried out or not. The absence of philosophy or, to say the same thing, the absence of natural reason can only lead to the destruction of cities. A millennium of Islamic history supplies enough evidence to prove Farabi right.

NOTES

1. The medieval Arab sources claim that Farabi spoke seventy languages. This is obviously an exaggerated figure, when it is not even certain that he spoke Greek, the language of his masters Plato and Aristotle. What is certain is that he spoke Arabic, Turkish, Persian, and Kurdish. See Ibn Khallikan, Wafayat al Al-A'yan, Vol. II, p. 100; H.K. Sherwani, Studies in Muslim Political Thought and Administration, p. 63.
2. Muhammad Ali Abu Rayyan, Tarikh al-Fikr al-Falsafi fil Islam. Alexanderia: Dar Al-Ma'rifa al-Jami'iyya, 1986, p. 242.
3. Philip K. Hitti, History of the Arabs: From the Earliest Times to the Present, 7th ed. London: Macmillan and Co. Ltd., 1960, Chs. xxiv–xxv, pp. 297–319.
4. The uprisings of the zinj (slaves) and the Qarmathians were most prominent in Farabi's time. The black stone of Ka'ba was removed by the Qarmathians and kept for fourteen years. The conflict between the Sunnis and the Shi'is with their various sects continued to drain the empire of its energy. See Mas'udi, Muruj Ud-Dhahab wa Ma'aden ul-Jawhar, Vol. 4. Beirut: Dar Ul-Ma'rifa, 1983, pp. 199–285; Ibn Khaldun, Tarikh, Vol. III. Beirut: Mu'assat al-A'lami, 1971, pp. 272–448; As-Suyuti in M.M. Abdulhamid, ed., Tarikh Ul-Khulafa. Cairo: Matba'at Us-Sa'ada, 1952, pp. 346–405; Hitti, p. 337.
5. Farabi, Fusul, Aphorism 57, p. 140.
6. Farabi, 'Risalat Fi ma Yanbaghi', in Friedrich Dietere ici, ed., al-Thamara al-Murdiyya. Leiden: E.J. Brill, 1890, p. 53 (13–16).
7. Ibid.
8. Farabi, 'Tahsil Us-Sa'adah', in Muhsin Mahdi, ed. and trans., Al-Farabi's Philosophy of Plato and Aristotle. Ithaca: Cornell University Press, 1979, p. 40.
9. See George Hourani, 'Reason and Revelation in Ibn Hazm's Ethical Thought', in Parviz Morewedge (ed.), Islamic Philosophic Theology. Albany: State University of New York Press, 1979, pp. 154–58. The thesis that Farabi harmonizes reason and revelation is adopted by E.J. Rosenthal, 'Some Observations on Al-Farabi's Kitab al-Mila', Etude Philosophique, pp. 65–74; Muhammad Y. Musa, Bayn al-Din wa al-Falsafa, 2nd ed. Cairo: Dar al-Ma'aref, 1968, pp. 56–63; Seyyed Hossein Nasr, 'The Meaning of Philosophy in Islam', Studia Islamica, Vol. 37,

1973, pp. 57–80; I. Madkour, 'Farabi', in M.M. Sharif, ed., *A History of Muslim Philosophy*, Vol. I. Wiesbaden: Otto Harrassowiz, 1963, pp. 454–57.

10. Unity in Farabi's sense must be understood as the unity between the intellect and its object of intellection to the point where the two become inseparable. This is expressed in Farabi's trinity of *'Aql* (intellect), *Ma'qoul* (rationally intellected), *'Aqel* (an intellecting subject who has intellected his object of intellection as an idea).

11. Albert Nasri Nader, ed., *Al-Madinah al-Fadila*. Beirut: Dar ul-mashreq-Mashreq, 1982, pp. 51, 57; Richard Walzer, *The Perfect State*. Oxford: Clarendon Press, 1985, pp. 95–97 (Engl.); see also Osman Amine, ed., *Ihsa'al-'Ulum*. Cairo: Maktabat al-Anglo Misriyya, 1968, p. 122–23.

12. Fauzi M. Najjar, ed., *Al-Siyasa al-Madaniyya*. Beirut: Catholic Press, 1964, p. 31 (1–11); *Al-Madina al-Fadila, op. cit.*, chapter 13, pp. 66–68.

13. *Al-Madina al-Fadila, op.cit.*, p. 62.

14. *Al-Siyasa al-Madaniyya, op. cit.*, p. 35 (4–6); Al-Madina al-Fadila, *op. cit.*, p. 66

15. D.M. Dunlap, eds., *Fusul al-Madani*. Cambridge: Cambridge University Press, 1961, Aphorisms 64, 65, 66, 67, 68, 77; pp. 147–49, 152. See also Farabi, 'Uyoun al-Masa'il', in *Al-Thamara al-Murdiyya*, pp. 57–58; 'Risalat Fusus al-Hilam', *op.cit.*, p. 98. Muhsin Mahdi, ed., *Kitab al-Milla wa Nusus Ukhra* (Book of Religion and Related Texts). Beirut: Dar al-Mashreq, 1968, pp. 89–92.

16. Farabi, 'Tahqiq Gharad Aristotales fi Kitab ma Ba'ad al-Tabi'ah' (Treatise on Aristotle's Aim in the *Metaphysics*), *Al-Thamara al-Murdiyya, op.cit*, pp. 34–35.

17. *Ibid.*, pp. 35–36.

18. See Farabi, Nukat Abi Nasr al-Farabi Fi ma yaseh wa la yaseh Min Ahkam al Nujum' (Farabi's Remarks on what Is True and Untrue in Astrology) in *Al-Thamara al-Murdiyya, op.cit.*, p. 105 (9–15); *Ihsa'al-'Ulum, op.cit.*, p.168.

19. *Ihsa al-'Ulum*, p. 54.

·20. Knowledge of first principles is more excellent than knowledge of moral precepts that are derived from these principles. That is the reason why Farabi relegates the art of *fiqh* and *kalam* to a status lower than the art of dancing. Farabi, *Al-Madina al-Fadila, op.cit.*, ch. 31, p. 138; Walzer, *The Perfect State*, p. 267. In *Ihsa' al-'Ulum*, p. 131. The art of *fiqh* is defined as the ability to deduce judgment on particulars, that were not clearly dealt with by the lawgiver, by using the general principles that constitute the basis for the opinions and actions of a particular religion. This is not contradictory to the Islamic understanding of the art of *fiqh* because it does not claim for itself more than what Farabi accurately ascribed to it; also *Kitab al-Milla wa Nusus Ukhra*, chapter 2.

21. See *Fusul al-Madani*, Aphorisms 25, pp. 120–21; 27, p. 122; 28, 29, pp. 122–24; 49, pp. 133–34. See also Farabi 'The Attainment of Happiness', in Mahdi, *Al Farabi's Philosophy of Plato and Aristotle*, p. 13, p. 28; Farabi 'The Philosophy of Aristotle, The Parts of His Philosophy, The Ranks of Order of Its Parts, The Position from which He Started and the One He Reached', *loc. cit.*, p. 92.

22. Farabi, 'Attainment of Happiness', *op.cit.*, p. 24.

23. *Ibid.*, pp. 24–25.

24. *Ibid.*, pp. 30–31.

25. See Al-Farabi, *Al-Tanbih 'Ala Sabeel al-Sa'adah* (Hyderabad: 1346 A.H.), p. 21. Avicenna, 'On the Division of the Rational Sciences', in M. Mahdi & R. Lerner, eds. *Medieval Political Philosophy*. Ithaca: Cornell University Press, 1972, pp. 95–97.

26. *Fusul al-Madani*, Aphorism 89, pp. 164–67; Aphorism 90, p. 168; Aphorism 93, pp. 169–70.

27. 'God will raise up, to suitable ranks and degrees, those of you who believe and who have been granted knowledge.' *Quran*: LVIII, 11; see also XXXXIII, 32; VI, 83.

28. *Al-Siyasa al-Madaniyya*, *op.cit.*, p. 84 (6–7); *Al-Madina al-Fadila*, *op. cit.*, p. 125; *Al-Thamara al-Murdiyya*, *op. cit.*, p. 53 (13–16).

29. *Attainment of Happiness*, *op. cit.*, pp. 43–44, 49; *Al-Siyasa al-Madaniyya*, *op.cit.*, pp. 35–36, 79; *Fusul al-Madani*, Aphorism 54, pp. 137–38.

30. Farabi, 'Fi Ma Yanbaghi', in *Al-Thamara al-Murdiyya*, *op. cit.*, pp. 53–54; Al-Jam'a, *op.cit.*, p. 26 (15–23).

31. Farabi, *Al-Jama'a*, p. 26 (11–15); '*Uyoun al-Masa'il*', in *Al-Thamara al-Murdiyya*, *op.cit.*, p. 57.

32. Farabi, 'Risala fi al-Milla al-Fadila', in A. Badawi (ed.), *Rasa'il Falsafiyya*. Benghazi: Manshourat al-jami'a al-Libiyya, 1973, pp. 33–36.

33. *Al-Madina al-Fadila*, *op. cit.*, p. 47; Walzer, *The Perfect State*, *op. cit.*, p. 71.

34. *Al-Madina al-Fadila*, *op. cit.*, pp. 47–53; Al-Siyasa al-Madaniyya, *op. cit.*, pp. 42–47; Ihsa', p. 5

35. *Al-Jama'a*, p. 23 (5–12). Fakhry, 'Ai-Farabi and the Reconciliation of Plato and Aristotle', *Journal of the History of Ideas*, Vol. 26 (1965), pp. 469–78.

36. *Al-Jama'a*, p.25 (17–19). Farabi uses here the Islamic concept of *bari'* in reference to God. It is used in the Quran in the sense of the creator from nothing, without the need for the Platonic forms as the model for the beings. See Ibn Manzour, *Mu'jam Lisan al-Arab*, under the term, bara'a. Also Murad Wahbadh, *Al-Mu'jam al-Falsafi* (Dictionary of Philosophy), 3rd ed. Cairo: Dar al-Thaqafa al-Jadida, 1971.

37. Farabi, 'Uyoun al-Masa'il, in *Al-Thamara al-Murdiyya*, p.58 (15–17).

38. *Al-Jama'a*, p.23 (13–19), (21–23), p.224 (15–17).

39. *Al-Madina al-Fadila*, *op. cit.*, pp.47–49; Al-Siyasa al-Madaniyya, *op. cit.*, pp.48–49; Walzer, The Perfect State, *op. cit.*, pp.89–93.

40. *Al-Madina al-Fadila*, *op. cit.*, p.57.

41. *Al-Jam'a*, *op. cit.*, pp.25 (23)–26(1–2); '*Uyoun al-Masa'il*, *op. cit.*, p.64 (20–23), p.65(1–3); Al-Siyasa al-Madaniyya, *op. cit.*, p.73 (9–17); *Fusul al-Madani*, Aphorism, 65, p.150; 'Fusus al-Hikam', p.68 (9–17), p.69 (1–5). Farabi uses the Quranic expression 'al-Lawh al-Mahfuz' or the eternal tablet of God's knowledge of all things including every fallen leaf. Farabi's attempt to harmonize the God of Islam with the God of the philosophers is not a complete success. An all-knowing providential God who emanates good and evil cannot hold man responsible for any evil deed that has been eternally decreed. Man's responsibility for his actions, man's free will in short, has a meaning only if God ceases to be all that he is in revelation. This line of reasoning may be the reason why the God of the mature Farabi began to move closer and closer to the God of Aristotle.

42. Al-Jama', *op. cit.*, p.26.

43. See Al-Madina al-Daila, *op. cit.*, chapter 7, pp. 55–56; *Al-Siyasa al-Madaniyya*, *op. cit.*, pp.45–48.

44. Fusul al-Madani, Aphorism 82, p.160.

45. *Ibid.*, Aphorism 6, pp.107–8.

46. *Ibid.*, Aphorism 7, pp.106–7; Al-Jama'a, *op. cit.*, p.21.

47. Al-Thamara al-Murdiyya, *op. cit.*, p.53 (4–7); *Fusul al-Madani*, Aphorism 13, p.112.

48. *Al-Madina al-Fadila*, *op. cit.*, p.102. Farabi calls the potential intellect here the affected intellect, or the hyle intellect.

49. 'If there were here beings that are images or forms that are separate from matter and can never be in matter, and once those beings are intellected they come into being as intellected presence.' Farabi, 'Maqalah fi Ma'ani al-'Aql,' in Al-Thamara al-Murdiyya, pp.39–45; also Fusul al-Madani, Aphorisms 30–34, pp.124–28. Compare with Aristotle, *The Metaphysics*, 1072b–1073b.

50. *Al-Thamara al-Murdiyya*, *op. cit.*, pp.46–47, 64; see also Ihsa', Aphorisms 30, 31, 35, 36, 38, pp.123–33; Mahdi, *Al-Farabi's Philosophy of Plato and Aristotle*, pp.16–29.

51. *Al-Madina al-Fadila*, *op. cit.*, p.125. Farabi offers an ingenious solution to a number of perplexing problems. Muslims believe in the truthfulness of all previous revelations, and yet claim that the revealed messages were corrupted. Islam is the final truthful manifestation of all previous revelations. Farabi does not seem to accept this argument completely. He accepts the corrupting influence of time, but does not attribute the basic differences between revealed religions to a malicious and wilful human act. Previous prophets received different messages because their abilities to unite themselves with the Active Intellect varied, and because prophets receive emanations from the Active Intellect mostly through their imaginative faculty.

52. It is noteworthy that Farabi uses two uniquely Islamic terms to describe the relationship between the philosopher or the 'virtuous man' and the ignorant or corrupt polities. The first term is the verb, *hurruma*, which connotes a religious injunction prohibiting the virtuous man from continuing to live in the midst of corrupt cities if there are 'virtous cities' in his time. The second term is the use of the noun, *hijrah* (emigration), which is traditionally associated with Muhammad's move from Mecca to Medina. The use of the word *hijrah* leads us to believe that Farabi considered himself to be either a prophet or worthy of prophecy. Compare with the argument of Abraham Joshua Heschel in, 'Did Maimonides Believe that he was worthy of Prophecy?', Arthur Hyman, ed., *Essays in Medieval Jewish and Islamic Philosophy: Studies from the Publications of the American Academy for Jewish Research*. New York: KTAV Publishing House, Inc., 1977, pp.134–63.

53. *Al-Madina al-Fadila*, *op. cit.*, p. 121; Walzer, *The Perfect State*, *op. cit.*, p. 237; emphasis added.

54. *Al-Siyasa al-Madaniyya*, *op. cit.*, p. 84(6–7); emphasis added. 'In the virtuous city…, the status of the king and first chief…is equivalent to God, who is the first Mudabbir (governing, dominating, ruling) of the beings.' *Kitab al-Milla*, *op. cit.*, p. 63 (18–20).

55. Al-Madina al-Fadila, *op. cit.*, pp. 123–25; Walzer, *The Perfect State*, *op. cit.*, p. 241, 245; Ihsa, pp. 121–23.

56. *Al-Madina al-Fadila*, *op. cit.*, pp. 125–26; Walzer, *The Perfect State*, *op. cit.*, p. 245. On Farabi's theory of prophecy, see E.J. Rosenthal, 'Some Observations on the Philosophic Theory of Prophecy in Islam', *Studia Semitica*, Vol. II, pp. 135–44; Rosenthal, 'Avicenna's Influence on Jewish Thought', *Studia Semitica*, Vol. I, pp. 298, 302; Rosenthal, *Political Thought in Medieval Islam*, pp. 122–26,

214 YUSUF K. UMAR

128–30; Musa, *op. cit.*, p. 57; Fazlur Rahman, *Prophecy in Islam.* London: George Allen & Unwin, 1958, pp. 57–60; M. Marmura, 'The Philosopher and Society', *Arab Studies Quarterly*, Vol. 1, No. 4 (Fall, 1979), pp. 309–22; R. Walzer, 'Al-Farabi's Theory of Prophecy and Divination', *Journal of Hellenistic Studies*, Vol. 77, part I (1957), pp. 142–48; Muhammad 'Abed al-Jabri, *Bunyat al-'Aql al-'Arabi* (The Structure of the Arab Mind). Beirut: Markaz Dirasat al-Wihda al-'Arabiyyah, 1986, pp. 450–54. Hans Daiber, 'The Ruler As Philosopher: A New Interpretation of al-Farabi's View', *Mededelingen Der Koninklijke Nederlandse Akademie Van Wetenschappen, Afd, Letterkunde Niewe Reks*, Deel 49, No. 4 (Jan., 1986), pp. 133–49.

57. *Al-Madina al-Fadila*, *op. cit.*, p. 126; Walzer, *The Perfect State*, *op. cit.*, pp. 246–47. Other secondary attributes include perfection in limbs, good understanding and apprehension, good memory, intelligence, fine speech, and knowledge. He must not crave food, drinking, sex, and wealth; must love the truth and truthful men and abhor lies and liars; he must be fond of justice and hate injustice and oppression; he must be of strong will, courage and determination. See *Al-Madina al-Fadila*, *op. cit.*, pp. 127–29; *The Attainment of Happiness*, *op. cit.*, p. 48.

58. *Al-Madina al-Fadila*, *op. cit.*, p. 249.

59. *Fusul al-Madani*, Aphorism 11, pp. 110–11. Compare with Farabi, *Falsafat Aflatoun*, p. 13 (1–3), p. 21 (3–10), where the perfect human being is the one who combines perfect theoretical knowledge with political knowledge, or the one who combines the science in the *Timaeus* and in the *Laws*. See also *Al-Siyasa al-Madaniyya*, *op. cit.*, p. 79 (11–17).

60. *Al-Madina al-Fadila*, *op. cit.*, p. 108.

61. *Ibid.*, pp. 112–13, 116; Cf *Al-Siyasa al-Madaniyya*, *op. cit.*, pp. 74–80; Amine's introduction to *Ihsa'*, pp. 45–46, *Fusul al-Madani*, Aphorism 52, pp. 135–36; 'Fusus al-Hikam', in *Al-Thamara al-Murdiyya*, p. 72 (4–8), (9–12), p. 75 (11–16).

62. This statement does not seem to consider Muhammad as an exception. The order which Muhammad brought is an image of the order Farabi would have brought. Farabi's political theory manifests a radicalization of the Shi'i concept of the imam, and manifests at the same time the Shi'i aristocratic and hierarchic world-view, a world-view that is dominated by the supremacy of election over selection.

63. *Fusul al-Madani*, Aphorism 93, pp. 76–77. The quoted text is Dunlop's translation. See also *The Attainment of Happiness*, *op. cit.*, p. 44. The 'vain philosopher', according to Farabi, is the '...one who learns the theoretical sciences, but without going any further and without being habituated to doing all the acts considered virtuous by a certain religion or the generally accepted noble acts.' The 'counterfeit philosopher' studies the theoretical sciences 'without being naturally equipped for them' whereas the 'false philosopher...is the one who is not yet aware of the purposes for which philosophy is pursued.' *The Attainment of Happiness*, *op. cit.*, pp. 48–49.

64. *Ihas'*, pp. 132–38.

65. *Al-Madina al-Fadila*, *op. cit.*, pp. 147–49. Compare with the depiction of the stages that Sufi initiates must go through to attain knowledge of God through an ascent from the letter of the revealed text under the guide of a teacher. Farid Ud-Din Attar (tr. with an introduction by Afkham Darbandi and Dick Davis), *The Conference of the Birds*. Middlesex: Penguin Books, 1984.

66. See Mahdi's translation of the Philosophy of Plato, pp. 65–66; Falsafat Aflatoun, p. 13 (4–11), p. 14(4–11), p. 16(1–7), (11–18); p. 19(12–16), p. 20 (1–14); p. 21 (11–17).

67. *Fusul al-Madani*, Aphorisms 25, pp. 120–21; 27, p. 122; 29, pp. 123–24.

68. *The Attainment of Happiness, op. cit.*, p. 31.

69. *Ibid.*, p. 49; pp. 32–35; pp. 35–60; pp. 36–39.

70. *Fusul al-Madani*, Aphorisms 27–29, pp. 122–24.

71. The number six is a possible indication that Farabi may have been an adherent of the Ismai'li offshoot of shi'ism. If we add six to the original rightful ruler the prophet Muhammad, we come up with seven. The Ismai'lis are known in the Islamic tradition as the 'seveners.' *Al-Madina al-Fadila, op. cit.*, p. 129. Cf *Al-Siyasa al-Madaniyya, op. cit.*, pp. 80–81. Farabi calls the second ruler here the 'king of the sunna' or the king according to the tradition. Cities that are on their way to perishing unless the process is reversed by the rise of virtuous men include the ignorant city, the corrupt city, the changing city, the city that has gone astray, the timorous city, and the democratic city. See also E.J. Rosenthal, 'The Place of Politics in the Philosophy of Al-Farabi', *Studia Semitica*, Vol. II, pp. 93–114. On democracy in Farabi and Islam, see Fauzi Najja, 'Democracy in Islam', *Studia Islamica*, Vol LI (1980), pp. 110–22.

72. *Ibid.*, p. 156.

73. *Ibid.*, Aphorism 77, p. 156 (p. 65-Eng.).

74. See *Al-Mu'Jam al-Sufi* (Sufi Lexicon) for a definition of zouq and *fana*', *al-hiss wa al-mushahada*. Farabi's rational Sufism manifests itself in practically all his writings. In *Al-Madina al-Fadila*, matter is conceived as the 'cause that distances our essence for that of the First Essence'. Man shares in the essence of the First cause in his rational faculty. Thus the more we are capable of separating ourselves from matter, our intellection of Him becomes more perfect. 'We draw nearer to Him by becoming an intellect in actu (rather than just in potentia). If we become completely separate from matter, what is intellected of Him in our mind becomes the most humanly possible perfection'. *Al-Madina al-Fadila, op. cit.*, p. 51. See also Al-Siyasa al-Madaniyya, *op. cit.*, p. 32 (6–12).

75. See Farabi, 'Risalat Fusus Al-Hikam', in *Al-Thamara al-Murdiyya, op. cit.*, pp. 69–71. On Farabi's understanding of the aim of philosophy as knowing God, see Fi Ma Yanbaghi in *Al-Thamara al-Murdiyya*, p. 53; see also *Al-jam'a*, p. 30 (17–20). Plato, Phaedo, 64Aff., 67E, 114C. On Plato's ideas on the soul, see Erwin Rohde, Psyche: *The Cult of Souls and Belief in Immortality Among the Greeks*, Vol. 2. New York: Harper and Row, Harper Torchbooks, 1966, pp. 463–89. See also Jacques Choron, *Death and Western Thought*. London & New York: Collier Macmillan Publishers, 1963 & 1973, pp. 47–52.

76. See *Al-Madina al-Fadila, op. cit.*, Chapters 20–21, pp. 87–92; Walzer, *The Perfect State, op. cit.*, pp. 165–75.

77. See *Al-Siyasa al-Madaniyya, op. cit.*, pp. 32–33. *Al-Madina al-Fadila, op. cit.*, chapter 22, pp. 101–4; Walzer, *The Perfect State, op. cit.*, pp. 196–210. See also Fusul al-Madani, Aphorism 6, pp. 106–7.

78. Farabi's doctrine of the survival of the theoretical faculty after death reflects the problematic nature of the conclusions that seem to follow from Aristotle's own philosophy. In the *Metaphysics*, 1070 a 19, Aristotle argues for the survival of theoretical reason too as the only part of the soul that survives man's death. See

Kenelm Foster and Silvester Humphries' translation of Aristotle's *De Anima: In the Version of William of Moerbeke and The Commentary of St. Thomas Aquinas*. London: Routledge & Kegan Paul, 1951 & 1959, paragraphs 732–39, p. 425ff; Aquinas's commentary on pp. 428–29. These paragraphs appear in Barnes' edition of Aristotle's works as 431 & 432. See also De Anima, 407, 412, 413a, 415a. In the Nicomachen Ethics, Aristotle seems to suggest that death is the 'most terrible of all things', because '...it is the end, and nothing is thought to be any longer either good or bad for the dead....'; see Nicomachen Ethics, in Barnes' Artistotle's *Collected Works*, Vol. 2, 115a 26–30, 1116b 20–24, 1117b 7–12. The same vagueness is noticeable in Plato's Apology (para. 40) where Socrates argues '...there is great reason to hope that death is good; for one of two things— either death is a state of nothingness and utter consciousness, or, as men say, there is a change and migration of the soul from this world to another.' The key phrase seems to be 'as men say', which is used in reference to life after death but not in reference to 'another place' where 'all the dead abide.'

79. *Fana* is defined by Farabi as the 'non-existence of a possible existent' or the non-being of contingent beings. See *Al-Siyasa al-Madaniyya*, p. 56. See also, p. 39 on the indestructibility of matter and the destructibility of the form.

80. *Al-Siyasa al-Madaniyya, op. cit.*, p. 83 (5–10), p. 87(5–17). Farabi uses the term, 'batalat', which means abolished, nullified. Among the wicked, Farabi lists those who cannot be guided or taught the virtues, the nawabet or the weeds among the inhabitants of the city, and those who are bestial by nature who must be treated as beasts—to be used if useful or destroyed if harmful.

81. Farabi, *Al-Madina al-Fadila, op. cit.*, chapter 19, pp. 80–86. Ibn Rushd, in order to reconcile philosophy with Ghazzali's charge of atheism for denying bodily resurrection, admitted the possibility that God, on the Day of Judgment, may endow souls with totally new matter that is unique to each soul.

82. *Al-Madina al-Fadila, op. cit.*, ch. 30, pp. 137–38; see Walzer, *The Perfect State, op. cit.*, pp. 265–67, esp. p. 267(1–6). See also Siyasa Madaniyyah, p. 82(5–15).

83. *Al-Madinah al-Fadila, op. cit.*, pp. 144–45.

84. See *Al-Madina al-Fadila, op. cit.*, pp. 134–36; pp. 137–38; pp. 139–41, pp. 102–3; *The Perfect State, op. cit.*, pp. 200–4, 206–10, pp. 242–44. These are the wicked souls of 'false philosophers' and 'false prophets'.

85. *Al-Madina al-Fadila, op. cit.*, p. 143; *The Perfect State, op. cit.*, p. 273.

86. *Al-Madina al-Fadila, op. cit.*, p. 143; *The Perfect State, op. cit.*, p. 273.

87. *Al-Madina al-Fadila, op. cit.*, p. 144; *The Perfect State, op. cit.*, p. 275.

88. 'Nukat Abi Nasr Fi ma Yaseh Wa la yaseh Min Ahkam al-Nujum', *Al-Thamara, op. cit.*, p. 106 (18–23).

10 Khomeini's Doctrine of Legitimacy

Majid Tehranian

There are few contemporary political leaders who have attracted as much attention, curiosity and bewilderment as Ayatollah Khomeini. At first glance, Khomeini appeared as an historical anachronism. He did not fit the stalk image of a twentieth-century revolutionary dictator. He defied the ordinary explanations of a despot craving absolute power. At the age of 89, when he died on 3 June 1989, he was too old to be considered as one in search of personal power, too frugal in his living style to be viewed as a fortune hunter, too independent of his family ties to be accused of building a dynasty, too diverse in his leadership style to be suspected of constructing a modern political party, and too much of a traditionalist to be considered as the architect of a revolutionary totalitarian state.

Andrew Young, the former United States Ambassador to the United Nations, called him—in a moment of enthusiasm in 1979—the equivalent of a modern day saint. Dariush Shayegan, an Iranian intellectual, likened him to Mahatma Gandhi. Oriana Fallaci, the Italian reporter/novelist, viewed him as a 'shrewd fanatic' (Fallaci, 1979, 1981). Mansour Farhang, a former Iranian Ambassador to the United Nations who served in Khomeini's early regime, labelled him as 'criminally insane.'[1] Contemporary novelist/reporter Naipaul perhaps captured Khomeini's contradictory images most poignantly in his reactions to two photographs of the leader he encountered in Tehran. The first showed Khomeini, '...as hard eyed and sensual and unreliable and roguish-looking as an enemy might have been portrayed.' The second revealed '...his old man's eyes held victory. No frown, no gesture of defiance, no clenched fist: the hands were the hands of the man of peace.'[2]

To understand Khomeini and his place in history, we are clearly in need of some historical perspective. Psychological categories and subjective impressions tend to lose their poignancy and relevance with rapidly changing circumstances. Indeed, the first two of the above characterizations of Khomeini have already been recanted by their authors, while the last three will probably seem remote with the passage of time. The purpose of this essay is therefore to focus on the phenomenon of Khomeinism rather than Khomeini, to examine the roots of Islamic fundamentalism of which Khomeini formed a vital part, to review the Shi'a Islamic *Ulema's* revolutionary role in Iran, and finally to put Khomeini's doctrines of political legitimacy and political leadership in that historical context.

THE HISTORICAL ROOTS OF ISLAMIC FUNDAMENTALISM

Fundamentalism, or perhaps more accurately, 'populism' is not a novel religious phenomenon in Islam, although its current political and ideological manifestations are new.[3] By contrast to Christian fundamentalism which is an ultra-conservative movement, Islamic fundamentalism is a peculiar melange of modernity and tradition, radicalism and obscurantism—more analogous to Christian Puritanism and its historic roots than to fundamentalism. To live strictly according to the rule of the *Shari'a*, the Divine Law of Islam, has been an aspiration commonly shared among Muslims for centuries. The *New Testament* incorporates the record of Divine Revelation, but the *Quran* is considered by Muslims as *the* Word of God to be obeyed completely and unconditionally. The *Shari'a* is thus based on four pillars: Quranic injunctions, the *sunna* (tradition) of the Prophet, *qiyas* (or the principle of analogy), and *ijm'a* (or the consensus of the Muslim community). While the first two are givens, the latter two have provided considerable room for interpretation and have led to the development of at least four generally acknowledged schools of law in Sunni Islam, the majority sect, and one in Shi'a Islam, the minority sect primarily found in Iran, Iraq and Lebanon.

There has been, of course, always a difference found among the five competing schools in their relative adherence to a strict versus a liberal interpretation of the *Shari'a*. The current puritanical revolutionary movement in Islam, however, cuts across that division and may be dated back only to the mid-nineteenth century.[4] In response to increasing western penetration, a Pan-Islamic movement rapidly spread throughout the Muslim world during the second half of the nineteenth century which could be considered as the political and religious forerunner of the current upheavals. This represented a threefold response to a threefold challenge from the West. In reaction to the external domination of the West, it called for pan-Islamic unity to resist military, political and economic subjugation. In response to the internal domination of western supported oligarchies and governments, it mobilized the masses for a series of liberal, nationalist and constitutional revolutions occurring in Iran, Turkey and Egypt at the turn of the century. In recognition of the decline and decay of religious faith, undermined both by superstitious accretions as well as secular tendencies, it also called for a new vitality and purification of the *Shari'a*. While there was considerable agreement among the *Ulema*, the learned men of Islam, and the faithful on the first two objectives, the third programme proved far more difficult than initially believed. Some shrewd though conservative members of the *Ulema*, like Shaikh Fazlullah Nuri in Iran, readily recognised the inherent contradictions between a divinely revealed law, the *Shari'a*, and the emerging constitutional forms of secular legislation for which other members of the *Ulema* had agitated. Others, like Mohammad Iqbal in Pakistan and Muhammad Abduh and Rashid Rida in Egypt, opted for a reformation of the *Shari'a* along a modernist path and outside the political sphere.

The Failure of Secular Ideologies

In the meantime, the secular ideologies of progress imported from the West, namely, nationalism, liberalism and Marxism, continued to penetrate the Muslim world.[5] In the political sphere, this meant the establishment of secular nationalist regimes by Attaturk in Turkey, Reza Shah in Iran, the Wafd in Egypt. These regimes tried to replace the *Shari'a* with western systems of law and justice, to secularize education, and to modernize the entire fabric of society. This transformation included a very important change in the position of women. In the economic sphere, the creation of centralized nation-state systems led first to the construction of economic infrastructures including transportation and communication, power, and banking systems and subsequently to the introduction of import-substitution industries and the increasing appendage of the national economies to the international capitalist market. In the cultural sphere, the increasing penetration of Muslim societies by imported western cultural artifacts and mass media led to increasing levels of ideological conflict among the competing traditional and modern world-views.

The secular ideologies of progress have largely failed to capture the imagination and loyalty of the masses on several grounds. First and foremost, these ideologies were foreign imports and lacked indigenous historic roots. The individuals and social groups that served as the carriers of nationalism, liberalism or Marxism have often represented social and cultural elites themselves alienated from their own cultural traditions through years of western residence or westernized education. Second, the increasing hegemony of the two world political and economic systems—as represented by the military, technological and economic domination of the United States and the former Soviet Union—had increasingly left little room for the autonomy of the liberal/nationalist or Marxist/nationalist movements. As illustrated by the cases of the Shah's regime in Iran, the Marxist regime in Afghanistan and the nationalist military regimes in Egypt, Iraq and Syria, an independent course of development has proved difficult if not impossible. And last but not least, the exodus of vast numbers of traditional Muslim peasants to the cities in search of employment and identity alongside a demographic revolution whereby those below the age of 20 make up 50 per cent of the population, have combined to create conditions ripe for revolution. The secular ideologies of progress, however, could not compensate these transient, alienated and exploited segments of the population for the decomposition of traditional religious ontological securities and social identity.

Fundamentalism as Counter-Modernization

The combination of these factors, in addition to a radicalization of the *Ulema* and a rising popular nostalgia for the lost innocence and cohesion of the past, have brought about an ideological revolution in the Muslim world that is at once revolutionary and obscurantist. What is going on in the Muslim world, however, is not without historical precedence. Most countries going through the initial phases of industrialization have experienced the phenomenon of counter-modernization, which might be called 'the Rousseau effect'.[6] It was perhaps the romantic revolutionary philosopher Jean Jacques Rousseau who first articulated a theory of counter-modernization. His formulation of the sense of popular disenchantment with the depersonalizing, alienating and abstracting effects of modern industrial society provided a revolutionary political philosophy that called for a radical attempt to recapture the innocence of 'the noble savage' and the natural hegemony of a golden past. Jefferson's call for rural democracy, Gandhi's advocacy of return to cottage industries in India, and Ayatollah Khomeini's zeal for a return to the purity and justice of pristine Islam are different ideological expressions of similar sentiments.

However, the past, even if it were ideal, cannot be brought back to life. Efforts to do so through persuasion will lead to romantic ideological lip service, as exemplified by the canonization of Jefferson and Gandhi in the United States and India. Attempts to recapture the past through violence and coercion, will ultimately result in a breakdown of society and all traditions of civility—including those of Islam. In this sense, Ayatollah Khomeini has been perhaps as effective in demythologizing Islam as the Shah was in demythologizing monarchy in Iran.

To say this, however, is not to consider fundamentalism as a political and ideological phenomenon that will soon wither away. Resurging Islamic fundamentalism draws on the conditions of foreign domination, elite exploitation, socio-cultural dislocation, mass mobilization and the continuing failure of the more progressive political ideologies and leaderships to provide viable alternatives. The Muslim world today stands in the twilight of tradition and modernity, suffering from the obscurantisms and inequities of both. Despotic modernization, either imposed by colonial or post-colonial secular elites, has often dislocated the traditional society without necessarily substituting a new rational and humane order. It has undermined the self-sufficiency of the indigenous economy without providing for productive interdependence; and it has destroyed the legitimacy of the old polity without constructing a new peace and justice. It has homogenized and depersonalized the old cultural patterns without a new sense of cultural autonomy and creativity. The obscurantism and timidity of traditional societies are thus mixed with the greed and ceaseless anxieties of modernity to produce atomized societies held together by the fears and shame of backwardness.

THE *ULEMA'S* REVOLUTIONARY ROLE IN IRAN

In Iran this increasingly dualistic structure of Muslim society, economy and polity revealed itself perhaps above all in the troubled ideological situation of the country prior to the Revolution of 1979.[7] We can best examine the salient features of this dualism in terms of the two competing religious and secular ideologies, structures, and processes of social communication—living autonomously side by side with immense frictions wherever and whenever they collided.

Secularization in Iran, as in the rest of the Islamic world, has faced the formidable obstacle that Islam recognizes no separation between spiritual and temporal authority. Muslims of all sectarian persuasions believe that Prophet Mohammad established an ideal Community of Believers in Medina within the short period of ten years from his exodus in AD 622 to his death in 632.

The inception of Christianity dates from the birth of Christ; however, the Islamic era does not begin with Mohammed's birth. It dates from the '*hegira*', the Exodus of Mohammad from Mecca to Medina. Muslims of the Sunni faith extend their conception of the ideal Islamic State to the period of rule by the four '*khulafa al-Rashidun*' (the Rightly-Guided Successors of Mohammad), while the Shi'a maintain that succession rightly belongs to Mohammad's cousin and son-in-law Ali, the fourth Sunni Caliph of Islam, and his direct descendants.

The differences in doctrine have been of considerable historical importance up to this day. Because the Shi'ites have often been in minority, they have generally provided in Islamic history a revolutionary ideological challenge to the established powers. Shi'ism was declared a state religion in Iran and gained a majority position during the sixteenth century. But its doctrines remained potentially revolutionary against any unjust temporal ruler.[8]

In matters of ideology and organization, Shi'ism continues to be distinct from Sunni Islam in two important respects. First, the doctrine of *imamat* in Shi'ism transfers the *temporal* as well as the spiritual authority of Ali to his direct descendants. Among the Ismaili Shi'ites, that authority has been transferred through the seventh Imam Ismail to his present descendant, the Agha Khan. In Iran, however, it is the 'Twelver' Shi'ites who dominate. For them, the transfer of power ceased with the disappearance of the twelfth Imam and is held in abeyance until he returns to save the world. In the meantime, all temporal power is considered to be illegitimate, to be tolerated only when and if it is exercised in accordance with the rule of the *Shari'a* as judged by the body of the *Ulema*. Shi'ism gives the *Ulema* a considerable veto power over the temporal authorities. It also maintains eschatological hopes for a second coming of the Mahdi, the twelfth Imam. Time and again, Mahdism has served revolutionary purposes in the Islamic world.

Secondly, the *Ulema's* position of strength in Shi'a doctrine is supplemented in Iran by the strength of the country's religious organization. Given the right cause, this communication network can mobilize vast numbers of people, as we have seen in Iran's three revolutionary movements in this century, including the Constitutional Revolution of 1905, the oil nationalization movement of 1950–53 and the Islamic Revolution of 1979, each imbued with religious indignation and inspired by a single-minded purpose.

The traditional autonomy of the *Ulema* from the state, buttressed by their independent sources of income from religious endowments and taxes, placed them very close to the mood of the people, giving them the position of a powerful counter-elite. Historically, the *Ulema* used this power to act as mediators between the ruling elites and the masses. However, their close association with the bazaar merchants and the liberal intelligentsia had always provided them with strong claims to political power. Under the Pahlavies, however, the relentless policy of westernization and secularization increasingly alienated the *Ulema* from the monarchy. The *Ulema's* religious, educational, legal and charitable institutions, wrapped into one integrated system, were considerably weakened by the encroachments of a secular and secularizing state.

However, another feature of the *Ulema's* religious organization—

namely, its polycentrism—gave them both the power to resist this repression and the ability to act when and if a unifying issue arose. The opportunity came after the bloody riots of June 1963 led by Ayatollah Khomeini and the radical *Ulema*. The *Ulema* and the monarchy were polarized as symbols for two diametrically opposed visions of the future of Iran. These two visions differed on almost every possible ground. The Islamic vision stemmed from an impulse to return to the purity and sacred justice of pristine Islam. The secular vision attempted to revitalize the pre-Islamic memories of Iranian nationalism in order to recapture the power and glory of Iran's imperial past. Not only did both visions thus clash in their reconstructions of the past but also in their utopian images of the future. The Islamic vision has been inextricably tied to Iran's cultural association with the Arabs and the rest of the Islamic world. The secular nationalist vision, however, wished desperately to wipe away all memories of Iran's subjugation to the Arabs, to purify the Persian language, and to revive pre-Islamic memories and political symbols. The responses to the western challenge have also been markedly different. Secular nationalism has rejected western political domination but has accepted and indeed welcomed western cultural values. In extreme cases, the former is enamoured by the western influences to the extent of what is called westomania, '*gharbzadegi*' while the latter feels threatened by the West to the extent of xenophobia. All these ideological rationalizations derived from the increasing gulf that separated the life-styles of the westernised elite and the deeply religious masses.[9]

A central element of the Pahlavies' cultural policy was the reconstruction of Iranian historical consciousness around the memory of its imperial past, and the destruction of everything that might stand in its way. The choice of the dynasty name of 'Pahlavi', after Iran's dominant pre-Islamic language, was itself symbolic. The organization of an Academy of Iranian Languages to purify Persian, the return to the grandeur and massive architectural style of the Achaemenids, the forced adoption of western clothes, and the deprecation of the country's traditional religious and lay clothing styles, the celebration of Persian kinghood on the 2500 anniversary of the Persian Empire and the 50th anniversary of the Pahlavi dynasty, the changes of calendar, first from the Islamic lunar to the Persian solar and then from '*hegira*' (1355) to '*Shahanshani*' (2535), were all aspects of the same policy of purification. Memories of the constitutional revolutionary period, and of the period of 1941–53, when a quasi-liberal parliamentary system was in operation, were severely repressed. The only major books on the history of the Mosaddeq era that remained in circulation were those of the Shah's autobiography, *Mission for My Country*, and a few histories which glorified His Majesty's role in the recapture of Azerbaijan and in the nationalization of oil.[10]

A nation without historical memory is a nation lost. Persians, however, have never had to rely entirely on historical documentation for their memories. This is why Ferdowsi's epic poem, *The Shahnameh*, and the legends of the martyrdoms of Hussein and so many other saints, are part of Iran's oral tradition of vivid drama and meaning.[11] But the cultural policy of historical vivisection did lead unwittingly to historical schizophrenia. Consider that 50 per cent of the population was illiterate, and 50 per cent was below the age of 20. Many were unable to remember the liberal constitutionalists. They did, however, have a strong memory of the martyrdom of legendary heroes, and they simultaneously acquired a religious and quasi-Marxist revolutionary ideology through information networks and underground publications.

In this context it was no wonder that for leadership, Iranian society turned to a sector least affected by the corrupting influences of modernization, namely the *Ulema*. Because the *Ulema* under the Pahlavies had been progressively stripped off their control over the legal, educational, charitable, and endowment (*waqf*) institutions while still retaining their spiritual powers through the mosque and *minbar* (the pulpit), they had both the cause and the means to stir up opposition. Twice in this century, the *Ulema* had entered into an alliance with the bazaar merchants and the liberal intelligentsia in campaigns to limit the monarchy. In the Constitutional Revolution of 1905–11 and the oil nationalization movement of 1951–53; it was the liberal intellectuals who led the way and the *Ulema* who provided the mass support, but the situation had radically changed in the meantime.[12] The riots of 1963, taking place in protest against 'the White Revolution', were the harbinger of the new politics to come. They were organized and almost exclusively led from Qom with Ayatollah Khomeini as its leading spokesman. They had been preceded by a visit paid to Qom by the Shah, in December 1962, during which he had castigated the radical *Ulema*, as 'obscurantist, backward, and lice-ridden', to be crushed if they resisted his enlightened reforms. This was followed by the referendum of January

1963 which was a shallow victory for the six-point reform. The latter was in fact rejected in the following June by massive riots. The ties between the monarchy and the radical *Ulema*, which had, since the coup of 1953, bound them together against the common threat of Communism, were finally severed. For the moment, the radical *Ulema* seemed to have been isolated from their allies in bazaar and liberal intellectual circles. Their allies in the National Front were truly bewildered during the riots of 1963.

This was the beginning of a relentless struggle between the radical *Ulema* and embittered monarchical regime. In interviews conducted by the author with some leading religious leaders in 1974, the issues emerged quite clearly.[13] To the *Ulema*, who were not necessarily a monolithic and homogeneous group, it seemed as though the entire trend of Iranian society was going against their sense of truth, goodness and justice. Their arch-enemies, the Bahais, the secularizing technocrats, and their foreign advisors were ruling supreme in every niche and corner—in the court, in the armed forces, in SAVAK (the secret police), in important branches of the civil bureaucracy, and in the burgeoning financial and industrial enterprises. Having usurped the educational, legal, and charitable institutions from their hands, the monarchical regime was intent on taking their prerogatives away even in family and religious matters. The new Family Law of 1967–74 introduced measures that undermined some of the fundamental tenets of Islam on marriage and divorce. The grant of rights of suffrage to women, in 1963, the organization of the Women's Corps in 1968, the appointment of women to highly visible public offices, but above all, the display of a decadent life-style and permissive sexual relations grieved the *Ulema*. The organization of a Religious Corps in 1971, the drafting of theology graduates for religious services under the auspices of the military, the plans for the organization of an Islamic University in Mashhad, the change of calendar from Islamic *hegira* to the Imperial *Shahanshahi*, the introduction of daylight saving time that trespassed the *Shari'a* time, all were further indications of the arrogance of the new omnipotent state. These measures were deeply resented by all factions among the *Ulema*, but it took the political, economic, and moral exhaustion of the new secular society and the determination and persistence of the Khomeini faction to dismantle the monarchical power.

It was not, however, the *Ulema* alone who rejected the secular trends. A national survey, conducted in 1974 among some 5,000 of a cross-section of Iranian society, revealed the dominance of religious beliefs and attitudes.[14] In another survey, conducted in 1974 among three traditionally secular and secularizing social groups in Iranian society, namely, the communication elite, the professional broadcasters, and the university students, the trend towards strong religious sentiments was already unmistakable.

Despite the repressive official attitude towards religion, there was growing support for the pre-eminence of the Divine Law of Islam and an egalitarian spirit suggestive of Islamic fundamentalism. The different nationalist orientations constituted a significant ingredient in this mix of ideological sentiment, and remarkably the same groups of respondents who indicated strong support for Islamic fundamentalism were still positively inclined towards the secular liberalism of the National Front. The monarchical regime's ideological interest in pre-Islamic and technocratic features of nationalism was not negligible, but support for these emphases was comparatively soft. The monarchy was apparently unable to control the developing ideological mix, and society's yearning for religious certainty was explicit in the rejection of ideologies of alienation, including nihilism, opportunism, cynicism and fatalism.

This ideological portrait of an important sector of Iranian society and opinion leadership, taken at a moment of material triumph, is revealing. It showed the strength of religious tendencies combined with nationalist preferences and the relative weakness of the government's ideological positions. But this portrait should not conceal the fact that each respondent had the opportunity of choosing a number of contradictory ideological positions. Thus, Islamic as well as secular and pristine, or pre-Islamic nationalist positions both scored relatively high. The combination of these positions may seem intellectually incompatible, but many respondents appear to have accepted them as emotionally valid and viable. The mosaic of cultural and historical forces which have shaped the modern Persian mind are represented in this portrait, revealing the ideological zones of national consensus as well as cultural cleavages, psychological dualisms and schizophrenia. Since the three groups of respondents represented three different generations, social strata, and levels of political access, the differences as well as the similarities were all the more significant. The underlying reality of this composite ideological portrait was the fact of an increasing social, economic, and cultural cleavage which cut across age, social class and politics.

The massive demonstrations in the autumn of 1978 were remarkable, among other things, for being predominantly made up of the younger generation and for the singular absence of any references to Mosaddeq, the charismatic liberal constitutionalist leader of the early-fifties. Instead, large portraits of Ayatollah Khomeini and the martyrs of the new urban guerrilla struggles were prominently displayed everywhere. The underlying theme of the demonstrations was the expectation of a second coming: For years, the greatest festival spontaneously celebrated by the people was neither Nowruz, the Persian New Year, dating to pre-Islamic Zoroastrian times, nor the birthday of the Prophet. It was, as banners throughout the country declared on those blessed occasions, 'the sacred birthday of His Majesty Imam Mahdi.' Two legitimacies, one spiritual and utopian, the other temporal and ideological, ruled Iran in the name of two competing regimes.

The emergence of two regimes with two belief-systems dramatically revealed itself in the two separate but intertwined modes of political communication. The secular view was profoundly westernized, and couched in the Faustian terms of a remorseless search for power by means of the mastery of science and technology. The Shah himself typified such an attitude in his love of gadgets, particularly military gadgets, his fetish for high, capital-intensive technology (e.g., nuclear energy, in a country endowed with immense resources of oil and natural gas), and in his messianic ambition to transform Iran within 20 years into the world's fifth major industrial power. Symbolic throughout, one of his first acts after returning to power in 1953 was to change the name of the Ministry of Defence to the Ministry of War. But all this show of strength was undermined by a tragic undercurrent of mysticism and martyrdom, which was ironically apparent in the constant appeal to the unseen powers who had seemingly protected his life in four assassination attempts, a steadfast call to meet his destiny, and in the end a resignation to accept the inevitable instead of engaging in a bloody counter-revolution.[15]

The same themes of power, blood, and martyrdom were obviously much more emphatic in the religious opposition's world-view. The unconscious choice of Dr. Mosaddeq and Ayatollah Khomeini as charismatic leaders in less than a generation reveals a profound continuity of historical archetypes. The historical consciousness of Iranians has always been deeply moved by the memory of those heroic martyrs who achieved positions of spiritual power through acts of defiance against tyrants, by shedding their blood to redeem the weak and the oppressed. The legendary Siyavosh in the 'Shahnameh', Imam Hossain in Shi'ite history, and Hallaj in Sufi memory, represent such archetypes. Dr. Mosaddeq's combination of (apparent) weakness and determination, and Ayatollah Khomeini's righteous yet (apparently) selfless cause, represented similar drives to power through righteousness and martyrdom.

KHOMEINI'S DOCTRINES OF POLITICAL LEGITIMACY

Within these terms of reference, the ideological and political significance of Ayatollah Khomeini rested in the innovations he introduced into the Shi'a doctrines of political legitimacy. These transformed Shi'ism from an oppositionist to a revolutionary force.[16] To be fully understood, these innovations should be considered from a historical perspective.[17] The position of Shi'a political doctrine vis-a-vis the state and established political power has been historically one of grudging tolerance, provided the ruling Shah or Sultan protects the *Shari'a*. Law and order have been considered by the consensus of the *Ulema* always preferable to conditions of lawlessness and violence.

In the early-fifties, for instance, the alliance between the liberal nationalists led by Dr. Mosaddeq and the radical *Ulema* led by Ayatollah Kashani broke down not only because of personal and ideological incompatibility but also due to increasing political in stability and the threat of Communism. Some elements of the *Ulema*, including Ayatollah Kashani who is considered by Khomeini and his followers as their hero, made an alliance with the monarchy in the *coup d'état* of 1953 in the hope of greater influence and political stability.[18] With the disaffection of Kashani from the restored monarchy, the tensions arose once again.

Following the death of Ayatollah Boroujerdi, the grand Shi'a Mujtahed in 1961, the last conservative links between the *Ulema* and the monarchy were ruptured and the tensions came into the open as never before. The monarchical regime tried unsuccessfully to transfer the seat of *marj'a taqlid* from Qom to outside the country, by cabling its condolences to Ayatollah Hakim in Najaf, Iraq. In the meantime, the continuing secularist policies of the state, particularly the reforms of the White Revolution, the continuing operation of the Fadaiyan-i-Islam guerrillas, the organization of new urban guerrilla movements under the aegis of Islam, and the increasing pauperization and radicalization of the clerical students in Qom—all led to the emergence of Ayatollah Khomeini as the dominant radical voice against monarchy.

The bloody riots of June 1963 were the most visible turning point in the mosque-state relations. Whereas before that date, the institution of monarchy and the Fundamental Laws of 1905, which had established the Constitutional Monarchy, had rarely been attacked, the ideological position of the radical *Ulema* thereafter directly challenged secular government. Khomeini's innovative ideas, reflected in his lectures in exile delivered in Najaf and published subsequently under a variety of titles including *Wilayat-e-Faghih* (*The Trusteeship of the Jurist*), met the needs of the hour.

In this ideological tract, Khomeini set forth his departure from traditional Shi'a views with a few polemical syllogisms. First, he argued, that the *Quran* has commanded Muslims to 'Obey Allah and Obey His Messenger and those of him who are first in command.' Second, Imam Ali and his male descendants up to the twelfth Hidden Imam are the rightful successors of the Prophet. Third—and here is a quantum leap from traditional Shi'a doctrines— they, and in their absence, the *fughaha* (the jurists of the *Shari'a*) who are the rightful representatives of the Hidden Imam, must, therefore, be obeyed in spiritual as well as temporal matters. Fourth, it follows that from an Islamic point of view, any form of government other than the direct rule of the *Shari'a* and its custodians, i.e., the Muslim jurists, is unconstitutional. Fifth, this applies especially to monarchy, which is at any rate an usurpation, and any form of parliamentary legislation which can only be sacrilegious. Because the Islamic Divine Law is given once and for all, Khomeini proudly declared that there is no legislation in Islam. He instructed: '...if at all, we should therefore have only a Majlis for planning.'

•In one great ideological sweep, Ayatollah Khomeini obliterated the traditional Shi'a doctrines of legitimacy which subtly made room for the co-existence of the temporal and spiritual authorities and a system of checks and balances. The assumption by Khomeini of the title of imam reserved in Shi'a theology only for Imam Ali and his eleven direct male descendants, was a symbolic gesture signifying this radical change. The new doctrine also provided much needed legitimacy for the new revolutionary leadership claims of a new class of young, pauperized, marginal and alienated clerics educated in the dialectics of Shi'a Islam, Marxism and Ali Shari'ati's syncretic ideas attempting to consummate this uneasy ideological marriage. Furthermore, this doctrine met the aspirations of the radical *Ulema* who felt they had been betrayed twice in this century by their liberal nationalist allies. While this doctrine provided a bridge to the growingly uprooted and marginal urban population, it also contained the seeds of its own future destruction. By assuming direct political responsibility for the government, the Shi'a utopia stood to lose much of its mystical appeal while the Shi'a clergy would be tainted by the inevitable corruptions of temporal power.[19]

Khomeini's doctrine of legitimacy attempted to address three important political functions by dealing with the long standing problems of authority (in the national domain), identity (in the personal domain), and legitimacy (in the political linkages between the state and the individual). All three problems have remained somewhat unresolved in the classical, medieval as well as modern Islamic political theory.

The problem of authority is an old one in Islam. It led, at the dawn of Islamic history, to Islam's First Civil War giving rise to the great schism between Sunni and Shi'a Islam. A belief in the unity of the spiritual and temporal authorities is, nevertheless, common to both main sects of Islam. Beginning with the Ummayads, however, secular dynasties largely took over the rule of the new Islamic empires. Reconciling a continuing belief in the unity of the temporal and spiritual authorities with the historical fact of secular domination, therefore, became a central problem of Islamic political theory. This problem has not been satisfactorily resolved to this day. However, three doctrines have emerged to attempt a resolution, i.e., the Doctrines of the Just Sultan (*sultan-i-a'del*), the Hidden Imam (*imam-i-qa'ib*), and the Trusteeship of the Jurists (*wilayat-i-faqih*). The last is Khomeini's chief contribution.

The doctrine of the Just Sultan was developed by the medieval *Ulema* to legitimate the authority of the secular rulers on the condition that they perform in accordance with the rules of the *Shari'a*. In the modern nation-state system, the same doctrine is invoked to legitimate the authority of the state if it does not infringe upon the authorities of the *Shari'a* and the *Ulema*. For the conservative *Ulema*, this provides a doctrine of authority that allows co-existence between religious and secular leaders, thus avoiding the evil that may ensue from political disorder and chaos.

The Doctrine of the Hidden Imam was developed to deny altogether the possibility of legitimate rule in the absence of the Hidden Imam—the Mahdi, the twelfth of Ali's direct descendants to be regarded as *imam-i-ma'sum* (Immaculate Imam). The doctrine has been embraced primarily by the Shi'a *Ulema* but also adopted by some Sunni *Ulema*. Imam Mahdi's disappearance at the age of fifteen provided Muslims with a messianic expectation of a second coming. Historically, this doctrine has served as a source of numerous uprisings against the established order in both the Shi'a and Sunni worlds. The nineteenth century Mahdist revolt in Sudan against the British, provides but one well-known example. The doctrine has also served as a source for the emergence of new sects, such as the Bahai. Generally speaking, the conservative as well as liberal perspectives in Shi'a Islam have adopted this position in order to pressure the state to conform to Islamic principles and precepts without acceding to its claims of legitimacy.

Khomeini's Doctrine of Trusteeship of the Jurists is a radical departure from the previous two doctrines. It essentially proposes a theocratic state. This doctrine calls for a fusion of the spiritual and temporal authorities within the Muslim jurists as the legitimate heirs to the authority of God, the Prophet, and the Immaculate Imams. In arguing his case, Khomeini draws from Quranic injunctions as well as the traditions of the Prophet of the Imams. The central Quranic injunction comes in the following sura frequently quoted by Khomeini:

In the Name of God, The Compassionate, The Merciful.
Verily God commands you to return trusts to their owners, and to act with justice when you rule among men. *Verily God counsels you thus, and God is all-hearing, all-seeing. O you who believe, obey God and obey the Messenger and the holders of authority from among you.* When you dispute each other concerning a thing, refer it to God and His Messenger; if you believe in God and the Last Day, this will be best for you and the result, most beneficial.[20] (emphasis added)

Khomeini then goes on to define what 'trusts' mean and who 'the holders of authority' are. He distinguishes between trusts pertaining to men (i.e., their property), and those pertaining to the Creator (i.e., the ordinances of the *Shari'a*). According to the Shi'a beliefs, following the death of the Prophet, rightful authority belongs to the designated successors of the Prophet—to Ali and his male descendants. To support his thesis that the *Fuqaha* (plural of *Faqih*, a jurist) have been collectively entrusted with the responsibilities of governance, Khomeini also quotes two reports by Abu Khadija and 'Umar ibn Hanzala on a ruling by Imam Sadiq Ja'far, the founder of the Shi'a Ja'fari school of law:

Abu Khadija, one of the trusted companions of Imam Sadiq (upon whom be peace), relates: 'I was commanded by the Imam to convey the following message to our friends [i.e. the Shi'a]: "When enmity and dispute arise among you, or you disagree concerning the receipt or payment of a sum of money, be sure not to refer the matter to one of these malefactors for judgement. Designate as judge and arbiter someone among you who is acquainted with our injunctions concerning what is permitted and prohibited, for I appoint such a man as judge over you. Let none of you take your complaint against another of you to the tyrannical ruling power."[21]

'According to this tradition', Khomeini concludes, 'the 'ulama of Islam have been appointed by the Imam (upon whom be peace) to the position of ruler and judge; and these positions belong to them in perpetuity.' Khomeini goes on further to make a distinction between the independent *fuqaha* and the servile *akhund*. The *fuqaha* 'are untouched by guilt', while the *akhunds* who joined the service of government in the past ages did not belong to our school. Not only did our *fuqaha* oppose the rulers, they also suffered imprisonment and torture on account of their disobedience.'

This doctrine has served as the cornerstone of the new Islamic state and constitution in Iran. Following a controversy in which several of the liberal supporters of Khomeini, notably Bazargan and Bani-Sadr, had to be repudiated for their opposition to the doctrine, the Constitution also designated Ayatollah Khomeini as the Supreme *Faqih*—the head of state, the commander-in-chief, and the main arbiter of legal and political disputes. Just before Khomeini's death, however, the problem of succession was dealt with by a constitutional revision that substantially separated the religious and symbolic functions of the *Faqih* from its secular and substantive functions. Following his death, the position of the *Faqih* was swiftly conferred by the Council of Experts on Ayatollah Khomeini, while Ali Akbar Heshemi Rafsanjani was elected to the newly-strengthened presidency. The office of the prime minister was abolished.

Since charismatic leadership can seldom be passed on, it is clear that the new *Faqih* does not enjoy Ayatollah Khomeini's prestige and power. By contrast, the presidency has gained considerably in effective power. If the historical precedence of the first Rightly-Guided Caliphs of Islam is any indication, the post of *Faqih* will not easily survive the rigors of politics. At the end, like the caliphate itself, it will be probably turned into a ceremonial function or completely abandoned. Under the best of circumstances, in any case, combining spiritual and temporal authorities has historically proved problematical. Witness, for example, the fates of the caliphate in Islam, the papacy in Christianity, and emperor worship in Japan.

The problem of 'identity' in Islamic political theories is similarly complex and subject to a variety of conservative, liberal and revolutionary interpretations. In this respect, the conservative and revolutionary Islamic perspectives come perhaps closer to each other than to the liberal views. While a liberal perspective sees no serious problem for a modern Muslim to hold multiple identities as a Muslim, an Arab, a Persian or a Turk, the conservative and revolutionary perspectives insist on the primacy if not the singularity of the Islamic identity. Revolutionary Islam may be also considered as neo-conservative in that it radically rejects any secular identities that might encroach upon the Muslim identity and loyalty of the believers. Khomeini's position on this question harks back to the early Islamic debate on the problem of *asabiyya*, or ethnic loyalty. In the modern context, *asabiyya* is interpreted as nationalism and national loyalty, and has been condemned by Khomeini and his strict followers as strongly as traditional tribal and ethnic loyalties.

Theories of legitimacy in modern Islam have similarly followed a diversity of perspectives that, in the interest of convenience more than accuracy, can again be labelled as conservative, liberal and revolutionary. The conservative views, such as those of the *Ulema* in Saudi Arabia and Pakistan, have been satisfied with the legitimacy of the state so long as the fundamental laws of the *Shari'a* are observed. These include, of course, an extension of those rules to all spheres of social life, including prohibitions of usury, alcohol, and sexual immodesty.

The liberal views, such as those of former prime minister, Mehdi Bazargan, and the late Ayatollah Shariatmadari in Iran, have emerged from a long tradition of an Islamic alliance with the cause of liberal constitutionalism. In this perspective, the fundamental cause of Islamic decline and decay has been perceived to be arbitrary rule by autocratic potentates. Islamic modernism, from Al-Afghani to Muhammad Abduh and Rashid Réda, thus supported a variety of constitutionalist movements in Turkey, Iran, and Egypt. However, to the extent that constitutionalism has meant some degree of secularization of law and education, the liberal perspective has held that some guarantees must be imposed upon modern legislators to observe the Islamic precepts. Iran's Constitution of 1909, for instance, provided for a committee of five *Mujahids*, or Shi'a *Ulema* with the right of issuing *fatwa*, i.e., religiously binding decrees, to oversee the laws passed by the *Majlis*. This provision was, however, never observed by the governments in power.

The revolutionary perspectives have thus evolved out of the failure of the liberal democratic programmes. To Khomeini, the words 'democracy' and 'liberalism' were anathema. In this connection, he wrote:

Islamic Government does not correspond to any of the existing forms of government. For example, it is not a tyranny, where the head of state can deal arbitrarily with the property and lives of the people, making use of them as he wills, putting to death anyone he wishes, and enriching anyone he wishes, by granting landed estates and distributing the property and holdings of the people. The most Noble Messenger (peace be upon him), the Commander of the Faithful (peace be upon him), and the other caliphs did not have such powers. *Islamic government is neither tyrannical nor absolute, but constitutional. It is not constitutional in the current sense of the word, i.e. based on the approval of laws in accordance with the opinion of the majority. It is constitutional in the sense that the rulers are subject to a certain set of conditions in governing and administering the country, conditions that are set forth in the Noble Qur'an and the sunna of the Most Noble Messenger. It* is the laws and ordinances of Islam comprising this set of conditions that must be observed and practised. Islamic government may be therefore defined as the rule of divine law over men.[22] (emphasis added)

From here, Khomeini goes on to argue that

> ...the fundamental difference between Islamic government, on the one hand, and constitutional monarchies and republics, on the other, is this: whereas the representatives of the people or the monarch in such regimes engage in legislation, in Islam the legislative power and competence to establish laws belong exclusively to God Almighty.... No one has the right to legislate and no law may be executed except the law of the Divine Legislator. It is for this reason that in an Islamic government, a simple planning body takes the place of the legislative assembly that is one of the three branches of government.[23]

It is clear from Khomeini's exposition in this treatise as well as from his subsequent practices that his doctrine of legitimacy focuses on the necessity for a Supreme *Faqih*. 'The qualifications essential for the ruler', he writes, 'derive directly from the nature and form of Islamic government. In addition to general qualifications like intelligence and administrative ability, there are two other essential qualifications: knowledge of the law and justice.' Furthermore, he asks rhetorically:

> Can we afford to sit nonchalantly on our hands while our enemies do whatever they want?...Is that the way it should be? Or is it rather that government is necessary, and that the function of government that existed from the beginning of Islam down to the time of the Twelfth Imam (upon whom be peace) is still enjoined upon us by God after the Occultation even though He has appointed no particular individual to that function?

Khomeini's doctrine of legitimacy thus presents a complex mix of tradition and modernity. In its essentials, the doctrine is grounded in the well-established Islamic traditions of unity of spiritual and temporal authorities, the primacy of the *Shari'a*, the necessity for the Islamic government to conform to the rules of the *Shari'a*, and the leadership of the *Ulema* as custodians of the Divine Law. In fact, he begins his treatise by asserting that '...the governance of the *Faqih* is a subject that in itself elicits immediate assent and has little need of demonstration...'[24] He goes on, however, for the next 120 pages to present a complex of rational and empirical evidence to support this self-evident truth!

The reason for this clearly lies in the fact that the doctrine has to contend with the other two indigenous doctrines of the Just Sultan and the Hidden Imam as well as with the doctrines of popular sovereignty borrowed from the modern West, hence Khomeini goes back to the classical Islamic views of the unity of spiritual and temporal authorities, while incorporating the medieval Islamic theories of *Madineh Fazeleh* (*the Virtuous City*). (See the chapter by Yusuf K. Umar in this volume.) He assigns the role of 'the philosopher-king' to the Supreme *Faqih*, while in a modern, pragmatic way recognising the need for organisation and leadership—a task he gives to the *Ulema* as a collective body. For Khomeini, therefore, the Ulema serve as the revolutionary vanguard of a party of pristine Islam dedicated to the overthrow of domestic, secular potentates and the foreign oppressors. Paradoxical as it may seem, he presents a revolutionary conservative whose cause elicits great emotional response among modern Muslims without, however, providing a satisfactory, theoretical and practical resolution to the complex, threefold problems of authority, identity and legitimacy in the modern world. His monist views defy the pluralist realities of that world.

KHOMEINISM: THE FUTURE OF AN ILLUSION

Islam, like many other great religions, has dramatically influenced the course of secular history by its spiritual, moral and political force. But in reconstructing a modern society, polity and economy, Islam faces essentially the same challenges as those confronting the secular ideologies. Dogmas, whether religious or secular in origin, are fundamentally at odds with modern, social, economic, and political problems which have mundane roots and demand ever-changing, corrective, and incremental legislation. Religious discourse seems best suited to responding to the spiritual longings and ontological insecurities of man, born out of his conditions of mortality, fragility and immorality. By contrast, the epistemologies of modern science and political ideologies tend to be better equipped for dealing with the problems of accelerating social and technological change which seems to be the lot of modern man.

Modern science, religion and ideology provide three symbolic structures, epistemologies and discourse strategies for the resolution or amelioration of the inherent contradictions and sufferings of the processes of social change. However, whenever one of these strategies of discourse tries to usurp the functions of the other two, we tend to get a depreciation of all three and the failure of each to perform its own unique integrative functions in its own sphere of competence. The language of science is primarily cognitive, its sphere of action primarily objective reality, its method of enquiry, trial and error, construction of hypotheses, empirical research or experimentation, its conclusions tentative and subject to the discovery of new evidence.

By contrast, the language of religion is affective. Its primary sphere of action derives from subjective truths and the human conditions of death, suffering and evil. Its methods of enquiry depend on faith and seeking, discipleship and mastership. Its conclusions are self-consciously universal and everlasting. By further contrast, the language of ideology is primarily normative/behavioural. Its primary sphere of action brings into focus interplays of the subjective and the objective in the political arena. Its method of enquiry encompasses both the dogmatic and the pragmatic. Ideology appeals to faith as well as to facts, commitment as well as to skepticism; and its conclusions are tied to class or group interests, as these accommodate the changing tides of fortune.

The modern world has been, however, peculiarly prone to three types of cognitive tyranny out of which a variety of modern totalitarian ideologies and dictatorships have emerged. We may label these three as the corruptions of science into *scientism*, transformation of political ideologies into *totalistic ideologies*, and the appearance of traditional religions in the form of highly politicized, *fundamentalist revivals*. Each doctrine is, of course, closely associated with the cultural and political domination of a particular elite in modern society. Scientism is not only what Paul Tillich has aptly called 'the tyranny of the cognitive language', but also the ideological expression of the rise of the scientific-technocratic elites in modern industrial society. The claim that positive science is and should be the final arbiter of all truth, including truths in religion, politics and the arts, turns science into a powerful secular religion with little tolerance for alternative epistemologies and truth claims.

By contrast, modern totalitarian ideologies in their leftist as well as rightist varieties represent the rise of mass society and mass movements in which the depersonalized and alienated individual 'escapes from freedom'[25] by complete abdication to the collectivity, as the nation, or the proletariat, and its political party and charismatic leader. Modern totalitarian ideologies such as Nazism, Fascism and Stalinism usurped the functions of science in their attempts to mould scientific theories, as in the case of genetics, to fit their own political preferences regarding Aryan superiority or the dialectics of nature. They also attempted to usurp the functions of traditional religion by establishing a new political eschatology with the nation or the class as the chosen people and Aryan domination or dictatorship of the proletariat as the new kingdom of God on earth.

By further contrast, religious fundamentalism in a variety of different historical contexts, whether one speaks of Begin in Israel, the Moral Majority in the United States, or Khomeini in Iran, seems to represent the backlash of the traditional sectors of the population, led often by politically disenfranchized clerical classes, against the alienating, abstracting, and corrupting pressures of modern mass societies. Fundamentalism's usurpation of the functions of science and ideology is represented by generally anti-intellectual postures and claims for direct state power. The search for identity, meaning, and chastity in a complicated world characterized by the multiplicity of psychic demands, plurality of epistemologies, and seductive pressures is common to most fundamentalist revivals. A return to the Golden Age and its positivist certitudes, as expressed in the Holy Scriptures and interpreted by fundamentalist religious leaderships, is a further common theme.

Khomeinism in Iran, however, has some peculiarly Iranian and Third World qualities as well. It springs out of the long years of Shi'a suffering as a minority sect, hence its passion for martyrdom and vindication by blood, and its deep ambivalence towards power. Khomeinism has drawn on a xenophobia born of Iran's humiliating experiences of foreign domination in recent centuries. It has built upon a cult of personality in the tradition of worship of Imams and saints and this more than anything else distinguishes it from Sunni Islam. The Khomeini regime has a clear memory of the traditional power and autonomy of the clerical class usurped by the modern bureaucratic state; it was born out of a reassertion of clerical authority vis-a-vis the modern scientific-technocratic elites. Its populism is rooted in the rising expectations and frustrations of the religious masses, and the utopian longings for the unity of the temporal and spiritual authority in the world.

How long can Khomeini's doctrine of legitimacy last? If we consider the progress of any revolutionary doctrine in three successive stages, namely, mobilization, legitimation and consolidation, Khomeinism in Iran has served the first two purposes admirably well but is facing serious difficulties with the third. Khomeini's doctrines were ambiguous enough to mobilize a vast cross-section of Iranian society and a wide spectrum of ideological and political interests, from liberals to nationalists, Marxists and a diversity of Islamic tendencies, against the monarchy. Once in power, however, the radical fundamentalist clerics found themselves in ideological and political conflict with all the other factions. In the eyes of his supporters, Khomeini's revolutionary charisma and insistence on a purist, positivist, anti-liberal, anti-nationalist and anti-imperialist Islam managed to legitimate the Islamic regime and its policies of militancy and repression. Khomeinism has in this sense represented a deepening of the class struggle in Iran, expressed in the rhetoric of revolutionary Islam.

The consolidation stage of Khomeinism has been marked by the establishment of an Islamic Constitution, granting full sovereign powers to the chief *Faqih* acting as a theocrat, and by the political struggles which led in 1979–81 to the complete elimination of the liberal nationalists, notably Bazargan and Bani-Sadr. However, to use Max Weber's well-known allegory, the routinization of charisma demands considerable institution-building and orderly procedures for legislation after the death of the charismatic leader. Given the premises of Islamic fundamentalism that confine legislation to the *Shari'a*, a well-developed and explicit body of traditional law, innovations necessitated by the requirements of a modern state will face enormous difficulties. This has already been the experience of the new legislative system; in conflicts between the *Majlis*, the *Ulema* and the Council of Guardians (*Shoray-e-Negahban*), the radical clerics bypassed the problem by direct appeals to the charismatic leader.

The successors to Khomeini have so far proved themselves adept at maintaining a balance between ideological commitment and pragmatic response to the pressing economic and political needs of the country. Rafsanjani's administration has fully committed itself to a programme of economic reconstruction and rapprochement with the outside world without repudiating its revolutionary objectives. Whether the clerical leadership can continue to withstand the pressures unleashed by a social revolution, however, remains to be seen. In the absence of any effective opposition forces, the most likely scenario is that the Islamic regime will continue to consolidate its power while softening its ideology. However, if the regime fails in its economic programmes, internal opposition may lead to a dismantling of the clerical leadership. The traditional polycentric authority of the Shi'a hierarchy may also reassert itself and provide legitimacy for a more secular, possibly military, takeover. In either case, the doctrine of Wilayat-e Faqih, which served a revolutionary purpose, will probably fade in memory and political efficacy.

CONCLUSION

The current upheavals in the Muslim world should be viewed in the light of the efforts of ancient societies and cultures to regain their sense of balance and dignity in the face of great adversaries and adversities. This generation of Muslims like all past generations is learning, through its own pains and sufferings, how to recreate its own traditions of civility along with new idioms of political and cultural expression. However, when religion is used as a direct instrument of state power, it risks the loss of both the majesty of moral law and the relevance of political expediency. Conversely, when the state is stripped off its spiritual foundations, it tends to lose legitimacy. The current fundamentalist revolt in the Muslim world represents a passion for certitude and a fetish of identity that would probably last as long as the challenges of overcoming foreign domination and domestic injustices remain. Islamic fundamentalism also represents perhaps the last moments of a proud medieval tradition before it gives birth to a modern Islam that will be more at peace with itself and the rest of the world. The place of Ayatollah Khomeini in history will most probably be judged on the basis of his contributions to this process.

NOTES

1. M. Farhang, Interview with McNeil/Lehrer Report, Public Broadcasting System,

September 1981; M. Farhang, 'Iranian Revolution Betrayed My Ideals', *Los Angeles Times*, as reprinted in *Pardis*, 21 November 1981.

2. V.S. Naipaul, *Among the Believers: An Islamic Journey*. New York: Alfred Knopf, 1981.

3. H.A.R. Gibb, *Modern Trends in Islam*. Chicago: The University of Chicago Press, 1950; G.H. Jansen, *Militant Islam*. London: Pan Books, 1979; E. Said, *Orientalism*. New York: Pantheon Books, 1978; E. Said, *Covering Islam*. New York: Pantheon Books, 1981; W.C. Smith, *Islam in Modern History*. New York: Mentor Books, 1959; M. Tehranian, 'Islam and the West: Dependency and Dialogue'. Paper presented at an international conference of media leaders, Rockfeller Foundations' Bellagio Study and Conference Center, Lake Como, Italy, 4–8 May, 1981.

4. M. Tehranian, 'Syyed Jamal ud-Din Afghani: A Study of Charismatic Leadership', an unpublished M.A. thesis, Harvard University, 1961.

5. M. Curtis, ed., *Religion and Politics in the Middle East*. Boulder: Westview Press, 1981; M. Mottahari, *Khadamat-i-motaghabel-i Islam va Iran* (Mutual services of Islam and Iran), in Farsi, Tehran, 1349/1950; M. Rodinson, *Islam and Capitalism*. New York: Penguin Books, 1974; M. Rodinson, *Islam and Marxism*. New York: Penguin Books, 1974; S.M. Taleghani, *Islam va Malekkiat dar mughayesseh ba nezamha-ye-eqtessadi-ye-gharb*. (Islam and Private Property in Comparison with Western Economic Systems.) Tehran, 1978.

6. M. Tehranian, 'The Curse of Modernity: The Dialectics of Communication and Modernization', *International Social Science Journal*, Vol. 32, No. 2, June, 1980.

7. S. Akhavi, *Religion and Politics in Contemporary Iran*. Albany: State University of New York Press, 1980; H. Algar, 'The Oppositionist Role of the Ulema in Twentieth Century Iran', in N.R. Keddie, ed., *Scholars, Saints and Sufis*. Berkeley: University of California Press, 1972; E. Abrahamian, *Iran: Between Two Revolutions*. Princeton: Princeton University Press, 1981; M.E. Bonnie & N.R. Keddie, eds., *Continuity and Change in Modern Iran*. Albany: State University of New York Press, 1981; M.M.J. Fischer, *Iran From Religious Dispute to Revolution*. Cambridge: Harvard University Press, 1980; H. Katouzian, *The Political Economy of Modern Iran: Despotism and Pseudo Modernism*. New York: New York University Press, 1981; F. Kazemi, ed., 'Perspectives on the Iranian Revolution', Special Issue, *Iranian Studies*, 1980, Vol. 13, pp. 1–4; F. Kazemi, *Poverty and Revolution in Iran: The Migrant Poor, Urban Marginality and Politics*. New York: New York University Press, 1980; M. Tehranian, 'Communication, Alienation, Revolution', *Intermedia*, Vol. 7, No. 2, March, 1979; M. Tehranian, 'Communication and Revolution in Iran: The Passing of a Paradigm', *Iranian Studies*, No. 13, 1980, pp. 1–4.

8. S. Amir Arjomand, 'Religion, Political Action and Legitimate Domination in Shi-ite Iran: Fourteenth to Eighteenth Centuries, AD', *European Journal of Sociology*, No. 20, 1979; Amir Arjomand, 'Shi'ite Islam and Revolution in Iran', *Government and Opposition*, Vol. 16, No. 3.

9. J. Al-Ahmad, *Gharbzadegi* (Westomania), in Farsi. Tehran, 1340/1961; A. Shari-ati, *Intizar, Madhhab e I-tiraz* (Expectation: The Religion of Protest). Tehran: Abu-Dharr, 1971.

10. M.R. Pahlavi, *Mission for my Country*. London, 1961.

11. P.J. Chelkowski, 'Iran: Mourning Becomes Revolution', *Asia*, May/June, 1980;

P.J. Chelkowski, ed., *Ta-ziyeh: Ritual and Drama in Iran.* New York: New York University Press and Soroush Press, 1979.

12. A.H. Hairi, *Shi'ism and Constitutionalism in Iran.* Leiden: Brill, 1977.

13. M. Tehranian, *et al.*, eds., *Communication Policy for National Development.* London: Routledge & Kegan Paul, 1977; M. Tehranian, *Socio-Economic and Communication Indicators in Development Planning: A Case Study of Iran.* Paris: UNESCO, 1981.

14. A. Assadi & M. Vidale, 'Survey of Social Attitudes in Iran', *International Review of Modern Sociology,* Vol. 10, 1980, pp. 65–85.

15. A. Jabbari and R. Olson, *Iran: Essays on a Revolution in the Making.* Lexington, Kentucky: Mazda Publishers, 1981.

16. R. Khomeini, *Kashf al-Asrar* (The discovery of secrets), in Farsi. Tehran, 1941; R. Khomeini, *Hokumat-e Islami* (The Islamic government), in Farsi. Jajaf, 1971; R. Khomeini, *Collection of Speeches, Position Statements by Ayatollah Ruhollah Khomeini.* Arlington, Virginia: US Joint Publications Research Service (JPRS 72717), 1979; R. Khomeini, *Islamic Government.* New York: Manor Books, 1979; R. Khomeini, *Sayings of the Ayatollah Khomeini: Political, Philosophical. Social and Religious.* New York: Bantam Books, 1980; Nigarandeh, *Barrasi va Tahlikli as Nahzat-i Imam Khumayni dar Iran* (Review and analysis of Imam Khomeini's movement in Iran), in Farsi. Beirut: Abd al-hafiz al-Basat, 1978.

17. J. Alpher, 'The Khomeini International', *Washington Quarterly,* Autumn, 1980; S. Amir Arjomand, 'Religion, Political Action and Legitimate Domination'; S. Arani, 'Iran From the Shah's Dictatorship to Khomeini's Demogogic Theocracy', *Dissent,* No. 27, winter, 1980; 'The Theocracy Unravels', *The New Republic,* 6 December 1980; S. Arani, 'The Toppling of Bani-Sadr', *The Nation,* 4 July 1981; W.G. Millward, 'The Islamic Political Theory and Vocabulary of Ayatollah Khymayni, 1941–63, and its Relation to the Islamic Revolution in Iran'. Paper presented at the 1979 MESA Annual Meeting, Salt Lake City, November, 1979.

18. K. Roosevelt, *Counter Coup: The Struggle for the Control of Iran.* New York: McGraw Hill Co., 1979; B. Rubin, *Paved with Good Intentions: The American Experience and Iran.* New York: Oxford University Press, 1980.

19. R.K. Ramazani, 'Constitution of the Islamic Republic of Iran', *The Middle East Journal,* Vol. 34, No. 2, Spring, 1980; R.K. Ramazani, 'Iran's Revolution: Patterns, Problems and Prospects', *International Affairs,* Summer, 1980.

20. R. Khomeini, *Islam and Revolution,* translated and annotated by Hamid Algar. Berkeley: Mizan Press, 1981, p. 87.

21. *Ibid.,* p. 96.

22. *Ibid.,* p. 55.

23. *Ibid.,* pp. 55–56.

24. *Ibid.,* p. 27.

25. E. Fromm, *Escape From Freedom.* New York: Holt, Rinehart & Winston, 1941.

Contributors

Barry Cooper is Professor of Political Science at the University of Calgary. He has authored or edited numerous books including *Merleau-Ponty and Marxism* (1979); *Michel Foucault: An Introduction to the Study of His Thought* (1982); *The End of History: An Essay on Modern Hegelianism* (1984); (co-edited with Allan Kornberg and William Mishler) *Resurgence of Conservatism in Anglo-American Democracies* (1988); *Papers in Political Philosophy* (1988); and *Action Into Nature: An Essay on the Meaning of Technology* (1989).

Ronald C. Keith is Professor of Political Science at the University of Calgary, editor of *Energy, Security and Economic Development in East Asia* (1986); and author of *The Diplomacy of Zhou Enlai* (1989); and numerous articles on China.

Anthony J. Parel is Professor Emeritus of the University of Calgary. He is the author of *The Machiavellian Cosmos*, Yale, 1992, and editor of *M. K. Gandhi: Hind Swaraj and Other Writings*, Cambridge, 1997, and *Gandhi, Freedom, and Self-Rule*, Lexington Books, 2000.

K. J. Shah, 1922–1994, was Professor and Head of the Department of Philosophy, Karnataka University, India. Educated at Trinity College, Cambridge, he edited, together with P. T. Geach and A. C. Jackson, Wittgenstein's *Lectures on Philosophical Psychology, 1946–47*, London: Harvester Wheatsheaf, 1988.

Majid Tehranian is currently Professor and formerly Chairman of the Department of Communication, University of Hawaii. He is the author (with A. Al-Marayati *et al.*) of *The Middle East: Its*

Governments and Politics (1972); *Towards a Systemic Theory of National Development* (1974); (with F. Hakim Sadeh and M.L. Vidale) *Communications Policy for National Development Planning: A Case Study of Iran* (1981); *Technologies of Power*; and *Information Mechanics and Democratic Prospect* (1989).

Yusuf K. Umar was Lecturer in Political Science, Mount Royal College, Calgary. Author of the unpublished doctoral thesis, *Strauss and Farabi: Persecution, Esotericism, and Political Philosophy* (1987), Dr. Umar died on 9 March 1991 after a short illness.

Robert X. Ware is Professor of Philosophy at the University of Calgary. He has taught Philosophy in China for two years. He has written on Marx, philosophy and politics in China, the theory of action, and the philosophy of language. His current interests include collective action and transitional socialist societies. He is an editor of the *Canadian Journal of Philosophy* and co-editor of *Analyzing Marxism: New Essays on Analysis Marxism*.

Index

Abdul Hamid, M.M., ed., *Tarıkh Ul-Khulafa*, 210n
Abrahamian, *Iran: Between Two Revolutions*, 242n
absolute reason (al-aql al-kulli), a concept of, 188
absolutism, patriarchical, 80
Abu Bakr As Sarraj, 185
Abu Bishr Matta ibn Yunus, 185
Abu Khadija, 233
Achaemenids, architectural style of, 224
Active Intellect (*Aqlfa'al*), 189, 190, 193, 196, 198, 200, 201, 202, 213n
Afghanistan, the Marxist regime in, 220
agathon, 35
Agha Khan, 223
ahimsa, the principle of, 177; *see also* non-violence
Akhavi, S., *Religion and Politics in Contemporary Iran*, 242n
Al-Afghani, 235
Al-Mu'tazz, 186
al-Sa'ada al-Quswa (supreme happiness), 195
al-Siyasa Madaniyya, 192, 207, 214n, 215n, 216n
Alarie, 59
Alexandre, Laurien, 'Democracy, Reform and Modernization', 136n
Alexandria, the philosophical school of, 185
Algar, Hamid, 243n, 'The oppositionist role of the Ulema in twentieth century Iran', 242n
Ali, 230, 233; the fourth Sunni Caliph of Islam, 222, 223

Ali Sharia'ati's syncretic ideas, 231
Alpher, J., 'The Khomeini International', *Washington Quarterly* (1980), 243n
American Revolutionary War of Independence, 31
Ames, Roger, *The Art of Rulership*, 84n
Amir Arjomand, S., 'Religion, Political Action and Legitimate Domination in Shi-ite Iran: Fourteenth to Eighteenth Centuries A.D., 242n, 'Shi'ite Islam and Revolution in Iran', 242n
Analyse & Kritik (1988), 138n
anarchist movement, the emergence of, 164
anti-Confucius campaign, 98
anti-Lin Biao, 98
anvıksıki (darsana or philosophy), 142, 143, 144, 145, 146, 147, 151, 161
appetitive faculty, 199
Aquinas, Thomas (St.), 13, 16, 18, 25, 29, 39, 41, 74, 174, 176
Arani, S., 'Iran from the Shah's Dictatorship to Khomeini's Demagogic Theocracy', 243n; 'The Theocracy Unravels', 243n; 'The Toppling of Bani Sadr', 243n
Archangel Gabriel, 200
arete, 37, 42; *see also* virtue
Aristotelian political philosophy, 18
Aristotelian *politikos*, 12, 65
Aristotle, 13, 15, 16, 23, 29, 30, 39, 40, 41, 42, 47, 58, 185, 210n; *Ethics*, 32, 36; metaphysics, 43n, 65, 67, 215n; observations on the practical implication of political philosophy, 37; *Politics*, 32, 33, 38, 46; *Problemata*, 57; *Theology*, 197

Arthasastra, 21, 22, 149, 165; and *Dharmasastra,* 156–58; the method of, 158–60
Arya Samaj, 164
As-Siyasa al-Madaniyya (The Political Regime), 186, 201
asabiyya, 234
'Asiatic' society, 81
Assadi, A. and Vidale, M., 'Survey of social attitudes in Iran', 243n
Ataulf, the Visigoth, 50, 58, 59
atheism, 163; Ghazzali's charge of, 216n
atmatustı (self-satisfaction), 149, 150, 156
Attaturk (Turkey), 219
Augustine (St.), 13, 16, 29, 49, 52, 59, 62, 67; *On the City of God Against the Pagans,* 45, 48; treatise, 49
Augustinian sacred history, 56, 60, 62
Augustinian theology of history, 51, 52, 53
Augustinian-Orosan construction, 57
Averroes, 25
Avicenna, 25; 'On the Division of the Rational Sciences', 211n
Azarbaijan, the recapture of, 225

Bahai(s), 226, 232
Bani Sadr, 233, 240
bari, the Islamic concept of, 212n
Basham, 173
Bau, M.J., 130; *Modern Democracy in China,* 138n
Bazargan Mehdi, 233, 235, 240
Begin (Israel), 239
Beijing Review (1988), 136n, 137n, 138n
Beijing University, questionnaire answered at, 121
benevolence, 123; the continuous existence of, 78; Mao's propogation of, 103; the question of, 107
Bentham, 13, 28
Bernadete, 48; *Herodotean Inquiries,* 68n
Bhagavad Gita (the), 20, 164, 165
Bible (the), 29
Bloom, Allan, *Closing of the American Mind,* 59

Bodde, Derk, 75, 77, 80; *Feudalism in China,* 85n and Clarence, Morris, *Law in Imperial China,* 84n, 85n
Bodhi tree, 28
Bombay, 164, 168
Bonnie, M.E. and Keddie, N.R., eds., *Continuity and Change in Modern Iran,* 242n
Book of Changes, 75
Boroujerdi, Ayatollah, 229
Bossuet, 51; Augustinian 'theology of history', 51; *Discours sur l' historie Universelle,* 48
bourgeois system, 103, 106; alleged spiritual pollution of liberalism, 109; democracy, 118; liberalisation, 84
Brhaspati, the followers of, 144
British colonialism, 164
British Parliament, 166
brute force, 171, 172, 173, 174, 180, 181
Buddha, 28, 34, 60, 64
Buddhism, Mahayana, 61, 62; rival schools of, 74
bureaucratism, a form of, 102
Burns, John P., *Political Participation in Rural China,* 138n

Calcutta, 164
Calgary Herald (the), 28n
Caliph al-Mu'tadid, 186
Caliph al-Wathiq, the reign of, 186
Canadian Dimension (1989), 135n
Canadian Journal of Philosophy (1981), 137n
capitalism, 97
caritra, 148, 149, 150, 156
Catlin George, 175; *In the Path of Mahatma Gandhi,* 182n
Charlemagne, the empire of, 48
chastity/*brahmacharya,* 170, 172, 177
Chatterjee, Margaret, *Gandhi's Religious Thought,* 182n
Che Guevera, 179
Chelkowski, P.J., *Iran: Mourning becomes Revolution,* 242n; *Ta-ziyeh: Ritual and Drama in Iran,* 243n

Chen Erjin's *China: Crossroads to Socialism*, 137n, 121

China, 13, 14, 38, 51, 52, 53, 60, 64, 74, 75, 82, 87, 88, 89, 94, 95, 96, 97, 106; democracy in, 113, 116, 118; the experiences and insights of, 17–20; impact of imperialism on, 90

China Daily (1986), 138n

China Spring, 116

China Spring Digest (1987), 136n

China's modernization, the dialectical relation of outside and inside in, 105–7

China's Youth News, 117

Chinese agrarian social order, Stalin's characterization of, 81

Chinese Communist Party, 19, 20, 78, 81, 93, 114, 118, 119, 120; leadership of, 131, 132

Chinese modernity, central paradox of, 97–101

Chinese People's Political Consultative Conference, 120

Chinese political system, 118, 119

Chinese politics, issue of 'idols' in, 100

Chinese Revolution, 104; the laws of, 93

Chinese tradition and modernity, 87

Cho-yun Hsu, *Ancient China in Transition* , 84n

Choron, Jacques, *Death and Western Thought*, 215n

Christian political philosophy, 18, 25

Christianity, 29, 40, 41, 42, 43, 48, 49, 50, 51, 53, 54, 59, 61, 62, 234; the ethics of, 164; the inception of, 222

Churchill, Winston, 174, 175, 182n

Cicero, 176

civil freedom and equality, the western concept of, 164

civilizational pessimism, 58

class struggle, Marxist-Leninist focus on, 94

clement, observation of, 66; *stromateis*, 69n

coercive force, 165, 172

coercive power, a science of, 163

collectivism, 126–28, 135

Colossians, 40

Commentary on the Politics of Aristotle, 28n

Communist neo-traditionalism, 18

Community of Believers (Medina), 222

comparative politics, depths of, 114–16

Comte, 62

Confucian ethics, 19

Confucian *junzi*, 12

Confucian theory, 74, 76

Confucian tradition, 83, 97; the liberal view of, 82; the place of law in, 74–78; politics, 20 .

Confucianism, 77, 96, 97, 107; aristocratic value associated with, 19; the different interpretative schools of, 74; modern fate of, 18; the narrow interpretation of, 83; the social doctrine of, 94, 108; the virtue-centred morality of, 123

Confucius, 13, 34, 38, 60, 64, 65, 67, 73, 90, 99, 103; *Analects*, 72, 76; *Great Learning*, 76; his political conservatism, 72; *Lunyu*, 71, 111n; the time of, 126

consciousness, European, 49; Islamic, 26; a subjective element of, 19, 108

consequentialism, 123, 124, 135

constitutional monarchy, 230

Constitutional Revolution of 1905, 223, 225 .

contemporary China, the dignity of law in, 74–80

contemporary philosophical inquiry, the Eurocentric tendency of, 7

Cooper, Barry, 15, 16, 17; *The End of History*, 68n; *The Political Theory of Eric Voegelin*, 68n

cosmic balance, pre-Socratic understanding of, 48

Coulborn, ed., *Feudalism in History*, 85n

Council of Guardians (*shoray-e-Negahban*), 240

counter-modernization, the phenomenon of, 221

Creel, H.G., *Chinese Thought from Confucius to Mao Tse-tung*, 84n; *Confucius: The Man and the Myth*, 84n
Cretans and the Spartans, the nomothetes of, 37
cultural relativism, the issue of, 7
Cultural Revolution, 18, 78, 79, 80, 82, 88, 89, 93, 100, 104, 109, 120, 130
Cunningham, Frank, 129; *Democratic Theory and Socialism*, 135n, 138n
Curtis, M., ed., *Religion and Politics in the Middle East*, 242n

Daiber, Hans, *The Ruler as Philosopher: A New Interpretation of al-Farabi's View*, 214n
danda, the exercise of, 144
dandaniti (arthasastra or the science of politics), 142, 144, 145, 151
Danielic monarchies, periodization of, 50
Daoist failure, 75
Daoist notions of eternal flux, 96
Daoist *Yinyang*, 105
Dariush Shayegan, 217
Darwin, Charles, 91
Dasism, 132
dating, Bristhlecone pine, 53; Carbon-14, 53
Dayanand Saraswati, 21
De Anima, 43n
de-anthropomorphism, 199
De Brabant, Siger, the heretical doctrine of, 58
de Gaulle, 174
de Santillana, Geiorgia and von Dechand, Hertha, *Hamlet's Mill*, 69n
democracy, 109, 235; bourgeois, 118; Chinese discussion of, 117, 118; collectivism vs individualism, 122, 126–28; conceptions of, 115, 133; conceptual differences, 122–32; contrasts in conceptions of, 113, 114; domain and degree of, 122, 129–31; dominant Chinese theory of, 134; dominant conceptions of, 118–22;

goods vs rights, 122, 123–26; Mao's theoretical conception of, 92; objective vs subjective interests, 122, 128–29; practice vs procedure, 122, 131–32; with Chinese characteristics, 116–18; *see also* proletariat democracy, socialist democracy
democratic centralism, the principle of, 119
democratic theory, Chinese discussions of, 115
Deng Xiaoping, 79, 80, 81, 82, 83, 90, 91, 92, 98, 109, 117, 120; *Fundamental Issues in Present-day China*, 136n, 137n
developmentalism, 135
Dewey, John, 115, 130, 132, 135n; 'Chinese National Sentiment: Transforming the Mind of China, 136n, 139n
dharma, 142, 146, 147, 155, 158, 161, 170, 171, 177; and *adharma*, 143, 144, 145; and law, 148–51; four-fold sources or characteristics of, 150; Indian, 12; sources of, 143, 149, 156
dharmanyaya, 150
dharmasastra(s), 20, 21, 142, 143, 156–58
dialectical thinking, Engel's three categories of, 104
dialectics, three laws of, 105; 'science' of, 94; scientific, 104
'dignity of law', 74
Dissent (1980), 243n
divine and human being, the inequality of, 41
divine determinism, 197
Divine Law, 236; Islamic, 230
Divine Legislator, the law of, 236
doctrine of progress, 146–47
Doctrines of the Just Sultan (*sultan-i-a'del*), 231
dogmatism, 104, 106, 200; a negative connotation of, 87
Dumont, *From Mandeville to Marx*, 162n
Dunlap, D.M., ed., *Fusul al-Madani*, 211n

education, English system of, 164
Egypt, 38, 53, 219; constitutional movements in, 235; the nationalist military regime in, 220
Elster, Jon, *Making Sense of Marx*, 138n
emanation, 196, 198, 199; the doctrine of, 200; rational, 203
Engels, 87
epikeina, 35
Epinomis, 65
epistome politike (political science), 36, 37
equivalences, 46, 66; language of, 65; the phenomenon of, 12
Erikson, Erik, 172, 173; *Gandhi's Truth*, 182n
essence, 101, 102, 108, 131
eternal recurrence, Nietzsche's doctrine of, 58
Eurocentric unlinear Christian construction, 51, 62
Eurocentrism, 63
European Journal of Sociology (1979), 242n
European political philosophy, 25

Fadaiyan-i-Islam guerrillas, 230
Faghih, 240
Fakhry, *Al-Farabi and the Reconciliation of Plato and Aristotle*, 212n
Fallaci, Olriana, 217
Family Law (1967–74), 226
Fang Lizhi, 136n
Fanon, Franz, 179
fanshen, 98, 108
Faqih, 230, 231, 233, 234, 236, 237
Farabi, 12, 23, 24, 25, 67; *Al-Jama'a*, 212n, 215n; *Al-Madina at Fadila (The Virtuous City)*, 186, 192, 201, 207, 211n, 214n, 215, 216; *Falsafat Aflaloun*, 214, 215; *Fusul al-Madani (Aphorisms of the Statesman)*, 186, 210n, 211n, 212n, 213n, 214n, 215n; *Harmonising the Opinions of the Two Sages, Plato and Aristotle*, 198; his God, 196–99; his political teachings, 201; his political theory, 186,
209; his Sufism, 206; his trinity of *Aql, Ma'quol, Aqel*, 211n; *Maqalah fi Ma'ani al-Aql*, 213n; *Risala fi al-Milla al-Fadila*, 212n; *Risalat fi ma Yanbaghi*, 210n, 212n; *Risalat Fusus al-Hikam*, 215n; *Tahqiq Gharad Aristotales fi Kitab ma Ba'ad at-Tabiah*, 211n; *Tahsil us-Sa'adah (The Attainment of Happiness)*, 185, 210n, 212n, 214n, 215n; *Uyoun al-Masa'il*, 211n, 212n
Farhang, M., *Iranian Revolution Betrayed My Ideals*, 242n
Farid ud-Din Attar, *The Conference of the Birds*, 214n
Fascism, 239
Fauzi Najja, 'Democracy in Islam', 215n
Fazlur Rahman, *Prophecy in Islam*, 214n
Fei Xiaodong, 81; *A Great Trial in Chinese History*, 85n
Feizi, Han, 77, 78
Ferdowsi's *Shahnameh*, 225
feudalism, 71, 78, 80, 82, 83, 89, 95, 96, 100; and China's legal tradition, 80–82; the Chinese concept of, 80; Weberian discussion of, 81
fiqh, the art of, 211n
First Cause, 193, 196, 197, 198, 201, 202, 207, 208, 215n
First Essence, 215n
First Existent, 194, 197
First Originator, 197
First Principle, 197, 206, 208
Fischer, M.M.J., *Iran from Religious Dispute to Revolution*, 242n
Foucault, the philosophy of, 14
Four Books and *Five Classics*, 90
French Revolution, 53
fuqaha (the jurists of the *Shari'a*), 230
Fundamental Laws of 1905, 230
fundamentalism, 218; as counter modernization, 220–22; Islamic, 218–22, 240, 241; religious, 239; *see also* Islamic fundamentalism

Gandhi, Mahatma, 8, 14, 21, 27, 217;

the canonization of, 221; his advocacy
of return to cottage industries, 221;
historical context of his political
*philosophy, 163–65; religious basis
of his political action, 177
'genius theory', 88
Gestalt, 54
Ghazzali, 198
Gibb, H.A.R., *Modern Trends in
Islam*, 242n
Gibbon, 59; *The Decline and Fall of
the Roman Empire*, 69n
Gnostic speculation, 55
God's omniscience and providence,
the subject of, 198
good and evil, philosophical conceptions of 190, 191
Gorgias, 38
Government and Opposition, 242n
Gramsci, Antonio, 19, 132; *Selections
from the Prison Note Books*, 139n
Great Leap Forward, 104, 106; feudal
excesses of, 100
Greek political philosophy, 15, 23; the
impact of, 25

Habermas, the philosophy of, 14
Hairi, A.H., *Shi'ism and Constitution-
alism in Iran*, 243n
Hakim, Ayatollah (Iraq), 229
Hanming, Shao and Wang Yankun,
Picking out the Pieces, 138n
Harding, Harry, 115; *Political Devel-
opment in Post-Mao China*, 136n
Hazard, Paul, 49; *La Crise de la Con-
science European*, 68n
Hegel, 13, 17, 53, 54, 55, 56, 57, 62, 125
Hegelian or Marxian type, dialectical
elaborations of, 58
Hellas, 38, 51; political philosophers
of, 34
Heraclitus, 38
Heritage Foundation, a forum of, 116
Herodotus, 43n, 47, 48
Heschel, A.J., *Did Maimonides Believe
that He was Worthy of Prophecy*,
213n
Hesiod, 38

hijrah, 213n
(The) Histories, 48
Hidden Imam (*imam-i-qa'ib*), 230,
231, 232, 237; the doctrine of, 232
hierarchy, Dumont's notion of, 162n
Hind Swaraj, 21, 22, 27, 28n, 165
Hinduism, 61, 62, 165, 176, 177; the
reform movement within, 164
hindutva, 22
Hippodamus (Miletus), 38
historical materialism, 18, 118, 125; the
institutions of, 20
historicism, 163
history, Augustinian conception of,
49; the historicist conception of, 17;
the materialist conception of, 96;
materialist view of, 19
Hitti, Philip K., *History of the Arabs*,
210n
Ho Chiminh, 179
Hobbes, 13
Hourani, George, 'Reason and Revolution in Ibn Hazm's Ethical Thought',
210n
Hu Shi, 105
human consciousness, the subjective
element of, 96
human happiness, 32, 33, 37, 186, 189,
195, 196, 197, 202, 204, 207, 208, 209
human nature, 17; a philosophy of, 15
Hungary, 92
hurrima, 213n
Hyma, Arthur, ed., *Essays in Medieval
Jewish and Islamic Philosophy*, 213n

ibda, the theory of, 197
Ibn Khaldun, *Tarikh*, 210n
Ibn Manzour, *Mu'jam Lisan al-Arab*,
212n
Ibn Rushd, 198
Ibn Sina, 198
Ihsa al-'Ulum, 211n
imaginative faculty, 191, 192, 196, 199,
202, 203, 206
Imam Hossain, 229
imamat, the doctrine of, 223
immortality of the soul, Farabi's views
of, 206–8

imperialism, 90, 95; Lenin's theory
of, 91
incarnation, 176
India, 13, 14, 27, 51, 52, 53, 60, 64,
221; the experiences and insights of,
20–22
Indian classical political philosophy, 20
Indian Maoists, 175
Indian National Congress, 164
indifference to possessions, the doctrine of, 175
individualism, 126–28
intellect, the different categories of,
200
*International Review of Modern
Sociology*, 243n
Iran, 219, 220, 221; constitutional
movements in, 235; deepening of the
class struggle in, 240; Khomeini in,
239; Shah's regime in, 220; Shi'a
Islamic Ulema's revolutionary role in,
218; Ulema's revolutionary role in,
222–29
Iranian historical consciousness, the
construction of, 224
Iranian Studies (1980), 242n
Iraq, 218; the nationalist military
regime in, 220
Islam, 13, 14, 51, 52, 61, 62, 165, 176,
186, 187, 188, 218, 219, 221, 222,
236, 237; under the aegis of, 230;
Divine Law of, 227; the experiences
and insights of, 22–27; opinions of,
209; rightly-guided Caliphs of, 234;
the sectarian conflicts of, 197; sects
of, 231; Sunni, 239
Islamic fundamentalism, 240, 241; the
historical roots of, 218–22; *see also*
fundamentalism
Islamic modernism, 235
Islamic political philosophy, 22, 25
Islamic political theories, the problem
of identity in, 234
Islamic prophet-legislator, 12
Islamic Revolution of 1979, 223
Israel, Begin in, 239
Israelite prophets, 34

Jabbari, A. and Olson, R., *Iran: Essay
on a Revolution in the Making*, 243n
Jansen, G.H., *Militant Islam*, 242n
Japan, emperor worship in, 234
Jaspers, Karl, 60, 61, 62; *The Origin
and Goal of History*, 69n
Jefferson, the canonization of, 221; his
call for rural democracy, 221
Journal of the History of Ideas (1965),
212n
*Journal of the Indian Academy of Philo-
sophy*, 149
Journey to the West, 110n
Judeo-Christian sacred history, the
expansion of, 53
judicial system, professionalization
of, 167
junzi, 72, 73; the notion of, 19
jurisprudence, divine, 24; Islamic sense
of, 26
Just Sultan, 237
justice, 22, 30, 32, 33, 36, 48, 55, 78,
205, 219, 221, 226; the meaning
of, 15

kalun, 35
Kama, 146, 147, 155, 161
Kangle, 149; *Kautilya's Arthasastra*,
162n
Kantianism, 123
karma, 176
Karma Yoga, 177
Kashani, Ayatollah, 229
Katouzian, H., *The Political Economy
of Modern Iran*, 242n
Kautilya, 13, 38n, 142, 144, 147,
148, 149, 151, 152, 153, 159, 161,
168n
Kazemi, F., ed., *Perspectives on Iranian
Revolution*, 242n; *Poverty and
Revolution in Iran*, 242n
Keddie, N.R., ed., *Scholars, Saints
and Sufis*, 242n
Keith Ron, 139n
Keith, Ronald C., 18, 19, 138n, *The
Diplomacy of Zhou Enlai*, 109n;
112n; *Mao Zedong and the Chinese
View of Modernity*, 136n

Khomeini, Ayatollah, 14, 217, 218, 221, 224, 225, 228, 229, 230, 232, 233, 235, 236, 237, 239, 241; the Council of Experts on, 234; the political theory of, 25–27

Khomeini, R., *Collection of Speeches, Position Statements by Ayatollah Ruhollah Khomeini*, 243n; *Hokumat-e Islami*, 243n; *Islam and Revolution*, 243n; *Islamic Government*, 243n; *Kashf al-Asrar*, 243n; *Sayings of the Ayatollah Khomeini*, 243n

Khomeinism, 237–41; the phenomenon of, 218

Khulafa al-Rashidun (the Rightly-Guided Successors of Mohammad), 222

kingship, 148; the institution of, 142

Laote, 60, 64

Laski, Harold, 175

law, divine origin of, 75

law and education, secularization of, 235

law, Shi'a Ja'fari School of, 233

Le Roy, Louis, 58

Lebanon, 218

Legalism, 73, 77, 78, 82, 83, the original argument of, 75; reinstatement of, 89; traditional, 19

legitimacy, Shi'a doctrine of, 230

legitimate and rightful Imam, the doctrine of, 186

Lenin, 138n

Lessing's Nathan, 62

Levenson, Joseph, 18; *Confucian China and its Modern Fate: A Trilogy*, 28n

Li Buyun, 79

Liang Ch'i-chao, *History of Chinese Political Thought*, 84n, 85n

Liang Qichao, 82

liberal constitutionalism, the cause of, 235

liberal democracy, institutions of, 166; Liang's interest in, 82

liberalism, 11, 14, 21, 25, 219, 220, 235; secular, 227; western 125

Liu Shaoqi, *Selected Works of Liu Shaoqi*, 138n

Locke, 13, 125

Loewith, Karl, 38

Lokayata, 142, 143

Los Angeles Times (1981), 242n

love force, 171, 172, 173, 180; *see also ahimsa*, non-violence

Machiavelli, 13, 19

machinery, 167, 168, 169, 170

MacIntyre, Alasdair, the philosophy of, 14

Macrobius, 176

Madineh Fazeleh (the virtuous city), Islamic theories of, 237

Madras, 164

Mahdi, Muhsin, ed., *Kitab al-Milla wa Nusus Ukhra*, 211n; ed. and trans., *Al-Farabi's Philosophy of Plato and Aristotle*, 210n; and Lerner, R., eds., *Medieval Political Philosophy*, 211n

Mahdism, 223

Majlis, 235, 240

Mansour, Farhang, 217

Manu, the followers of, 144

Manusmrti, 143, 156, 157, 158

Mao Tse-tung, 'The Chinese Revolution and the Chinese Communist Party', 111n; *see also* Mao Zedong

Mao Zedong, 14, 19, 81, 84, 94, 95, 96, 117, 120, 121. 124, 125, 126, 128, 130, 131; and Chinese modernization, 108; as a dangerous Trotskyite, 105; *Books of History*, 90; concept of man, 99; explanation of metaphysics, 102; mass line, 83; methodological collectivism, 127; 'On Contradictions' and 'On Practice', 91; 'On the Correct Handling of Contradictions among the People', 92; 'On the Ten Major Relationships', 92; 'Reform our Study', 91; revolution, 18; theory of contradictions, 79, 81; *see also* Mao Tse-tung

'Mao Zedong Thought', 82, 97; Manuism-Leninism, 87, 90, 93

Maoism, 87; rival schools of, 74

Maritain, Jacques, 174; *Man and State*, 182n; the writings of, 17

Marmura, M., 'The Philosopher and Society' in *Arab Studies Quarterly* (1974), 214n

Marsilius, *Defensor Pacis* of, 58

Marquise du Châtelet Lorraine, 48, 49, 50, 51, 53

Marx, Karl, 13, 17, 55, 56, 57, 62, 81, 87, 109n, 124, 125, 127, 137n, 219, 220; *Economic and Philosophical Manuscripts*, 55; social theorizing, 127

Marxism, 14, 100, 128, 231; China's experiment with, 17

Marxism-Leninism, 20, 104, 107; Mao's brand of, 87; nationalist adaptation of, 91; 'sinification' of, 81, 87

Mas'udi, *Muruj Ud-Dhahab wa Ma'aden ul-Jawhar*, 210n

materialism, Mao's acceptance of, 97

medicine, the professionalization of, 167

Mehnert, Klaus, 'Mao and Maoist: Some Soviet Views' in *Current Scene* (1970), 112n

Meisner, Maurice, 95, *Marxism, Maoism and Utopianism*, 110n

Mencius, 77, 99; democratic ideology of, 124

Merton, Thomas, 177; 'A Tribute to Gandhi', 182n

Mesopotamia, 38, 53

Meyer, Eduard, 59

Mill, John Stuart, 13, 91, 123

Miller, Richard, 137n

Millward, W.G., 'The Islamic Political Theory and Vocabulary of Ayatollah Khymayni', 243n

Misch, George, 55; *The Down of Philosophy*, 68n

Mission for my Country, 225

modern free press, 166

modern government, 'science' and technology in, 101–5

modernity, 8, 11, 15, 17, 21, 94, 96, 97–101, 107, 163, 164, 165, 166, 167, 168, 170, 218, 221, 222, 236; the 'baleful' effect of, 27; the

epistemological and ontological foundations of, 14; European, 25; the flowering of, 13; Gandhi's rejection of, 26; Gandhi's term for, 22; Mao Zedong's view of, 26, 93–97; western idea of, 20, 26

modernization, 93; Mao's strategy for, 97

'modesty compatible with reality', 96, 103

Mohammad Iqbal (Pakistan), 219

Mohammad (Prophet), 222; the transfiguration of, 53

moksa, 146, 155, 156, 161

Mommsen, 59

Montesquieu, 59, 91

Moon, Penderel (Sir), 165; *Gandhi and Modern India*, 181n

Morewedge, Parviz, ed., *Islamic Philosophic Theology*, 210n

Morris, Clarence, 75, 77

Mosaddeq, 228

Most Noble Messenger, the *sunna* of, 235

Mottahari, M., *Khadamat-i-mota ghable-i-Islam va Iran*, 242n

Muhammad, 23, 200

Muhammad Abed al-Jabri, *Bunyat al-Aql al-Arabi*, 214n

Muhammad Abduh (Egypt), 219, 235

Muhammad Ali Abu Rayyan, *Tarikh al-Fikral Falsafifil Islam*, 210n

Muhammad Y. Musa, *Bayan al-Din Wa al-Falsafa*, 210n

Mujahids, 235

Muslim *Failasauf*, 34

Muslim society, dualistic structure of, 222

Muslim *umma*, 23

Mu'tazilites, 199

Nader, Albert Nasric, ed., *Al-Madinah al-Fadila*, 211n

Naess, Arne, 114

Naipaul, 217; *Among the Believers: An Islamic Journey*, 242n

Najjar, Fauzi M., ed., *Al-Siyasa al-Madaniyya*, 211n

Nandy, Ashis, ed., *Science, Hegemony and Violence: A Requiem for Modernity*, 28n

Nathan, Andrew J., 125, 135; *Chinese Democracy*, 136, 137n, 139n

The Nation (1981), 243n

National Endowment for Democracy, 116

nationalism, 25, 26, 219, 220, 234; Iranian, 224

'natural justice', the pre-modern western notion of, 12

'nature' and 'virtue', twin foundations of, 15

Nazism, 239

Necessary Existent, 194

Needham, Joseph, 75; *The Shorter Science and Civilisation in China*, 84n

negation of negation, 104, 105

Nehru, Jawaharlal, 170

'new bourgeoisie', 93

The New Republic (1980), 243n

(The) New Testament, 16, 218

Nibelungenlied, 58

Nicomachean Ethics, 28n, 216n

Niebuhr, 59; *The Meaning of Revolution*, 43n

Nielsen, K. and Pattern, S., *Marx and Morality*, 137n

Nielsen and Ware, Robert, eds., *Analyzing Marxism*, 138n

Nietzsche, 58

nihilism, 227 ·

non-violence, 163, 170, 171, 172; *see also ahimsa*

Nubians and Scythians, the ways of, 47

nutritive faculty, 199

Obscurantism, 218, 221, 222

October Revolution, 107

oil nationalization movement of 1950–53, 223, 225

olive tree, 28

Omegaminus, 61

On Democracy, 116

order of being, the experiences of, 35

Orosian myth of continuity, 59

Orosius, 48, 50, 58, 59; *Seven Books of History*, 69n

Orwell, George, 175, 176; 'Reflections on Gandhi' in *Partisan Review* (1949), 182n

Osman Amine, ed., *Ihsa'al-'Ulum*, 211n

Pahlavi, M.R., *Mission for My Country*, 242n

Pakistan, the *Ulema* in, 234

pan-Islamic movement, 219

patriarchal socialism, 18

Paul (St.), 40

People's Daily (Renmin Ribao), 117, 124

people's democratic dictatorship, 119

perfect man, 191, 196; Farabi's conception of, 201, 202

perfection, 195, 196, 204, 205, 206, 207, 209

Persia, 53

phenomenology, preface to, 54

philosopher king, 237; Platonic, 12

philosopher prophet, 24

Philosophic wisdom, the principle of, 25

philosophy and divine revelation, parallelism between, 193

Philosophy and Phenomenological Research (1944), 69n

philosophy and political philosophy, a dialectical relationship between, 189

philosophy of history, 47, 48, 51, 55; Voltarian principles of, 53

Plato, 13, 16, 23, 28, 29, 35, 36, 39, 41, 47, 65, 67, 197, 204, 210n; aphorism, 39; *Republic*, 33, 34, 35, 49, 66; *Timaeus*, 58

Poland, 92

Politesse, 51, 52

political legitimacy, Khomeini's doctrines of, 229–37

politics, European vision of, 16

politikos, 37; Chinese, 38

polycentrism, 224

Pope Gelasius, 45

popular sovereignty, 25; the doctrines of, 237
Posterior Analytics, 30
pragmatism, 103; bourgeois, 105
primitive accumulation, 92
professionalization, 166, 167
proletariat, 91, 239
proletarian democracy, 118; *see also* democracy
prophecy, 176; Farabi's theory of, 199
prudence, the meaning of, 15
purusartha(s), 142, 146, 158; the terminology of, 143, 161
Pythagorean belief, 201

Qarmathians, 210n
Qin Shihuang, 89, 97, 98
Quran (the), 187, 218, 235

radicalism, 218
Rafsanjani, Ali Akbar Heshemi, 234; his administration, 240
Raghavan Iyer, *The Moral and Political Thought of Mahatma Gandhi*, 181n
Raghavendra Rao, K., 'Kautilya and the Secular State' in *Journal of the Karnatak University*, 162n
rajasasana, 148, 149, 156
Ramazani, R.K., 'Constitution of the Islamic Republic of Iran' in *The Middle East Journal* (1980), 243n; 'Iran's Revolution: Patterns, Problems and Prospects' in *International Affairs* 243n
Rashid Rida (Egypt), 219, 235
rational faculty, 191, 199, 202, 206
reason, 188, 189, 191, 192, 199, 291; theoretical, 203, 206, 209, 219n
reason and revelation, conflict between, 192; relationship between, 22
rectification, 96, 98, 104
religion, meaning of, 176; the virtue of, 177
religious corps, the organization of, 226
resurrection, 176, 206, 207, 208, 216n
revelation, 41, 54, 65, 187, 188, 189, 190, 191, 192, 193, 196, 200, 201, 202, 203; divine, 218; the God of, 196

revolution, colonial theory of, 91
revolutionary doctrine, three stages of, 240
revolutionary, Islam, 234; totalitarian state, 217
Reza Shah (Iran), 219
(Rg Veda the), 143
Rightist empiricism, 105
rights, conception of, 153–56
Rodinson, M., *Islam and Capitalism*, 242n; *Islam and Marxism*, 242n
Roosevelt, K., *Counter Coup: The Struggle for the Control of Iran*, 243n
Rosenthal, 'Avicenna's influence on Jewish thought, 213n; 'The Place of Politics in the Philosophy of Al-Farabi' in *Studia Semitica*, 215n; *Political Thought in Medieval Islam*, 213n; 'Some observations on Al-Farabi's Kitab al-Mila', 210n; 'Some Observations on the Philosophic Theory of Prophecy in Islam' in *Studia Semitica*, 213n
Rostovtzeff, Michael, 59; *Social and Economic History of the Roman Empire*, 69n
Rousseau, Jean Jacques, 13, 91, 221
'Rousseau effect', 221
Roy, Ram Mohun, 164
Rubin, B., *Paved with Good Intention: The American Experience and Iran*, 243n
Rubin, Vitaly, *Individual and State in Ancient China*, 84n
rule of law, 82, 84
Ruskin, John, *Unto this Last*, 164
Russia, 48

sadachar (the conduct of good man), 149, 150, 156
Sadiq Ja'far (Imam), 233
Said, E., *Covering Islam*, 242n; *Orientalism*, 242n
Saif ud-Dwala, the Shi'ite Prince of Aleppo, 185
Salman Rushdie, 26
samanya dharma, 149, 157; *see also* dharma Samaveda (the), 143

Samkhya, 142, 143
Sarvodaya, 22, 170, 173
satya, the principle of, 177
satyagraha, 22, 164, 170; the truth of, 173
Saudi Arabia, the *Ulema* in, 234
Savak, 226
Schram, Stuart (Professor), 81, 97; *Mao Tse-tung Unrehearsed*, 110n, 112n; *Mao Zedong: A Preliminary Reassessment*, 109n; *The Political Thought of Mao Tse-tung*, 109n
Schwartz, Benjamin, *The World of Thought in Ancient China*, 84n
sciences, and their relationship, 142–48; the goals of, 146; the importance of, 117; Marxist-Leninist conception of, 101
scientism, 238
secular ideologies, the failure of, 219–20
secularization, 222, 223, 235
'seeking the truth from the facts', 90, 91, 93, 99, 103, 105, 106, 109; Mao's dialectical conception of, 108
Selected Works of Mao Tse-tung, 91
self-reliance, 94, 97, 98, 100, 106, 108
sense-perception, 196, 202, 206
sensory faculty, 199
Sermon on the Mount, 177
Seven Books of History against the Pagans, 48, 50
Seymour, James D., *China's Satellite Parties*, 137n
Seyyed Hossein Nasr, 'The Meaning of Philosophy in Islam' in *Studia Islamica*, 210n
Shah, K.J., 21; 'The Concept of Dharma', 149
Shahnameh, 229
Shaikh Fazlullah Nuri, 219
Shama Sastri, 149
Shari'a (Islamic law), 23, 186, 187, 219, 229, 230, 231, 240; the fundamental laws of, 234; the jurists of, 26; the ordinances of, 233; the primacy of, 236; the rule of, 223
Shariatmadari Ayatollah (Iran), 235

Sharif, M.M., ed., *A History of Muslim Philosophy*, 211n
Sherwani, H.K., *Studies in Muslim Political Thought and Administration*, 210n
Shi'a Islam, the dialectics of, 231
Shi'ism, 222, 223, 229
Shi Ji (Book of History), 72
The Shorter Oxford English Dictionary, 27
Shue, Vivienne, *The Reach of the State: Sketches of the Chinese Body Politic*, 138n
Smith, Adam, 91
Smith, W.C., *Islam in Modern History*, 242n
Smrti, 149, 150, 156
Snow, Edgar, 88; *The Long Revolution*, 109n, 110n
social harmony, Confucian emphasis on, 94
social peace and happiness, the attainment of, 15
socialism, 11, 14, 25, 78, 92; Marxist, 21; patriarchal, 18; with Chinese characteristics, 83
socialist democracy, 83, 90, 117, 119; *see also* democracy
socialist spiritual civilization, 18, 83, 84, 109
Socrates, 15, 33, 38, 165, 204; Phaedrus, 54
soul force, 171, 172, 173, 174, 180; *see also* non-violence, *ahimsa*
South Africa, 164
Soviet ideological preference, the rejection of, 104
Spathari, Elizabeth, 28n
Spencer, 91
speculative mysticism, 56
Spengler, 58, 60, 62; 'Going-Down of the West', 57; his preface, 59
spoudaios, 36
sruti (the vedas), 143, 149, 150, 156
Stalin, 92, 101, 102, 105, 109n
Stalinism, 239
Stalinist 'personality cult', 100
statecraft, 21, 23, 24

Statesman, Plato's myth in, 58
Stoics (the), 29
(*The Story of My Emperiments with Truth*, 171
Strauss, Leo, 11, 29, 31, 33; the writings of, 17
Straussian way, 198
Subjectivism, 104
Sundan, Mahdist revolt in, 232
Sufism, 25; rational, 206–9
Summa Contra Gentiles, 39
Sundararajan, 'The *Purusartha* in the Light of Critical Theory' in *Indian Philosophical Quarterly*, 162n
Sun Wukong, 89
survival of the theoretical faculty, Farabi's doctrine of, 215n
Svadharma, 177
swaraj, 172, 173, 174, 175, 227; Gandhi's concept of, 170, 171
symbolism, 46, 50, 63, 64, 66, 68
symbolization, 62, 65, 66, 67, 68
synoptic gospels, the ethic of, 177
Syria, nationalist military regimes in, 220

Taleghani, S.M., *Islam va Malekkiat dar mughayesseh ba nezamha-ye-eqtessadi-ye-gharb*, 242n
Taoism, rival schools of, 74
Taylor, Charles, the philosophy of, 14
technology, 25, 167, 168, 169, 170, 173; foreign, 106; naive, 106
Tehranian, Majid, 25, 26; 'Communication Alienation, Revolution' in *Inter Media* (1979), 242n; 'Communication and Revolution in Iran' in Iranian Studies (1980), 242n; 'The Curse of Modernity' in *International Social Science Journal* (1980), 242n; *Islam and the West*, 242n; *Socio-economic and Communication: Indicators in Developmental Planning*, 243n; 'Syyed Jamal ud-Din Afghani: A Study of Charismatic Leadership', 242n
Tehranian, Majid, et al., eds., *Communication Policy for National Development*, 243n

Thales formula, 41
Theaetetus, 43n
'theistic rationalist objection', 193
theological debate, Farabian contribution to, 199
Theosophical Society, the founding of, 164
Thucydides, 38
Tillich, Paul, 238
time of troubles, 64
tiyong, the idea of, 107
Tolstoy, Leo, the writings of, 164
totalistic ideologies, 238
Toynbee, 60, 61, 62, 64; *A Study of History*, 57, 62, 69n
tradition, 8, 12, 13, 14, 30, 32, 43, 82, 83, 96, 218, 221, 236; Buddhist, 27
transcendent spiritual destiny of humanity, Christian or Jewish doctrine of, 58
trayi (the three vedas), 142, 143, 144, 145, 147, 151, 161
'Tree of Utility', 28
Trusteeship of the Jurists (*Wilayat-i-faqih*), 230, 231, 241; Khomeini's doctrine of, 232–33
truth (*satya*), 170, 171, 172, 186, 188, 192
truth about the whole, the search for, 187, 189, 191
truth force, 171, 172, 173; *see also* non-violence, *ahimsa*
Turkey, 219; the constitutional movement in, 235

Ulema, 223, 224, 225, 226, 229, 230, 231, 234, 237, 240; the leadership of, 236; radicalization of, 221; revolutionary role in Iran, 222–29; Shi'a, 232, 235; Sunni, 232
Umar, Y.K., 23, 237
Umar ibn Hanzala, 233
umma, 26
United States, 121; moral majority in, 239
Unnithan, T.K.N., 172; *Change without Violence*, 182n
Upanishads (the), 20, 55

Upas tree, the metaphor of, 27
utilitarianism, 123; Mao's concept
of, 95

Varnas and asramas, 143, 149
Vartta (the science of the means of
livelihood), 142, 144, 145, 146, 151,
161
Vedanta, 171
Vico, 59; New Science, 60
virtue, 16, 17, 19, 21, 37, 38, 45, 46, 47,
73, 76, 77, 97, 98, 123, 152, 176, 195,
199, 200, 203, 204, 205, 207; the
cosmic immanence of, 74; dianoetic
and ethical, 36; the philosophy
of, 15
virtue of religion, the practice of,
175–76
visesa dharma, 149; see also dharma
Vivekananda (Swami), 164
Voegelin, Eric, 12, 14, 41, 63, 64;
'Equivalences of Experience and
Symbolization in History' in
Philosophical Studies (1981), 69n;
From Enlightenment to Revolution,
68n; The New Science of Politics,
43n; Order and History, 68n, 69n;
writings of, 17
Voice of America, 116
Voltaire, 48, 51, 52, 54, 57; 'Softening
of Morals', 51, 53
voluntary poverty, 177; the virtue of,
173–75
voluntary suffering, 174
Vyavahara, 148, 149, 150, 156

Wafd (Egypt), 219
Walder, Andrew G., Communist
Neo-Traditionalism, 28n
'walking on two legs', 106
Walzer, R., 'Al-Farabi's Theory of

Prophecy and Divination' in Journal
of Hellenistic Studies (1957), 214n;
The Perfect State, 211n, 212n, 213n,
214n, 215n
Wan Li, 117; 'Making Policies Demo-
cratically and Scientifically', 117
Wang Gungwu, 'The Chinese', 110n
Wang Hanqing, 79
War Measures Act (Canada), 119
Ware, Robert X., 18, 20
Watson, Burton, trans., Han Fei Tzu,
85n
Weberian assumptions, 107
We-ch'ang conference, 105
Westomania (gharbzadegi), 224
Whitehead, 41
White Revolution, 225; the reforms of,
230
Women's Corps, organization of, 226
Wong, David B., Moral Relativity,
137n
Woodcock, George, Gandhi, 183n

Xenophon, 29, 47; Cyropaedia, 43n

Yajnayavalkyasmrti, 143
Yajurveda (the), 143
Yang Yichen, 85n
Yoga, 142, 143
Yohanna ibn Hailan, 185
Young, Andrew, 217
Yu Guangyun, On the Objective
Character of Laws of Development,
137n

Zetema, 66, 67, 68
Zhang Yongming, 79, 85n
Zhao Ziyang, 118, 119, 120, 129, 130
Zhou Enlai, 118
zinj (slaves), the uprisings of, 210n
Zoroaster, 34, 61